inaccessible

RICHARD LAYNE

Softcover version:
ISBN 10: 1-59152-118-1
ISBN 13: 978-1-59152-118-1

Hardcover version:
ISBN 10: 1-59152-119-X
ISBN 13: 978-1-59152-119-8

Published by Richard Layne

Cover photo: The elbow of the approach to Hole in the Wall, Glacier National Park
Back cover photo: Belly River canyon, Glacier National Park

Maps created using TOPO! software ©2011 National Geographic Maps.

Designed by Laurie "gigette" McGrath, graphicsbygigette@bresnan.net

For more information, write Richard Layne, 621 Madison Avenue, Helena, MT 59601,
or email: rclayne@mt.net

You may order extra copies of this book by calling Farcountry Press toll free at (800) 821-3874.

sweetgrassbooks
a division of Farcountry Press

Produced by Sweetgrass Books.
PO Box 5630, Helena, MT 59604; (800) 821-3874; www.sweetgrassbooks.com.

The views expressed by the author/publisher in this book do not necessarily represent
the views of, nor should be attributed to, Sweetgrass Books. Sweetgrass Books is not
responsible for the content of the author/publisher's work.

Printed in the United States of America.

17 16 15 14 13   1 2 3 4 5

dedication

For my wife, Carleen, the beautiful lady.

Without you holding down the fort and keeping the lights on,
none of this would have been possible.

For my mother, Kathyrne, under overwhelming odds Mom,
you showed that the fight is less about winning
and more about not quitting.

To my seven siblings, Charles, Almer, Connie, Greg, Tom,
Christine, and Robin, regardless of the route each of us has
taken it was under the same roof together that we learned.
I would not trade anything for what each
of you has brought to my life.

acknowledgments

After nearly one year inside what I have come to call the black hole—my office in the basement—what I came up with, the public will never see. A metamorphosis has taken place as the result of a group of people who in great tolerance were able to get through numerous reads and influence the outcome of this book.

My wife, Carleen, had to show the greatest of tolerance each day as I reemerged to join the living while my mind was obviously somewhere else. Hers was a tough stance as the initial reader, questioning grammar, confusing phrases, and so much more.

I want to thank Kelly Weber, Cinda Holt, Sean Connolly, and Linda Knoblock, who effected further changes with their sometimes dead-on nose punches, which in turn altered the story into even greater readability.

Will Harmon, editor at Farcountry Press, showed me why writers fawn over their editor. I am astounded at his insight.

Laurie "Gigette" McGrath, graphic artist with decades of experience, showed her expertise in the first 22 seconds creating a book cover that had three words (two of them being my name), a cover that spoke volumes about the content of the book.

I want to express my gratitude to Kathy Springmeyer at Farcountry Press and Rick Newby for their support and helpful suggestions.

I would also like to thank all my "Friends of Bill" who have stood by me since 1979 when no one else could or would. In particular and without a doubt, Clancy Imislund, my mentor, who continues to show me how to quit biting the hands of others while they attempt to render assistance.

The influence of Jim Whitlock is indispensable. Ex-Marine, ex-Boy Scoutmaster, ex-photographer, ex-writer, and ex-mayor, he revealed to me the bounty of expedition-type trips into the backcountry of Montana and Idaho, and never mind the damn season.

I would be remiss not to mention Bud and May Richard, who anchored me down each time I came home from Vietnam and beyond.

Finally, I would like to thank the men of old, from Daniel Boone to Joe Cosley, who continue to influence where and how I travel. And all the other writers too numerous to mention who provide the grist for the voracious reader I have become—if I didn't devour books, I wouldn't be the storyteller I seek to be.

table of contents

May 2011 Trip: Hole in the Wall

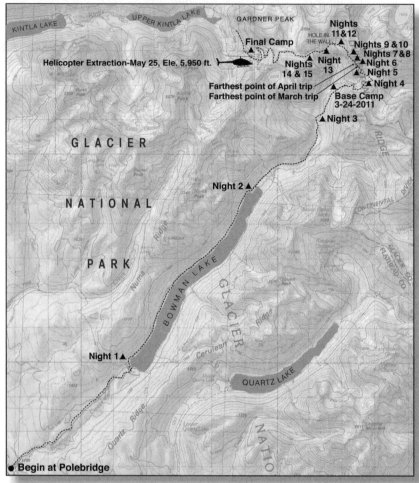

TOPO! © 2011 National Geographic

February 2011 Trip: Belly River

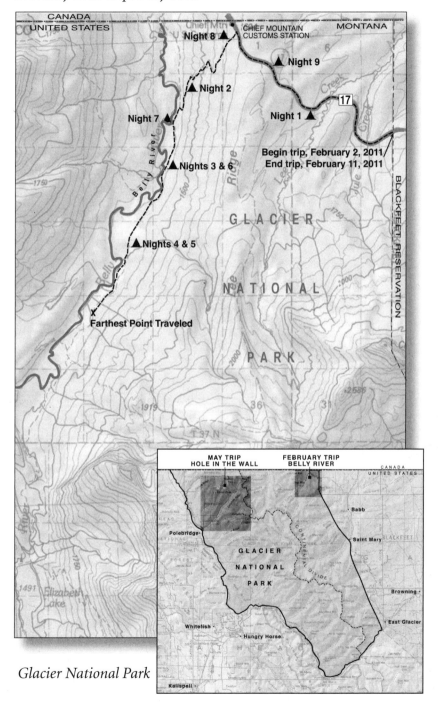

Glacier National Park

1 • rising to the challenge

In the predawn light on May 15, 2011, the swirling clouds lifted—and my heart sank. In the distance, my destination beckoned: Hole in the Wall, a large, snow-filled, bowl-shaped cirque rimmed by ragged, black peaks and saw-toothed arêtes. From where I stood—alone, beyond help, beyond reason, in front of my tent just west of Brown Pass—I knew that the gleaming, untracked snow of Hole in the Wall awaited, an oasis of gently rolling terrain in an otherwise near-vertical world. The distance from my camp to Hole in the Wall was a mere three-quarters of a mile. But I knew that those 4,000 feet were tilted 70 degrees or more, punctuated by cliffs, ravines, and avalanche debris. The snow there was deep and untested—poised to crack, primed to fail. The pit of my stomach went hollow with fear.

The only reason I was standing in this spot was to traverse the slope ahead and enter Hole in the Wall. During summer, hikers stroll here on a well-worn trail cut back into the steep angle of the mountains' flanks, skirting cliffs and contouring easily into the cirque, then on to Boulder Pass and the Kintla Lakes drainage to the west. But May in Glacier's high country is still winter. Seven months of accumulated snow rest uneasily on the mountains, temperatures dive well below freezing, and fast-moving storms dump more snow on the unstable slopes. Park rangers and managers had warned that Hole in the Wall was inaccessible during winter; no one had ever entered the cirque under winter conditions. No one was crazy enough to try. If the deep snow and miserable weather didn't stop an intrepid backcountry traveler, surely the trackless plunge of the traverse from Brown Pass to Hole in the Wall would bring a person to his senses. The sheer slope offered no protection, no safe haven. In short, if you didn't fall to your death, one of the frequent earth-shaking avalanches would surely finish the job.

But I needed to reach Hole in the Wall. If I hoped to succeed in my larger dream of crossing the entire length of Glacier National Park in the winter, I had to prove that this traverse was survivable. The death trap ahead was the keyhole that unlocked Glacier's Livingstone Range and the northwestern end of the route across the park.

My timing could not have been much worse. During the winter of 2010-2011, a La Niña weather pattern hurled storm after moisture-laden storm at Glacier's peaks. By May, the snowpack was 200 percent of average, and the forecast called for yet another train of low-pressure systems to dump more snow. Hole in the Wall's reputation as unassailable seemed secure for at least another year. A sane person would have turned around. I gathered my gear and stepped forward.

Why take the risk? Why even contemplate such a trip in the first place, never mind the even crazier scheme of crossing the entirety of Glacier, alone, in the winter? A simple "Because it's there" wouldn't suffice. If the challenge before me was at all about this particular place, it was even more about a lifetime of rising to challenges, a lifetime of defying the odds as others saw them.

Apparently, this ambition started at an early age during my first year in Arkansas. Among my belongings is a black-and-white photograph from 1952 of a baby boy, clearly less than a year old. He wears a white cloth diaper, nothing else. The infant stands midway on the stairs of a porch, either going up or coming down. On the back of the picture in my mother's handwriting is the name "Richard." This early climbing career was nearly cut short, however, by a bout of infectious colitis. Two neighbor children had died from the colitis, and my mother was caring for their ailing mother, which is likely how I caught the disease. I wasted away for six weeks, until finally, when I was 11 months old, we left Arkansas for Missoula, Montana, where my mother had been born and raised. During the long bus ride north, my mother fed me laudanum-laced sugar water to quiet me, so she could get some rest. When we arrived in Missoula, an aunt asked her doctor for a prescription that finally cleared the colitis. But I bear the scars to this day with a hernia that stretches from my sternum to my lower abdominal muscles. With a weakened immune system, getting grievously sick became a part of my life. In the coming years, I sometimes missed weeks of school.

Other forms of trouble, mostly self-induced, soon developed. Shortly after arriving in Montana, I nearly drowned in a milk bucket on my grandparents' dairy farm, saved at the last moment by my mother. Not long after, I followed my two older brothers to an irrigation ditch. Again, mom came to the rescue. Frantically searching in muddy water up to her neck, she somehow found me and yanked me to the surface. I have no conscious memory of any of these incidents. Yet to this day, I have trouble burying my face in a mummy sleeping bag or walking on ice-covered lakes.

I was the third of eight children. We grew up in a world of poverty surrounded by people with plenty in the Bitterroot Valley. In the late winter of 1960, we lived for one month without electricity; the only light came from candles my mother made from animal tallow. My youngest sibling was six months old when we moved again, this time without our father. By then we had already felt the hunger that went with an empty larder.

Our home for the next three and a half years was three miles from the nearest town. For the first time we knew enough stability to cease going hungry. Nearby pastures and farm fields held an ample supply of Chinese pheasants and an occasional jackrabbit, and local streams provided ducks and trout. We also had a large garden, and across the creek bordering the west side of our yard was a chicken coop that was restocked with 50 chicks and 16 poult turkeys every spring. We also had rabbits and pigs. Our outhouse, a two-seater, had doubled in size.

There was electricity, and eventually a black-and-white TV that sometimes worked. In the boys' bedroom were two sets of bunk beds, one large bed, a boys' community dresser, and a woodstove. The living room held another woodstove, and a third in the kitchen was both a cook stove and water heater. The water heater was almost large enough to get a shower, located in the girls' room. We also finally connected to the rest of society with a telephone.

During that first summer without our father (who was soon enjoying free meals at the Montana State Penitentiary), my mother picked strawberries, raspberries, and blackberries for a farm one mile from our home. She took my two older brothers to help. My younger sister and I cared for our younger siblings, with the two youngest still in diapers. My mother's income, supplemented by government welfare checks, also included medical assistance, a fact that soon became public information. Some of my classmates at school took that to mean we could afford the mental and physical punishment they then inflicted on me. By 1964,

I felt like a lower class of human being, which created a smoldering, but growing fire within me.

In this rural setting, the two older brothers and two of the younger brothers teamed with each other as duos. I tried to tag along with the elder two, although often spurned as too young. Less often, I joined the younger two. Through the years however, I began to go out alone. Growing up in a rural mountainous setting, "going out" meant visiting the river bottom or hiking into the mountains. We lacked money for school activities or fun in town. Even when we eventually moved into the town of Hamilton, population approximately 3,000, our idea of fun usually took us outside city limits.

Throughout my adolescence, evidence mounted that years of illness and deprivation were taking their toll physically and mentally. In 1965, faced with the prospect of a second try at seventh grade, I went into a tailspin. Since I had also repeated the first grade, I was two years older than my classmates, although physically smaller than many of them. My new classmates also included a younger sister. Regardless of my efforts, it seemed I would always fall short. Unwilling to fully resign myself to this fate, I resisted. Unfortunately, the harder I fought, the worse my situation became. My fear of others grew, particularly when they were in groups. For relief, increasingly I wandered the nearby canyons and mountains alone.

If 1965 was a bleak year for me, it also brought a special opportunity—a one-week backcountry trip with the Boy Scout troop from Corvallis, a small town north of Hamilton. I lacked the gear the other boys had, and I suffered during the long, cold nights, but I secretly swooned over the experience. I now had a dream: to spend more time traveling in the backcountry. All I had to do was get some of the gear the others possessed—boots, backpack, tent, cookware, and sleeping bag.

A childhood of hardships had taught me how to live with what little was immediately available. We couldn't afford winter gloves or mittens, so I made do with old socks. A heavy coat was an impossible luxury, so I learned to dress in layers. I found that dead grass stuffed into my shoes could soak up water when a foot went into the creek. Cattails and haystacks offered insulation against the cold. For overnight trips, my kitchen was a cast-iron skillet, which sometimes dug into my back, while my larder consisted of flour or cornmeal, salt, pepper, russet potatoes, and sometimes bacon. Fishing gear gave the promise of protein.

Although I was deeply embarrassed by these makeshift provisions at the time, they became a great asset in later years, a wellspring of self-reliance and assurance in adverse conditions. When taxed to the limit, these life lessons would more than once save my life.

In 1969, two months short of my 18th birthday, I dropped out of high school and abruptly decided to leave town. The U.S. Army offered a way out. The recruiter assured me that if I signed a three-year contract, the Army would train me as a helicopter crew chief. If they fell through on this promise, I could get them on a breach of contract and receive a discharge.

Beyond my very small sphere of attention, I was vaguely aware of the protests and civil unrest against the enormously unpopular Vietnam War. Young men were burning their draft cards, enrolling and loitering in college, and even hiding in Canada—anything to escape the military draft. From where I stood, they looked desperate to avoid a step down into what looked like a step up for me. Over the radio, I listened to a young woman belt out a goodbye song, a country-western singer question Suzy about where the playground was located, and another crooner complaining about one being the loneliest number, which was something I had known for too long. Mostly though, time was tight and I was desperate to get the hell out of a world with no hope.

"And when would you like to leave?" the recruiter asked. "As soon as possible? Is five days too long to wait? It is, but okay?"

When I entered Army basic training, I weighed 155 pounds, and my height at five feet nine inches was as tall as I would ever get. For the next two months, the drill instructors pummeled 150 of us through physical exercise and not enough to eat. On average, most trainees lost weight, some upwards of 40 pounds. I, on the other hand, gained 10 pounds.

The recruiter and the Army held up their end of the contract, even after I decided it was no longer necessary. While I was going through helicopter mechanic training in Alabama, I discovered that the Army was paying already active soldiers to reenlist for six years as helicopter crew chiefs, with a reenlistment payout of $10,000. At the time, that was the highest reenlistment bonus, reserved for critical jobs. By all that I could see, the only thing critical about the helicopter crew chief was there were not enough people signing up. I came cheap. The Army got me for three years with an initial paycheck of $96 per month.

Five months and eight days after enlisting, I arrived in Vietnam.

While waiting at the Long Binh Army base a few days later for permanent assignment, an Army officer asked if any of the several hundred of us would like to volunteer for long-range patrol or Special Forces duty. No one stood up; I too stayed seated. Still feeling like I was on the edge of nothing, my inaction left me feeling soiled. That would be the last time I would say no to avoid combat. Nothing I did, however, eased the load of baggage that came with me when I entered the Army.

In another month, I was beginning to adjust to a monsoon season and copious quantities of red mud several miles south of the Demilitarized Zone, when I volunteered for permanent perimeter guard duty. Eighteen months later, I could look back on surviving several crises, including riding a destroyed helicopter to the ground and a short visit to Laos, where a day earlier enemy gunfire had downed one of our helicopters.

In July 1970, I was nine months inside Vietnam when the Army gave me a 30-day leave. I flew home to Montana. On my return to Vietnam, I brought back pictures and showed them to the small group of my buddies. When we got to the photos of a couple friends and I prepared to go backpacking, my buddies couldn't hide their surprise, which in turn embarrassed me. Leave was supposed to be spent pursuing women, letting your hair grow, and drinking. The thought of leaving the war zone for 30 days and spending any of it in the backcountry seemed ridiculous. In Vietnam, the men often talked about life back home—the women, the food, and the amenities we had taken for granted. There was never any talk, however, about hiking into the backcountry. My buddies yearned to get back to civilization; that sounded good to me, too, but I also craved wilderness. Despite the dangers, I often sought solace during the daytime alone at the bunker, on the perimeter, and sometimes further afield.

Always one to buck the norm, I volunteered for an extra six months in Vietnam. As I prepared to put in for a second six-month extension, the Army said no. On that terrible day in April 1971, one month before I was due to leave Vietnam, the unit's captain saw the rejection written across my 19-year-old face. He put a hand on one of my shoulders, and in a soft voice said, "Someday you will thank me for this, Layne." Sixty days earlier, he had shown nothing but anger and disdain for me. If I was already easy to dislike, my disgusting drinking bouts further drove people away. After the destruction of my helicopter, I arrived as a volunteer at our temporary forward base on the dangerous Khe Sanh plateau located in the northwest corner of South Vietnam. With no alcohol available up there, my sober but abnormally risky actions (such as removing Claymore mines off a perimeter that was on fire or driving an overloaded two-and-a-half-ton truck down a muddy and slimy hill, which no one else was willing to do) soon changed the captain's opinion of me. Now back at our rear area, he probably thought he had just saved my life. It also revalidated that the captain's opinion of me had gone through a revision while we were at Khe Sanh, in spite of my resumed drinking once we returned to our rear base.

That backpacking trip in 1970 was the last one for 13 years. In July 1983, I was divorced with three children. Although unaware of it at the time, I was in the last week of a 15-year drinking binge. No longer employable, I was homeless except for my tolerant but reluctant family members. I asked a brother-in-law to loan me some backpacking gear, a .357 revolver, and several boxes of bullets. Then I attempted to get sane and sober in the one place that had been my comforter since I was a teenager, the Selway-Bitterroot Wilderness. My plan was to return to civilization only to resupply for the remainder of my life. Failing at that, perhaps I would be able to use the pistol to remove the horror that was my life.

Alcoholism is a powerful illness. The mountains did not betray me, but only partly relieved the pain. The first two days I traveled to the end of one canyon and climbed the wall into the next. I woke up dry and comfortable, but to a steady rainfall. The drizzle gave me the excuse I wanted, and I declared I had to get the hell out of there. Five hours and two inadvisable creek crossings later, I sat in a bar near Stevensville with a drink in my hand, suffering from a mild case of hypothermia.

I gradually pulled my life together. In July 1993, remarried, I accompanied my wife, Carleen, a native Montanan, on her first-ever trip into the backcountry. We entered Idaho's Selway-Bitterroot Wilderness for a four-day trip. To make her as comfortable as possible, I borrowed a lightweight tent. I also purchased two closed-cell sleeping pads, lightweight kitchen gear, cheap but genuine hiking boots, ponchos, and two (until then unheard-of) internal frame backpacks. This was far more than I had ever taken into the backcountry. For all of that, at the end of each miserable day Carleen was comfortable and warm inside the tent. Meanwhile I had just rediscovered the security of the mountains and a way to travel in them year-round. In spite of nonstop rain (except when it was snowing), a sprained ankle, and extensive off-trail travel in the jungle of fallen timber, she loved the experience.

During the ensuing years, Carleen and I went on trips of up to two weeks duration in all four seasons. She took to the backcountry like an old hand. Learning quickly, soon she could read a map and compass and was at ease traveling off-trail deep into the wilderness. She also learned to locate water in seemingly dry areas. In August 1999, I thought I lost Carleen when, in a solo test, I sent her through trees and heavy brush in a specific direction for water, using a compass for navigation. She re-appeared an hour later bubbling with excitement, having successfully navigated alone and found the water. Her enthusiasm almost removed the "scared to death" lump lodged in my throat. Shortly after that, we began to carry two-way radios.

In December 1993, with ongoing equipment improvements and additions, Carleen and I began taking more serious winter trips. But in 1996, a particularly hazardous trip into the deep snows of the Selway-Bitterroot made us reconsider the risks. Thereafter, our winter trips together were restricted to the lower elevations of the Selway River canyon on the western side of the Selway-Bitterroot Wilderness, where we repeatedly saw buttercups blooming near the end of January.

Camping gear had changed drastically since I was a teenager. With the stronger and lighter gear came the sense of being able to travel in the most remote areas I could find, and in the worst sort of weather. No matter how bad the day or extreme the environment, I felt that inside the tent was comfort, food, warmth, and security. (Soon enough the outside conditions would permeate the interior of my tent and almost take my life, while removing any residual sense of invulnerability.)

Through the years, the trips grew more difficult until finally I approached a magazine editor with the idea of crossing the Bob Marshall Wilderness in winter and then writing about it. I was unable to say no when she suggested instead that I attempt a winter crossing of Glacier National Park. With multiple years of winter travel inside the Selway-Bitterroot, Bob Marshall, and Scapegoat Wildernesses, I thought that if it was at all possible to make the crossing, I might be the one to do it. I started making winter reconnaissance trips into Glacier, using an ice axe and crampons for the first time. Ultimately, I found myself perched just below the Continental Divide at Ahern Pass staring at an impossible route forward and unable to retreat. I survived what would have been a lethal fall with a well-placed ice axe and then a long night in a tent listening to avalanches roar all around, waiting to be crushed and swept away by the enormous cornice hanging above my campsite. Horrified at the precarious circumstances and utterly exhausted, I swore that if I survived I would never do such a trip again.

Through sheer stubbornness and luck, I did survive, crossing Ahern Pass against all odds. As I drove homeward, I made a phone call to my mentor of 18 years, who resided in Los Angeles. With a growl, he said, "Well, I hope you got that out of your system." As soon as I heard those words, I realized that I had spoken too soon in my despair below the cornice on Ahern. Like a thirsty man whose lips had just touched cool sweet water, I was already yearning for more.

Originally, I sought the backcountry for relief from my fear of people. Now the challenge of staying alive while trekking where few or none have ventured has trumped that reason. Moreover, it is almost impossible to experience quiet solace on the side of a mountain while fearing the next snowpack-shaking avalanche. In the nearly two decades since I returned to the backcountry, old age is nipping at me. The prospect of never again getting to stand atop Ahern or Blodgett Pass in a howling blizzard is in sight. To me that thought is awful, so I continue to resist the inevitable.

Which is how I came to be on the doorstep of Hole in the Wall.

2 • the goal: hole in the wall

May 15, 2011, had turned into a warm and beautiful spring day, the kind that stokes the fires of spring fever. Lying on my back, I stared at the deep blue sky and billowing white clouds. After all the storms I had endured in the three trips since February, the clear weather was wonderful. Today was the sixth day of my fourth and final trip in the northwest region of Glacier National Park during the winter of 2010 to 2011. The mid-afternoon sunlight was bright, with the temperature easily above 50 degrees F. My face was sunburned, even though for at least half the day my direction of travel had put the sun at my back.

Memories of this slope were still fresh from a month earlier. It had been storming for three days, with two more of the same waiting in the wings. I had plowed through three feet of fresh powder on top of a snowpack that was already 200 percent above average. On that April day, I stood inside a scattering of trees on the southern edge of this 60-degree slope. Through the clouds, winds, and snowstorm, I inspected the steep mountainside from the safety of the trees. With clarity, I had seen two things. The first was the avalanche that would have started if I stepped onto the plunging, treeless slope. The second was the verification I needed that, with the right gear and conditions, it was reasonable to approach Hole in the Wall across this same slope. Intent on accomplishing that goal in better conditions, I backed off the slope and backtracked the 20 miles out of the park.

According to the National Park Service, no one had ever traversed this approach and accessed Hole in the Wall in winter conditions. They declared the route impassable. One employee dissented with the park service view, but only after he learned I would be using technical climbing gear.

Now I was 500 feet and four hours into the three-quarter-mile traverse. For every 100 feet of progress, there was 700 feet of traveling back and forth ferrying gear. At the end of each relay, I dug a small flat into the snowpack for the two ferried loads. It was progress, but at a price.

Lying on the slope, as I began to relax and catch my breath, I realized how tired I was. I really should have taken a 10- or 15-minute break two hours earlier. I would have done so, except there had been no safe spot to rest on the steep slope. Shortly after I began the traverse, chunks of snow, ice, rocks, and even some mud started to fall intermittently off the cliffs that towered above the naked slope, compliments of the rapidly warming sunlight. It had only been in the last 100 feet that I had entered an area relatively safe from the falling bombs.

I reflected on how quickly my thinking could change. Just minutes earlier, I had planned to continue across the traverse for another couple of hours before making camp. Accomplishing that would have given me a total of 700 or 800 feet traveled for the day, about one-third of the total distance across the technical portion of the approach. Now I decided that if I ever stood up again I was going to dig out a large flat nearby and make camp. For the second time since March, I was in complete agreement with the park service about this mountainside. I looked beyond my left leg, buried to the knee in the snowpack, and stared longingly at the rope nine feet away and out of reach. If only I had clipped into the rope, I would not now be lying upside down on a near-vertical slope, left foot stuck in the once-hidden hole that had felled me in the first place.

As near as I could tell, that hole was the only reason I had not shot down the slope 300 feet and over the cliff to my death. I expected the hole to lose its grip on my leg at any moment. Still resting but getting ready to move, I decided that if I survived this, come tomorrow I would pack my gear and go home. The decision sounded suspiciously like the scoundrel's bargaining prayer, "God, if you get me out of this one . . . I will never do this again."

It was a lesson well learned. Some 68 hours later, still on the approach, my next fall was much worse, except this time I was clipped to the rope.

An Introduction to the Park

My winter trips of 2011 had their beginnings in December 2005, when I was in the process of planning a winter route to cross Glacier National Park. One crisp December morning I approached a neighbor, who was a regular backcountry visitor of the park. Since I had never been in Glacier, I thought I would talk to him about a possible route. His first recommendation was a strong statement to stay out during the winter. Seeing that I intended to go anyway, he soon pointed a finger at 7,100-foot Ahern Pass.

Later, in my office, I found the pass on the topographic map software on my computer. I also spotted a much tamer looking Stoney Indian Pass that topped out at 6,908 feet several miles north of Ahern. I immediately went against my neighbor's second recommendation and pointed myself toward Stoney. During the ensuing two months, I continued to prep for the trips, which included studying the maps. It was during that time that I spotted Hole in the Wall several miles west of Stoney Indian Pass. The name was immediately captivating and odd, like something from a bad B Western movie. More intriguing were the contour lines on the topographic map showing one helluva bowl in treeless avalanche terrain, with the eastern trail into it traversing a wall 2,000 feet above the canyon floor.

In February 2006, during my second trip into the Belly and Mokowanis River canyons, I almost froze to death. Too intimidated to continue the route, my next four trips were aimed at Ahern Pass. After successfully crossing Ahern's lethal, exposed cliffs and frequent avalanches, I again approached my neighbor, this time inquiring about Hole in the Wall. He instantly pointed out that dynamite had been a major ingredient for building the trail in the near-cliff terrain. I left the conversation with the impression that I must never go near that location during the winter. I backed off, but never quite put that spot on the map out of my mind.

During the spring of 2009, I started working on the most difficult challenge I would ever face, one that said if I could complete it, then I should retire. It would involve snowshoeing 900 miles along the spine of the Rocky Mountains. While there were many dangerous bottlenecks along the entire journey—particularly within Glacier—by my reckoning, if only one location blocked me from successfully completing the trip it would be Hole in the Wall, just 30 miles from the finish line. For this reason, I knew at some point I would have to access the cirque prior to attempting the longer journey.

An Autumn Scouting Trip

In the latter days of August 2010, I decided to plan a second winter crossing of Glacier. The trip would begin at the Belly River and end at Kintla Lake. Along this route, I would have to cross Stoney Indian, Brown, and Boulder Passes. The real target, however, was Hole in the Wall. I wanted to cross the entire park, at the same time attempting to access this high-elevation cirque because I needed a genuine test of my endurance. And I harbored a strong desire to make it over Stoney Indian Pass. There were also some winter ghosts to exorcise from the near-fatal February 2006 trip in Belly and Mokowanis River canyons.

Unlike the first crossing four years earlier, this time I was determined to know what I was getting into before winter arrived. I had no doubt this route would be less forgiving than the one that had taken me from the Belly River on the east side to McDonald Creek on the west side of Glacier in 2006. I left during the last week of September. On the third day, I crossed 6,908-foot Stoney Indian Pass and arrived at the backcountry campground at Stoney Indian Lake west of the pass. My neighbor back in Helena had been right that this area was one big avalanche chute, though I noted it was less dangerous than Ahern Pass. While timing would be critical, travel through the area was doable. I moved on—so far, so good.

The route zigzagged north and west along upper Waterton Valley and Olson Creek, both broad enough to present minimal avalanche hazard. At the summit of 6,255-foot Brown Pass, the Boulder Pass Trail intersected with the Bowman Lake Trail. To the right, Boulder Pass Trail cut across the huge and almost treeless south face of 9,406-foot Chapman Peak. Below the trail and extending west from the pass, a mile-long bench of small rolling hills and stunted pine trees suggested that most of the area was repeatedly hammered by avalanches. Though still hidden around the curve on the trail one mile ahead, Hole in the Wall was less than one and three-quarter miles distant. Beyond that, the Boulder Pass Trail threaded cliffs to the pass itself just north of 8,528-foot Boulder Peak. Even this late in the season, its ragged wall, 4,000 feet above the canyon floor, held shimmering snow and ice fields reflecting the autumn sun. The scene was both breathtaking and discouraging.

My topographic map indicated that beyond the steep ridgeline that hid Hole in the Wall, the terrain was far steeper than the area around the Brown Pass bench. Decades of using this type of map, whose contour lines were in 40-foot increments, was difficult to unlearn, which was precisely what the Glacier National Park maps required. The contour lines on the park map were in 80-foot increments, deceptive for someone accustomed to the more finely detailed maps. The 40-foot increments would have shown the steep angles of the slopes. By doubling the footage between the lines, the park map hid 70-foot cliffs and distorted my ability to discern the true angle of the slopes. I couldn't read the terrain while sitting in my office back in Helena; I needed to see it firsthand. Before I left Brown Pass, as I compared the map to the view of Boulder Peak, my doubts grew about being able to access Hole in the Wall during winter. The first one-third mile of the bench was the most dangerous. In that area, Chapman Peak towered nearly 3,200 feet above the bench. As high and dangerous as the peaks were around Stoney Indian Pass, nothing over there compared to this. Just before I went around the curve of the ridgeline, I turned around and looked once more at Brown Pass and the bench. I could not know that the incoming winter's powerful avalanches would alter that view for the next 50 years.

As I went around the bend, the angle of the slope was approximately 45 degrees. In spite of that, I was encouraged to see a scattering of 12- to 24-inch-thick trees. They would provide a safe launch point to begin the traverse. On the other side of the trees and bushes, my heart dropped, and all that fresh encouragement disappeared. The sedimentary rock and dirt face of the approach, was a jumble of 60- to 80-degree angles with numerous cliffs, some hundreds of feet high. To have any hope of traversing the approach, it was obvious that I would need more than an ice axe and crampons. How much more weight in climbing gear would I need to add to what would be an already heavy load?

And how would I explain this to Carleen? She was a homegrown western Montanan and knew about Glacier's shocking 100-foot-deep snowdrifts and cliff-like mountainsides. The fatal mauling of backpackers by grizzly bears in 1967 had cured her of any desire to visit the park's backcountry. Nor had Carleen's fear of the park subsided with my reports from the trips I took in 2006. If anything, her disquiet increased, particularly after seeing the photographs. That same trepidation had her making phone calls to park personnel when I went overdue by one day, something she had done only once when I went overdue in a wilderness. Now I needed to find a way to explain to her the ease of a route that had never been accomplished, which also happened to require technical gear if I was to have any chance to get across. While I could trivialize the details of the terrain, and neglect to show certain photographs, I would be unable to hide the equipment purchases.

I also got a first look at what the map was unable to show below the trail. If I fell, I would have 2,000 feet of tumbling drop space to contemplate where I had gone wrong. The beautiful autumn scenery was unable to hide a terrain that would show little forgiveness in a fall during the winter. I tried to shake the view by reminding myself that this was only a scouting trip.

Several minutes into the traverse, I came around a second and smaller ridgeline. The trail cut into a cliff and ravine 200 feet ahead, and then made a sharp left turn. Without a doubt, this elbow-like area was the most treacherous part of the approach. Up to here, as hazardous as it would be when covered in snow and ice, the approach seemed feasible. Yet even if the rest of the approach was passable, this nearly vertical ravine could be a death trap. The map showed that the indentation continued to nearly the top of the ridge, a quarter mile away and 1,600 feet above me. The avalanches here would be powerful and frequent.

I filled my water bottle from the small stream splashing onto the trail and continued up the path. Several feet beyond the elbow the trail skirted a large overhang, forming a sizable cave 10 feet deep in the cliff face. If I could get this far, the cave might provide a safe haven for the night. The hollow in the cliff could spell the difference between living and dying. As I walked away, I wondered who I was fooling. To shelter in the cave meant that I would have to get there first.

Several minutes later and 1,000 feet beyond the elbow, I entered the sparsely treed, one-and-a-quarter-mile-wide bowl of Hole in the Wall. The scene was spectacular. Like a fortress wall, the peaks and scoured ridgelines loomed over the tiered cirque. High on the flank of 8,883-foot Mount Custer, snowfields fed meltwater into a crevice—the headwaters of Bowman Creek. The rivulet collected other runoff and meandered across the base of the bowl before spilling off the lip of the 1,600-foot cliff to the floor of Bowman Creek canyon far below. Perched so high above the canyon, the cirque felt cut off, orphaned. I recalled the somber tone of the park rangers when they said that, after some heavy snowpack years, the area remained inaccessible into August.

I stopped at a fork in the trail. To the left, a dead-end spur trail dropped 300 feet into the main bowl to the backcountry campground a half mile away. On this scouting trip, I would follow the main trail to the right, staying high on the side of the bowl in a gradual ascent to Boulder Pass. As I continued to survey the cirque, I noticed the southwestern edge of the bowl held trees that were larger than saplings—a zone of relative safety from avalanches in this otherwise exposed terrain. I made a mental note: this is where I would ascend the 1,200 feet out of Hole in the Wall to Boulder Pass.

My attitude about the route had clearly changed. Just minutes ago back on Brown Pass, I was fairly convinced that the traverse to Hole in the Wall would be too dangerous in winter. Yet as soon as I entered the beautiful autumn bowl, I began to make a mental inventory of what equipment I would need to make the traverse. Over the next several months, I felt pangs of hesitation and even dread about the pending attempt. From that day in the bowl forward, however, I never had a doubt that I would do all I could to return in the snowpack.

A La Niña Winter

Before I left on the scouting trip, the National Oceanic and Atmospheric Administration (NOAA) announced that another La Niña weather pattern would dominate through the winter. For western Montana that normally meant more storms and moisture interspersed with brief but intense cold spells. In September, NOAA was yet unable to predict how strong or long the La Niña would be.

By the end of October, 20 inches of snow blanketed the ground at 6,400-foot Flattop Mountain, 11 miles southeast of Hole in the Wall. On December 1, the snowpack had grown to 49 inches. Though somewhat alarmed, I knew the weather could change. Many times I had seen winter start strong and then ease off after December 1. Later that month, NOAA declared that the La Niña event was strengthening. The winter storms continued unabated through December and January.

On December 11, I headed for the park with a 12-day supply of food and fuel and a plan to be gone for 9 days on the route to Stoney Indian Pass. As I drove north, the thick and low-hanging clouds of the latest storm clung to the peaks along the Rocky Mountain Front while above me was winter's fierce blue sky. There was a gusting crosswind, which dared me to be a sightseer as I drove.

Being the weekend, there was no one at Glacier's Hudson Bay Ranger Station in St. Mary on the east side of the park. A few days earlier, I had called for a permit, which was supposed to be in the permit box located next to the main office door. The box was empty. Although I had been vague with the park employee about my timing, I blamed the park service anyway. With grinding teeth, I continued north past Babb and then on the Chief Mountain Highway. Alone inside the van, I threatened aloud to head into the backcountry without the permit. I knew however, I would eventually go to Apgar on the west side of Glacier and get one issued.

Before I headed west though, I wanted to check the condition of the snowpack at the winter trailhead for the Belly River canyon. At the closed gate, which was also the border between the Blackfeet Indian Reservation and the park, the snow was approximately three feet deep with at least one foot of fresh powder on top, perfect for having a damned miserable trip.

There was also something wrong with my nasal passage and throat. As I drove away from the gate I decided that rather than go to Apgar, I had better head the 240 miles back home. As it turned out, I had the beginnings of a nasty cold.

The storms kept coming and building the snowpack. With every storm, my worry inched upward as the already above-average snowpack grew. By mid-January, I wondered if the trip had become an impossible venture. I briefly considered a postponement until the following year. Then I shrugged the thought off. There was more riding on this than a mere crossing.

With the snowpack continuing to pile up and no new information to alter my thinking, I kept coming back to the same ending: the possibility of abandoning Hole in the Wall when I arrived there from the Belly River, except that meant I would be abandoning the real reason for the route. Without the cirque, the trip would be worthless.

A small window opened beginning February 2 when there would be two days of travel before more weather set in. There would also be a five-day window before subzero temperatures arrived. That ought to be enough days to prepare my body for the intense cold. Carrying a load of over 90 pounds, I would be returning to the Belly and Mokowanis River canyons, and if conditions permitted, Stoney Indian Pass.

3 • old man and the winter

February 2: A Tough Beginning

I drove away from Helena in the dark, just after 4 A.M. with the temperature 11 degrees below zero. The forecast called for a mostly sunny day with a high of 33 F. in Belly River canyon. A high-pressure ridge accompanied by subzero temperatures had shoved the latest storm out a few days before, but not before it dropped another foot of snow. I was certain I would be pushing powder from the trailhead. Since part of the reason for this trip was mental and physical training, I was looking forward to the challenge the fresh powder would likely provide. I could only hope it wouldn't prevent me from scouting the route over Stoney Indian Pass. While I knew the chances were slim, I was also hoping the snowpack would soften today and then harden into a crust overnight. Wearing the large Atlas backcountry snowshoes, and given the heavy load I would be packing, a firm crust would allow me to travel 6 to 10 miles per day.

I had been driving north for 30 minutes, dictating notes into my audio recorder when the machine went dead, the result of two depleted lithium AAA batteries I had forgotten to replace. To compound the problem, the spare batteries were also dead, depleted during a trip in October. While there were alkaline spares inside the van, they would last only a short time in the cold. I also had five untouched lithium batteries stored in my more than 90-pound backpack, although three were spares reserved for the head lantern. Another forgotten item was the latest avalanche report. That was less concerning, because by the time I arrived in avalanche terrain, the report would likely be obsolete.

In preparing for each trip, I would pack and repack the load. This trip had been no exception. I had added some items missed on the previous outing and removed a few, such as the weighty tripod and head. In the darkness of my warm vehicle, I now wondered what else I had forgotten.

I drove for an hour under a star-filled sky and was on the plains of the Rocky Mountain Front when the chinook crosswinds arrived. Within minutes the temperature increased by 30 degrees. I arrived at Hudson Bay Ranger Station on the east side of the park four hours after leaving Helena.

Although the park employees more loosely enforced the park's permit system during the winter, they were still insistent about having dates and locations for each night I spent in the backcountry. I told the permit writer I would try to make it the 21 miles to Stoney Indian Pass in five days. I knew that such a distance would be impossible in unconsolidated powder snow. Even with a good crust to walk on, I wondered if I was strong enough to complete the 42-mile round-trip—and 2,800-foot elevation gain—in the nine days allotted.

If I did make it though, I would achieve my goal of seeing firsthand almost one-third of my planned route across Glacier in winter. The next step would be to inspect the western third of the route, scouting the approach to Hole in the Wall, entering from the west side of the park at Bowman Lake. If I succeeded as well on that western leg—reaching Brown Pass and a clear view of the cliffs and avalanche paths guarding the inner approach to Hole in the Wall—then I would finally have the knowledge necessary to attempt crossing Glacier National Park in winter conditions. To be possible though, these first two trips would each have to work with almost no hitches. Frankly, I had never had a series of trips without encountering problems. Yet I remained hopeful.

Winter weather was a critical factor in my decisions about when, where, and how far I would travel on any given trip into Glacier's backcountry. Temperature extremes, high winds, and heavy snowfall all could conspire against my plans. As it turned out, I could have picked a better year than the La Niña winter of 2011 to attempt the crossing. A steady stream of storms battered the park, continually adding to the already above-average snowpack. More importantly, the lengthier a trip, the less I could count on predictable forecasts. The longer I ventured into the backcountry, the more exposed I would be to the fast-moving La Niña storms and potentially lethal weather. Nevertheless, based on my previous two winter trips in the area, I placed the first camp on the permit at Belly River Ranger Station, 9.4 miles from the trailhead. Accomplishing that, I would enter the Mokowanis River canyon and try to get to the upper end of Glenns Lake, another 7.6 miles, by the second or third day. Beyond Glenns Lake was where I would encounter avalanche terrain as I attempted to summit Stoney Indian Pass 4 miles beyond the lake.

Just before 11 A.M., at the closed gate on Chief Mountain Highway two miles east of Chief Mountain, I hefted my backpack and started walking toward Chief Mountain Customs Station three miles ahead. The customs station marks the Canadian border and also the location of the summer trailhead for the Belly River Trail. Fittingly, for the start of such an audacious plan as mine, the Belly River trailhead is also one of two locations that through-hikers on the Continental Divide Trail use as the beginning or end of their route, the other being Goat Haunt on the southern end of Upper Waterton Lake. Just to reach the summer trailhead, I first had to cover three miles in the rolling hills separating Glacier's jagged peaks from the eastern prairies. Like a winding white snake, the snow-covered road gently ascended and descended north through aspen and pine forest.

With approximately three feet of snowpack, which included at least one foot of fresh snow, the first day of my less-than-realistic clockwork plan immediately began to unravel. At each step, the 300-pound combined weight of my backpack and me shoved the snowshoes through the powder, and then partially broke through the crust beneath. Within minutes, the warm sun in the open areas combined with plowing through the snow had me drenched in sweat. I soon shed the jacket and fleece vest. It took an hour to travel the three-quarter-mile, 100-foot descent from my van into the draw of Jule Creek.

The huge, heavy backpack was torturous. A few minutes after beginning the climb out of Jule Creek, I began to think that, in these conditions, 20 pounds less on my back would have been ample for a strength and endurance trip, and never mind trying to get to Stoney Indian Pass. To make things worse, the sciatic nerve that had plagued me for a year and a half on my left side had flared up. I had little doubt that the heavy load combined with my inconsistent exercise since October had plenty to do with the problem.

Nearly two hours and barely over a mile from where I started, I halted at Lee Creek Bridge, removed the backpack, and sat on it. An hour's rest later and still tired, I left the backpack behind and packed a trail two miles through the powder, arriving at the summer trailhead at the customs station one hour later. During the return trip to my backpack, I decided to hold off using the trail until the next morning.

With thin clouds now covering the western sky, I set up camp a third of a mile beyond Lee Creek Bridge, 50 feet off the road and on the edge of a meadow. Disgusted, tired, in pain, and discouraged, the thought of abandoning the trip came strongly. In five and a half hours of travel, I was little more than a mile from the van. Was I too old and out of shape for such a trip?

Shortly after crawling into the tent, my anger emerged and I caustically recalled the part of the trip that concerned physical and mental training.

"If that's what this trip is all about," I howled, "then the first day has been one helluva good day."

Too tired to cook and with no appetite, I nevertheless crammed down a cold supper. Regardless of how the food got into me, within a short time its effect was soothing and soon had me thinking more rationally.

Later I gave more serious consideration of the effect my age had on the day's travel. Three years earlier on a winter trip in the Selway-Bitterroot Wilderness, by the end of each day and into the following morning, I had felt this same weakness. Discouraged with the daily experience, I nevertheless groused at growing old gracefully, and completed the trip. Although I covered a distance of 150 miles and spent 40 days in the Selway-Bitterroot that winter, the experience left me indelibly marked by the signs of old age.

Now at the end of my first day back in Glacier National Park, fed and warm in my sleeping bag, I balked at the thought of quitting. With a packed trail through the powder to the trailhead, I told myself aloud that the next day would be easier, and gave friendly counsel that the first day was always the most difficult.

As if on cue, I was jolted back into the moment by severe leg cramps. I had let myself get dehydrated. Now each time I got rid of a cramp, I gulped down a couple mouthfuls of water. Sometime after midnight, a headache arrived as a final reminder to drink more water.

February 3: Belly River Canyon

The forecast for the night and following day called for breezy weather. That turned out to be understated. Through the night, the wind drifted snow into the trail I had built, filling much of it. The next morning, it took me an hour and forty minutes to arrive at the Chief Mountain Customs Station and Belly River trailhead. During that time, I decided that besides Stoney Indian Pass, even Cosley and Glenns Lakes were out of reach. Getting to the Belly River Ranger Station in the canyon below would have to be enough. This also meant I would have to make an additional trip at a later date to get a look at Stoney Indian Pass. Disheartened, I refused to turn around and go home, still holding out for a possible improvement in snowpack conditions. Besides, slogging through the soft snow was certainly providing the strength and endurance training I was after.

I rested for 25 minutes before I stepped into the snowpack that covered the Belly River Trail. The valley floor was less than two miles away and 760 feet below the parking lot at the trailhead. I immediately began to plow through powder in a forest that still had snow on the Douglas-fir and lodgepole pine tree branches. Less than an hour later, I emerged out of the thick forest of the upper portion of the canyon wall and into small clearings—and deeper snowdrifts. I dropped the backpack and started packing a trail.

As the day wore on, the opaque clouds of that morning thickened in the west. Now able to see the Belly and Mokowanis River canyons, I watched the storm build. By 3 P.M., it had consumed everything behind 7,933-foot Pyramid Peak, which was only one mile west of the Belly River Ranger Station. Hidden inside the storm were Cosley and Glenns Lakes. Behind Glenns Lake and 2,000 feet higher was Stoney Indian Pass. Already traveling in at least two feet of old snow with a foot of fresh powder on top, I wondered how much deeper the snowpack would be inside the Mokowanis River canyon, not to mention atop Stoney Indian Pass. Knowing the forecast and seeing what was happening six miles away further convinced me that the forecast might have fallen short.

The wind continued its relentless blowing; intermittent raindrops began to smack my face. If the temperature dropped, soaked gear that froze would be dangerous. In the meantime, the warmer temperature converted the powder into a wet, clingy, and heavy snowpack. Back to being discouraged, I again thought about turning back. I dropped the backpack for the second and final time that day where I would build the second camp. Before setting up camp, though, I finished packing a trail to the canyon floor.

This camp was 150 feet up the canyon wall inside a semi-open stand of aspen trees. My disgust at the location was worse than the previous night. On my first winter trip into Glacier five years earlier, I had camped 100 feet from this same spot. On that occasion, I had traveled five hours to arrive here from my vehicle at the gate on Chief Mountain Highway. Now, on this day, I traveled for six hours and covered only three miles. Later, inside the sleeping bag, I recalled that on that first trip in 2006 there had been so little snow the snowshoes went unused for the entire trip.

February 4: Belly River Canyon Floor

Morning arrived with no letup in the wind or warm temperatures. Half an hour after leaving camp, I entered a cluster of large cottonwood trees on the canyon floor four miles north of the Belly River Ranger Station at the foot of 9,762-foot Gable Mountain. This river valley at some points was half a mile wide and nearly level to just past the ranger station. Though I knew it was a stretch, I was hoping by the end of the day to be at Belly River Ranger Station.

The wind and spring-like temperatures created another day of wet snowpack to push through. I dropped the backpack twice and packed trail. During the first leg, the weather careened from sunshine, to rain, snow, and snow pellets, all in a nonstop wind. Oddly, yesterday's storm on the peaks looked no closer, while east of me on the plains and sometimes over my head was a cloudless sky.

The barometric pressure continued to drop. My altimeter eventually showed an elevation 250 feet higher than the topographic map for the same location. With the inevitable storm coming, I thought I was ready. Snowfall I could live with, but I was less confident about my ability to survive in colder temperatures.

In spite of the storm buildup, I continued to hope there would be a crust to walk on the next day. For three days, I had either pushed through powder or slugged it out with wet snow, while much of the trail I packed was a foot-deep trough.

On the second leg, returning to my backpack, I ran out of steam. As I passed a small stream near the former Threemile Campsite, I decided to retrieve my backpack and set up the night's camp at the edge of a grove of aspen trees. With the creek flowing through a thick stand of Douglas-fir trees 100 feet away, tonight I would have water without having to melt snow.

At one and a half miles beyond the previous night's camp and less than six and a half miles from my van back on the highway, the distance was disgraceful. Now, almost certain that even the Belly River Ranger Station was out of reach, I decided to press on one more day before I turned back.

Four months earlier, I had made a late autumn trip on this same trail. Two families, including two toddlers, had trekked in behind me. We spent the night at Gable Campground near the ranger station. They had needed part of a day to travel the six miles from the parking lot and summer trailhead. Now with the Gable Campground still three miles away, I gloomily reflected on that autumn day, and thought about how old and fat I was. If conditions remained unchanged by the next morning, I would be unable to get there in four days. Tired, I fell into a restless sleep at 6:30 P.M.

4 • the snowstorm

February 5: The Storm

I woke up hungry at 11 P.M. and ate a day's ration of peanuts. I stayed awake for another three hours, then slept and rose late at 7 A.M. Unaware of what had taken place overnight, as I prepared to light the stove I opened the top of the vestibule for venting. Snow spilled through the hole onto the stove, pillow, sleeping bag, and the back of my neck. I finally stopped cursing after I had a flame on the stove. With the coffeepot on, I opened the vestibule a little more and looked around. Three inches of snow had fallen.

After 21 hours in camp, it was noon when I left. In the continuing snowfall, I felt great, although I had reasons enough not to. As I began to trek up the nearly smothered trail I had packed the previous day, I realized I had been wrong about how much snow had fallen. There was closer to one foot of fresh powder. In the open areas, barely able to discern my one-foot-deep tracks of the day before, I needed an hour to travel the half-mile trail. At the top of a rare small climb in that area of the canyon, I dropped the backpack where yesterday's packed trail ended and continued another two miles up the canyon, plowing through the powder like a young man. I turned around at a small stream a half mile short of Gable Campground and began the return trip to my backpack.

I had been packing trail for three hours, feeling strong. But before I reunited with my backpack, I ran out of steam. I pressed on, retrieving the backpack and soldiering down the trail again toward Gable Campground, but it was too much. Snow continued to fall, filling the day's tracks. Doubting that my packed trail would exist the following morning, I nevertheless abandoned the last mile and made camp in an aspen grove near another nameless creek.

Inside the tent, I castigated myself for yet another low-mileage day and the entire trip's travel. In five hours, this new camp was a mere one and a quarter miles beyond the previous night's camp. Were my days of winter travel over? In four days, except for cinching the waist belt tighter, the end of each day felt the same. Granted, I was pushing through powder and carrying 90 pounds, but in my mind these were thin excuses for how little I was accomplishing. In particular, I focused on my age, which only fed my discouragement.

Throughout the night, I listened to the snowfall build up and slide off the tent. With the rising barometric pressure, eventually the storm would dissipate and the forecast temperature drop would happen. For tonight, though, the snow buildup on the roof and sides of the tent kept the interior warm. I slept without my customary fleece cap and vest.

February 6: More Snowfall

After nine hours of sleep, I was up a little after 5 A.M. Like the day before, I had the normal two cups of coffee and hot stew breakfast while I took my time preparing for the day. The slower pace came from the increased soreness in my body. My knees were swollen and painful. The sciatic nerve in my hip was now troublesome not just on the trail but also in the tent and the sleeping bag. My shoulders hurt, and my hands would go numb if I kept my elbow bent for an extended period or while lying on either of my sides in the sleeping bag. When I laid flat on my back, the small of my back was increasingly painful.

The skin on my fingers was also splitting. Inconsequential the day before, overnight they had become painful. I had been applying barrier cream, but apparently not enough. Such skin splits are normal during winter trips. Skin is soft and pliable because of the moisture on the skin. In the low-humidity winter environment, this moisture evaporates rapidly off the skin, leaving it dry and brittle, opening the door for painful splits, which eventually bleed. The condition can become debilitating enough to be dangerous. Five years earlier inside this same canyon, my fingers became so sore I had trouble lighting a fire on the stove, tying my boots, and managing a host of other everyday tasks that required the use of my hands.

After finishing the coffee, I applied more Badger Healing Balm and did so again after washing the dishes. I also pulled on a pair of heavy-duty nitrile gloves. This recent addition to my backcountry winter gear had proved to be a vital one. Besides helping keep my skin from cracking, they had other uses.

I could briefly hold hot containers, handle the camera and lens in subzero temperatures, dig around in the snow, or place my hands into a cold stream without the instant danger of frostbite. So far, in my experience they had but one downside, in that my skin became too soft inside the gloves. Eventually they would also take on a repulsive odor. I could live with the smell, but injured hands were dangerous.

This was the fifth morning, turnaround day. I balked at the thought. I had packed a trail up the canyon more than one mile beyond this point, and goddamned if I would let it go to waste. However, on a hunch of where the day would actually go, instead of breaking camp, I shoved approximately 40 pounds of gear into the backpack and crawled out of the tent.

On the other side of the camp, the trail I worked so hard to engrave one and a half feet deep into the snowpack the day before had disappeared beneath the overnight snowfall. Amazed and a little disgusted at the sight, I hefted the load and began pushing through the powder toward Gable Campground.

The barometric pressure had risen through the night, creating an apparent elevation drop of 235 feet. Through thinning clouds around the peaks to the west, I could see hints of blue sky. In the windless calm, the scene 300 feet from camp was breathtaking. I sacrificed some of my energy and ascended a treeless, 25-foot knoll on my left to photograph the canyon.

My feet were cold 20 minutes later when I dropped back down to where my trail once was. For 10 minutes, I struggled through deep powder. After 500 feet, I came to a gasping stop and asked myself why I was continuing up the canyon. With nearly two and a half feet of snow dropped in the last 36 hours, how would the exit be quicker than it took to get in? Obviously, I was going the wrong way. Beneath an increasingly open sky, I began to repack the trail down the canyon, bypassing my partially buried camp.

Almost four and a half hours after leaving camp, I noticed that the barometric pressure was falling again when I turned around at Threemile Campsite. I arrived back at my previous night's camp six hours after leaving it. Tired, I was ready to quit. As I approached the tent, I boiled over in anger and snarled that I had now packed the trail three times in some areas of the canyon and was going to travel across some of the same ground six times. This trip had come straight off hell's game board. Meanwhile, more goddamned snow was in the offing. The chill in the air was also indicative of a cold night ahead. I was asleep by 7:30 P.M.

5 • arctic cold revisited

February 7: The Third Snow

Overnight, the temperature dropped below zero, compelling me to stay in the sleeping bag until 7:45 A.M. Much of the drinking water in the 96-ounce bladders froze despite their close proximity to my body. Although the barometric pressure was rising once again, when I looked outside I was discouraged to see that nearly another foot of snow had fallen overnight.

In addition to the normal morning activities, I spent the rest of the morning thawing equipment. As I took down the tent, I had to use a shovel to dig it out of the snow and ice. In the process, I accidentally scraped a pole sleeve on the side of the tent. That earned me a one-inch tear in the nearly new fabric. Then using the heat of my armpits, I thawed the frozen tent pole joints, which took time. Since it was too cold to stand still while thawing the poles, I paced and repacked the trail to the stream's edge. I stayed warm, the poles finally came apart, and in the process, I re-created the nearly buried trail. The downside was that it took one and a half hours to break down and pack the tent.

By the time I was ready to go, the temperature was approximately 9 F. and it was 3 P.M. Several minutes later, I left the fresh trail and crossed the small stream. Actually, it was more of a barely controlled fall across the 6-foot-deep ravine. I slid down the bank easily enough, but the stream's thin ice instantly broke beneath my snowshoes. I stepped quickly and scrambled up the other side of the ravine, which luckily enough was less steep. Somehow, I managed to avoid accumulating much slush and water. In the arctic cold, ice-bound snowshoes would add more weight on my already taxed legs and feet and increased resistance as I plowed through the snow. I was fortunate to clamber out of the creek without a real dunking.

A day earlier, I had crossed without any complications, but then my load had only been 40 pounds instead of nearly 90.

It came as no surprise that much of the trail from the day before no longer existed. A couple of times, I came close to dropping the backpack to repack the trail. In one open and nearly level quarter-mile leg through a meadow, I plowed through the powder for forty-five minutes, stopping every six to eight minutes. After two and a half hours and one and a quarter miles, I arrived at Threemile Campsite. Although I failed to grasp it on this day, a week later I would realize that, with increased endurance, this sixth day of travel was vastly better than the first few days.

With darkness less than an hour out, and the temperature dropping fast, I was careful but quick to set up camp. Constant movement was crucial until I could get in the tent and fire up the stove. In my last act before crawling into the tent, I filled two bladders of water at the nearby stream, which was rapidly freezing from the rocky bottom upward, an indication the temperature had gone subzero.

February 8: The Enemy of My Enemy

That night the arctic cold came for a visit. I woke up several times and jogged inside my sleeping bag to warm myself. The failed sleeping system consisted of a down mummy sleeping bag with a rating of zero degree's Fahrenheit stuffed inside a zippered fleece blanket. Both layers were inside a light bivy sack and lay on two pads, which for their part kept the frozen ground from sucking the heat out of my body. Near midnight, I pulled on a fleece jacket and then added a lighter fleece vest. While the extra layers helped, I still had to jog in place several times until I got up at 6 A.M.

Although they lay next to my body through the night, the water bottle and bladders were frozen solid. That happened only when the temperature was colder than 20 degrees below zero. The cold had also affected the digital thermometer in my altimeter watch. The manufacturer boasted that the thermometer was accurate down to 19 degrees below zero, which explained the obviously wrong reading of 9 F. That also meant I did not know how cold it was. Real cold! I slipped the watch into a pants pocket and began the process of getting it warm, dry, and once again functioning accurately. I also decided that I had had enough. When I got back to civilization, I was going to buy a thermometer that gave indoor/outdoor readings simultaneously and was capable of accurately reading the temperature down to at least 40 degrees below zero.

There were two important functions in the watch for extended backcountry winter travel: an altimeter and a thermometer. The altimeter kept me informed of what sort of weather was coming, thereby giving me a chance to prepare or get out of the way. In a lesser role, and in conjunction with a topographic map and compass, the altimeter was also a navigation aid. Although the altimeter was more vital, it was still important to have an accurate temperature reading.

In light of how vulnerable this device was in winter conditions, I would have replaced it many years before. However, I had found nothing on the market that had all of the functions I wanted, including the ability to upload the daily logs onto the computer back in the office.

Like a day earlier, I walked down a nearly snow-filled trail while I thawed the tent poles in my armpits, except this morning took less time. That was probably attributable to only spending one night in this camp, thereby minimizing the moisture buildup. At 11:20 A.M., I hefted the backpack and continued down the Belly River canyon. I traveled 150 feet to the end of the fresh trail and stopped. Unlike the day before, there was now three days of snow on top of the trail I had laboriously packed earlier in the trip. Pushing through it with this load was out of the question. I dropped the backpack and was back to packing trail.

Because of the trouble with the watch earlier, with the exception of the thermometer, I quit watching for weather changes. Besides, I decided the cold was here to stay for a while. In the early part of the walk, the clouds still covered most of the sky, with many hovering on the higher peaks. They were also an indication of how fortunate I had been last night. With the clouds came lingering warmth, but that was about to change. In the first 25 minutes after leaving camp, the clouds dissipated and, for the first time since the trip's first day, there was more sky than clouds. The sun eventually emerged, and within minutes the temperature rose enough that I began shedding layers of clothing.

Blue sky and snow—beautiful, yes, but also a reminder that I had been in this canyon before under similar conditions. Just eight days shy of five years ago, I nearly froze to death one interminable night here. The similarities brought the memory back fresh and raw. With that in mind, today I would put in an extra effort to get off the Belly River canyon floor. It would be better to be on the canyon wall rather than down here when the real cold arrived this evening.

Half an hour later, I was a quarter mile short of beginning the climb when I entered an open flat near a bend in the Belly River. Surrounded by scattered limber, Douglas-fir, and cottonwood trees, the small meadow was a white paradise. With the additional asset of the open water of the river, it was also a nice place to set up a camp. As I continued on, I was unaware that the elevation on the altimeter read 4,396 feet (a fact I would later discover back at my office going over the trip log). I began the climb 15 minutes later.

For another hour and fifteen minutes, I pushed through deep powder until I was too tired to continue. With 400 feet ascended, I was over halfway to the parking lot. In light of what kept happening to my packed trails, I had some misgivings about having made it so lengthy. The past five days had shown my exertions would be a waste if I did not use the trail the day I packed it. Nevertheless, I justified my actions with the high barometric pressure indicated by the calm and now nearly cloudless sky. All that was coming for at least the next 24 hours was a whole lot of cold.

I was back at the flat next to the Belly River in 45 minutes. Tired from the exertions of pushing through the powder while ascending, I decided to use the meadow for the next camp. I packed a path to the river's edge for access to water and stomped a campsite 200 feet away. Soon finished, all I needed to do was travel one mile and retrieve the backpack, return and erect the tent, and then get everything inside. In my exhaustion, the task looked daunting. I had also missed that in two and a half hours, according to my altimeter, my location had gained another 45 feet of elevation.

When I arrived at the backpack, the last of the clouds had finally dispersed. I was now certain the coldest temperatures of the trip would arrive tonight. As I pushed toward the camp, the memories of my efforts to get out of this canyon in February 2006 flooded my thoughts. Punctuated by hunger and exhaustion, I broke down, afraid I was about to experience a repeat or worse. I wiped my eyes without stopping.

Arriving at the new campsite, I kept moving. Although too tired to notice my altimeter readings, the elevation had increased another 30 feet at this spot in the last hour and a half. An hour later, with two freshly filled water bladders, I threw the last of the gear into the tent. A few minutes earlier, at 5:30 P.M., the sun had disappeared behind Glacier's peaks and the temperature immediately dropped below zero.

Although the 2006 experience had better prepared me, I was unable to convince myself that this was going to be anything less than a repeat of that near-death nightmare, particularly after what had happened the previous night. In the tent, I hustled with the necessary prep of getting the gear stowed and dinner cooked. At 7:45 P.M., as I settled into the sleeping bag the fear bubbled over again and the tears returned, but only briefly. Exhaustion and a full stomach soon put me to sleep. For the next four hours, with the piercing cold biting at my cheeks and lips, I woke at least once every hour and jogged in my sleeping bag. After midnight, I awoke with a need to go to the toilet. For that, I had a sealable freezer bag, except the only way I could use it was to open the sleeping bag.

Several minutes later and buried again in the bag with the lost heat rekindled, I quit jogging. In the sudden quiet, for a moment I thought I heard a familiar whisper in the distance. Wondering if I just imagined what I heard, I stayed quiet and listened. Several seconds later, I heard the sound again, this time much closer and convincing. Somewhere out there a wind was pushing through the trees! Shocked, I wondered how that could be. Then I realized I had not kept up with the altimeter since I woke up the morning before. The wind meant that the barometric pressure was dropping again—warmth! Shaking off the mistake of negligence, with rising hope I wondered if it would drop into the canyon and blow out some of this awful cold.

Less than a minute later, I had an answer. The gust arrived in the branches of the sparsely populated trees around the camp and broadsided the tent. When a shelter shook that hard, it was reasonable to be worried. Tonight though, I breathed a sigh of relief and thanked the powers that be for the wind, as indeed the enemy of my enemy became my friend. Within a few minutes, my face, feet, and torso were warm. I checked the thermometer. The reading was 18 F. More than an hour later, my excitement subsided and in spite of the noisy flapping of the tent shell, I fell asleep.

February 9: The Harshest Days

Although it was too soon to complain about my newfound friend, the gusting wind woke me throughout the remainder of the night. When I awoke at 5 A.M., I knew it was time to get up. Nevertheless, being toasty warm and comfortable I laid my head back for just a few more moments.

The next time I woke was at 8:15 A.M. Shocked, I got going quickly. But I was not destined to get comfortable anytime soon. I was preparing to light the stove when I realized going outside was going to have to happen immediately. It had been 48 hours since my last bodily evacuation, and my digestive system made it clear that this was as long as it would go. The need came on so quickly I vacated the tent with only wool socks on to protect my feet. To make matters worse, the wet flushable wipes were frozen.

This was one of those rare moments I was glad to be alone. Back inside the tent, my imagination promptly conjured up the nightmarish scene another person would have been stuck with that morning inside the tent as I thawed the wet wipes.

Although unsure how low the temperature had dropped the night before, the one-quart saucepan of water was frozen solid, as were the two water bladders and 16-ounce water bottle. Except for the saucepan, all the other items had spent the night against my body and covered by a coat. Rarely did I see that happen. It was obvious that the temperature had dropped beyond 20 degrees below zero again. That also meant that when the wind arrived, the temperature had jumped nearly 40 degrees.

Many years before, I had learned to have a full pan of water ready to thaw on the stove. After melting the ice, I could then go through the process of thawing the bladders and bottle in the hot water of the saucepan. If I was unable to thaw the bladders, the only recourse would be to carry the full, frozen bladders in an already monstrously heavy backpack. Today, I had plenty of fuel. On the much longer planned crossing of Glacier, however, with fuel at a premium, the added weight of full, frozen bladders could prove disastrous.

Finally comforted by the first cup of steaming coffee, I reflected back on what I had seen while outside. The wind had done its work. Besides the nearly snowless trees, sections of the trail leading out of camp no longer existed. Where the trail penetrated the cottonwood tree grove 200 feet away, the deep groove of the trail partly reappeared. Perhaps fate had given me a break and left portions of yesterday's packed trail unfilled.

By midmorning, I realized that my lateness in rising, the time spent thawing the frozen bladders, and having at least a partially filled trail meant that the soonest I would make it back to the van on the highway was the next day. Breaking camp and preparing for the day ahead in winter conditions generally required four hours. On this day, travel began at 12:45 P.M.

With a nonstop steady wind interspersed with gusts, my new friend from the night before soon fell off its pedestal. In one hour, I ascended a mere 200 feet up the wall. Half an hour later, I stopped in a small clearing to catch my breath. The gusts slammed into me so hard I had trouble standing. I turned to face the wind and saw a repeated scene from the second day;

a storm that Glacier's peaks seemed to be holding back from clobbering me. Inspired by their protectiveness, I kept going.

Two hours after leaving camp, I was 400 feet into the ascent with the end of yesterday's trail just behind me. I dropped the backpack and went back to packing trail, climbing for 15 minutes before turning back. By the time I got back to the backpack, drifting snow in the numerous open areas had buried much of the freshly made trail. When I arrived at the upper end of the fresh trail with the backpack, a total of 45 minutes had passed, while only rewarding me with 100 feet of ascent.

I dropped the backpack three more times, having learned to travel a maximum of 10 minutes before turning back. The three feet of new snowfall over the 72-hour period was now drifting. The consistency of the snow was also changing; it was thicker and far more difficult to push through. By 4:30 P.M., I was more exhausted than at any other time in the eight days I had been messing around with this damned canyon.

A few hours earlier, I had surmised I would probably spend one more night in the Belly River canyon, albeit on the wall. When I finally staggered to a halt, too tired to go any farther, the sun was setting. I was also back in the Douglas-fir and lodgepole forest, which meant the road was close. In five hours, according to my map and altimeter, I had ascended only 600 feet and traveled less than a mile and a half. (Wrong yet again, I had failed to account for the changing barometric pressure when calculating my travel. I had underestimated by 100 feet in elevation and a half mile in distance. Given the adverse conditions, the discrepancies were huge.)

The fatigue was so great that all I wanted to do was crawl into the sleeping bag and go to sleep. Instead, I cooked some stew and forced myself to eat. The food eaten this evening was going to affect how well I would do the next day. I was asleep by 8:30 P.M.

February 10: Old Man Muscles

I woke up at 3 A.M. hungry, so out came a bag of peanuts. I was soon back to sleep, but arose for the day at 5 A.M. Just over four hours later, with the temperature a warm 23 F., I was packed and ready to continue up the trail. Rather than hefting the load, I began to pack the trail from the edge of camp.

Half a dozen steps later, I noticed the tiredness from the day before was still in my leg and buttock muscles. My body was still recovering in spite of

12 hours in camp and 8 hours of sleep. I figured I knew what was wrong. Yesterday's harshness combined with the lack of enough food or water was affecting today's travel. The forced eating before going to sleep had fallen way short of what I needed. Nor were the peanuts in the middle of the night going to offset the punishing activity of the day before. Couple all that with what I had taken to calling "old man muscles," and this morning's weakness was explained. No matter, I still had to push on as far as I could with what I had. In 15 minutes of travel, I found out I had spent the night only a fifth of a mile and 80 feet below the snow-covered parking lot at the Chief Mountain Customs Station.

As far as I am concerned, there are two types of powder snow. The first is what initially falls out of the sky. Get enough of this, and I did, and it becomes difficult to travel through. The second type is nothing more than a slight metamorphosis of the first, but it's far more difficult to travel through. Subfreezing temperatures combined with a whole lot of wind are the two necessary ingredients to create the change. All those gorgeous snowflakes blow about and slam into each other, breaking down into something similar to ugly-clingy powder. They cling to each other creating a crust, of sorts, on the surface.

This crust is different from the solid surface created by the seesaw affects of warm and cold temperatures. Like a properly prepared and baked piecrust, under the slightest pressure this wind crust will crumble. That is when the snowshoe will drop through into the powder beneath. Since the snowshoe is normally moving forward when the crust breaks, snow piles up on top of the front of the snowshoe, weighing it down. In deeper snow, I tend to stop with every other step and shake the snow off before taking another step. When the snowshoe drops down less than a foot, however, I just barge through. Except that weak excuse for a crust then has to be broken through from the bottom upward. This slower travel is maddening and quickly exhausting. I soon found that the Chief Mountain parking lot and highway were awash in wind crust.

I dropped the backpack on the road and continued to plow up it. Over the next three hours, I dropped the load three more times and ascended 160 feet before arriving on top of the ridge with the backpack, a mere three-quarters of a mile south of the customs station. Exhausted, I would go no farther that day. Tremendously disappointed that I would need yet another day to arrive at the vehicle, at 2:50 P.M., I trudged another 400 yards and built camp in the lodgepole forest on a knoll 50 feet east of the road.

Inside the tent, I did what I could to undo the damages of the day. While traveling, I had continued to stuff snow into the 16-ounce water bottle and then kept it inside my shirt and against my chest to keep the snow melting. Nevertheless, I was unable to stay hydrated. Now inside the tent, within a short time the dehydration cramps attacked again.

Today, in less than five hours, I was all in. My travel for the day was less than one and a half miles of forward progress, an average of one-quarter mile per hour. With over two miles and two valleys still in front of me, based on today's travel I would need six hours to get back to the trailhead. The thought revolted me, and the resultant discouragement was overwhelming. How in the hell did I get so old so fast? Was it even possible to get into good enough shape to access Hole in the Wall, much less attempt crossing the entirety of Glacier in winter? On this evening, I was doubtful.

Although I had food and fuel for another three days, I would be officially overdue as of tomorrow. Carleen, already worried, would hold off for another 48 hours before she made the call to the park service.

Lots of sleep was crucial, but so was water and nourishment. I started slugging down food immediately, melting snow, and drinking large quantities of water. All right, I had old man muscles and was out of shape. Was it also necessary to starve and dehydrate them?

Although tired, I had trouble sleeping. Each time I woke, as if I was in an echo chamber, the voice in my head informed me that I was too old and out of shape to continue such trips.

6 • exit from belly river canyon

February 11: Fresh Resolve

I arose before 5 A.M. Once a hot cup of coffee was warming my hands, my situation stopped looking so bad. My thoughts of quitting disappeared. Okay, I'm no spring chicken. But I'd be damned if I would lay a weary arm on that coffin 20 or 30 years early.

I also had a plan. Yesterday's mistakes could create a different set of tracks for today. More than the full water bottle, there would also be a partial bladder for the trail. Each time I dropped the backpack or picked it up while packing trail, I would suck a couple mouthfuls out of the extra water. For nourishment, the fruit and peanuts were still there. In addition, I still had three and a half English muffins, which I was going to slather with the remaining peanut butter. Combined, the muffins and peanut butter would provide me with an extra 1,600 calories. Old age might pull me down before I arrived at the van, but I would do everything I could to make sure my body had plenty of water and food.

With a mild temperature of 30 F. and shortly after 9 A.M., I stepped back onto the road. I was delighted to see that most of the trail that I had packed the afternoon before toward Lee Creek Bridge still existed. Nevertheless, the easy travel ended 20 minutes later where the trail ended. With the backpack still on, I tried punching through the wind-packed snow as I continued the one and a quarter miles and 328-foot elevation loss to the bridge. I made it only a few feet, dropped the load, and returned to packing the trail through the powder.

At 43 minutes, I was 300 feet short of Lee Creek Bridge. I had planned to turn around at the bridge, but the wind had swept much of the snowpack off the road here. When I got back to the backpack, I stuck to the plan and pulled out the water and sandwiches. I hefted the load 20 minutes later and arrived at the end of the trail half an hour later. I had needed two hours to get the backpack here. As discouraging as that should have been, my spirits were up.

With plenty of energy still in me, I now walked with the load rather than first packing a trail. Unsure of how far I would go before I dropped the load again, every little bit of forward progress I made without traveling over the same ground three times was a tremendous relief. On the south side of the bridge, I spotted my tracks from 10 days before. Once again, in deep snow, I traveled on top of the windswept and crusted tracks.

Around the curve beyond the bridge, I spotted the first two of four cross-country skiers as they popped up over the next ridge approximately a fifth of a mile away. I was relieved to see other people for the first time in 10 days. A couple minutes later we halted in front of each other. As it turned out, they were traveling to Belly River Ranger Station. All were young summer employees of the park, presently laid off and performing volunteer work in wolverine studies. A friendly lot, the one woman in the group thanked me for the trail from the gate on the highway to this spot. I bantered with them about that for a minute, letting them know my preference was to have had it the other way around for the last several days. Hearing my description of how I packed the trail for most of the trip, there was a momentary stirring as they glanced at each other.

The elder of these young travelers, and possibly the one in charge, was David Smith, a strapping 30-year-old. Three and a half months later, I would see him again under very different circumstances.

They had recently gone to Glacier's Goat Haunt Ranger Station via Waterton Townsite in Canada for the same reason as this trip. Besides finding their actions admirable, I had an additional interest in where they had been. I listened to them talk about taking a single day to arrive at Goat Haunt from Waterton Townsite. Encouraged, I once again got back to thinking about crossing Glacier rather than about the last 10 days of getting my butt kicked.

I hiked the final one and a quarter miles in 75 minutes. When I arrived at the gate blocking the road, standing on a snowdrift, I threw my right leg over the metal bar of the gate, and then with a sigh of relief plopped my body and backpack onto it. For several seconds I thought I was going to take a break before completing the final 50 feet to the van. Like so much of the trip, being wrong would continue on this side of the gate as well. A gust of wind slammed into the load and me. A moment later, I was lying prone in the snowpack on the other side of the gate, and the trip was over.

Officer Jeremy Kelly of Homeland Security (Border Patrol) was in his patrol vehicle waiting for me. At least I like to think that was what he was doing. We grinned at each other as we met up.

I first met this man five years earlier. When I had exited the park at the end of my second trip in 2006, the temperature was 15 degrees below zero at the closed gate. As it turned out, he had been sitting there for the last three afternoons and into the evening waiting for me to exit. Two days before that, while crossing the river near Belly River Ranger Station, I had broken through the ice. Suddenly I had found myself fighting for my life in subzero temperatures. Then the night before I exited, with a broken stove and damp sleeping bag, I thought I was going to die when the temperature plummeted to near 40 degrees below zero. At the time, what I had just gone through was unknown to him, although in those frigid conditions he correctly figured I had had a tough go of it. When I heard what he had been doing, I had broken into tears. As a result, since the early evening of February 17, 2006, the Border Patrol/Homeland Security has been on my good guy list.

As I got out of my trail gear and retrieved the lighter clothing and footwear for some civilized comfort, I talked about this trip and the trips planned for later this winter. When I got to the part where I would cross the international border into Canada to resupply, Officer Kelly took issue with the plan. He thought it would be a good idea to have an alternative route without a border crossing, and to use it. He was very clear in his statement that if I crossed the border, I would have trouble with both Homeland Security and the Royal Canadian Mounted Police.

Although I said nothing, I immediately thought about those four young and unemployed people who had crossed the closed border a few weeks before. It has always been my impression that outside of an emergency, the laws extend to all in an equal manner.

Kelly's information was discouraging. In front of me were at least two more trips before taking on the challenge of crossing Glacier, all of which might already be impossible. Now I faced getting in trouble with American and Canadian authorities. The new information increased the already problematic logistics and peril, but until I came up with an alternative, I would continue to plan the crossing.

Summary of the Trip

I later found out that during the cold spell, the Many Glacier SNOTEL site in Glacier recorded a low of 27 degrees below zero, while Hudson Bay Ranger Station recorded 30 degrees below zero. In a nonsensical way, where the failure of the sleeping system was concerned, the information made me feel better.

Back in Helena, I had trouble reconciling the trip. There was no doubt the effects of getting old would continue. Was I already too old for these types of trips? While some people clearly thought so, I was unsure. The next trip might provide an answer, although I would return only after a crust had formed on the snowpack.

There were also some other issues from the trip that I needed to put to rest. I began the trip weighing 206 pounds, approximately 30 pounds overweight. The backpack had weighed over 90 pounds. Additionally, from the gate the snowpack had been tough to get through, while the three feet of fresh powder that fell during the trip increased the difficulty. I finally concluded that carrying that much weight on a crust-less snowpack would probably have slapped anyone silly. Even Joe Cosley, from more than 80 years before and known for his extraordinary feats of snowshoe travel, had expressed some reluctance about traveling in the powder of Belly River canyon. (For more on Cosley, see *Belly River's Famous Joe Cosley*, by Brian McClung, Life Preservers Publishing, 2009.)

I concluded the condition of the snowpack was the major reason for the difficulty of the trip. Since I would be waiting for a strong crust to form on the snowpack before I returned, any difficulty in the next trips would have to come from a different direction. As it turned out, that is precisely what would happen.

7 • the original intent and date

Fear and Hesitation

After the February trip, my intent was to return sooner than I did, but a succession of storms delayed me. The first of two trips planned for March was a seven-day trek to summit Stoney Indian Pass. The second, another seven days, was to begin on about March 21 at Polebridge and head toward Brown Pass and Hole in the Wall. Once the second was completed, I planned to deliver a cache to Waterton Townsite in Waterton Lakes National Park, Canada. Yet getting across the closed international border at Goat Haunt was still problematic. Another problem with this plan was the additional 16 miles it would add to an already lengthy winter trip. Nevertheless, until I could improve on it, I would stick to the original plan.

On March 10, as I left Helena, I knew bad weather was a possibility, but I took a chance anyway. I arrived at the gate on Chief Mountain Highway in a downpour. With two feet of slushy snowpack on the closed portion of the road, I canceled the trip.

Rather than return to the eastern side of the park for another attempt at Stoney Indian Pass, I thought it was best to stay with the scheduled trip to the Brown Pass area. The winter days were fast ebbing, and I still had yet to see the real target of the route, Hole in the Wall. But this meant that, when I embarked on the ultimate trip across the entire park, I would not see Stoney Indian Pass under a snowpack until I got there. This also meant that, on the chance that I would need all my technical gear on the pass, I would carry every ounce of it from the Belly River trailhead rather than leave it at Waterton Townsite with the cache.

I planned to be gone for approximately one month. After the Brown Pass trip, I would return to the eastern side of the park, obtain the necessary permits at Hudson Bay Ranger Station, deliver the resupply cache at

Waterton Townsite, and then return to the Belly River trailhead and begin the park-wide crossing.

I left Helena in the late afternoon of March 20. As I drove north up the Seeley and Swan Valleys, I worried about the cloud-laden peaks on the Swan Range. When storms hit, I knew that the park usually received the lion's share of the moisture in this area. The forecast near Brown Pass called for a 60 percent chance of snow. Given what I could see happening on the Swan Range, 100 miles south of Hole in the Wall, I worried about how much more snow was falling in the park.

The plan was to pick up the permit, which I did, and then spend one night with friends near Bigfork. The following morning I would begin the trip. I ended up spending two nights with the friends. I had a couple of reasons for doing that, weather supposedly being the foremost. In reality, fear held me back that extra day.

8 • a different trip

March 22: A Death on Bowman Lake

I left Bigfork at 1 A.M. and arrived at the Polebridge trailhead three hours later. After arranging my backpack, I left the trailhead at 5:30 A.M. still in darkness. Traveling in the dark, the LED head lantern effectively lit the way, but the narrow beam of light only somewhat alleviated my fear of hungry grizzlies that would now be emerging from their winter snooze. The ski grooves on the road to Bowman Lake indicated substantial use by cross-country skiers. I usually give skiers the courtesy of not snowshoeing on their tracks, but here I appreciated the packed trail. (On several occasions, skiers in the backcountry have voiced their gratitude for the trail I've provided with my snowshoes. In the long run, it all balances out.) Walking on the grooved trail, in spite of a backpack weighing over 90 pounds, I made good time on a crust where the snowshoes broke through infrequently.

An overcast day, it was still getting light two hours into my walk. Although the road parallel's Bowman Creek, I traveled two miles on the winding road and through an old burn before I left the North Fork Flathead River Valley behind. My entrance into Bowman Creek canyon brought me into a mature climax forest of Douglas-fir and lodgepole pine trees.

The six miles to the lake on the snow-covered dirt road created the illusion that it was more level than the three miles on Chief Mountain Highway. In reality, I covered a vertical gain of 600 feet and a drop of 100 feet compared to Chief Mountain's gain of 395 feet and loss of 420 feet. I was elated at the difference between this and the slow slog of the Belly River canyon trip in February. I even dared to believe I could go beyond the foot of the lake today. I arrived at Bowman Lake Campground in four hours.

Although the permit called for me to spend the night at this location, that was supposed to have happened on March 21, yesterday. Today the permit had me at the head of the lake. Even if I had the energy, I would have been unable to travel that additional six and a half miles on this day. The sciatic nerve on my left hip had flared up again. I dropped the backpack and briefly considered setting up camp, but the pain subsided quickly and I decided to continue.

I am no fan of walking on ice. In my mind's eye, I see me breaking through it and holding my breath for a very long time, while unsuccessfully trying to claw my way back to the surface. As a toddler, I almost drowned twice, although I have no conscious memory of either event. As an adult, I stay off the ice. To punctuate my fear, during a phone call before the trip, a park ranger informed me of a previous incident in which cross-country skiers broke through the ice near the lake's north shore.

My only alternative was the weakly crusted snowpack that covered the trail inside the trees along the north shore. Faced with walking on a crust that would only partially hold my weight or on the lake ice, I hesitated. Then I spotted some deer on the ice near the north shore one mile up the lake. A few minutes later, I headed for the ice.

The foot of the lake was located in rolling foothills. On the north side, Numa Ridge rose 1,500 feet, while on the south side Cerulean Ridge was 1,000 feet above the lake. Glacier's world-renowned canyon walls and peaks were three miles farther east. I decided to set up camp once the peaks and steeper canyon walls were on either side of me.

I arrived at a partial elk carcass 10 minutes later. All that remained was about a quarter of the hide, some bones, and numerous predator tracks, both coyote and wolf. I was a little surprised to see that anything remained of the animal. Generally, scavengers and carnivores would clean even a large elk within a short time. Perhaps, as I guardedly looked around, a short time was all that had passed.

As I traveled farther onto the ice, my confidence in its strength increased. So much so, I decided to walk a straight line through the curvature of the lake, thereby cutting the distance to the upper end. That also meant I would gradually cross the lake twice. As I got farther from shore, however, my confidence dropped until, with visions of me gurgling under the ice, I lost my nerve and altered my course back to the north shore. Thereafter I stayed between 40 and 70 feet offshore.

By 11 A.M., with my hip hurting again, I ran out of steam and stopped for a break. I also had eaten nothing since the previous evening. Somehow, I kept ignoring the oft-repeated lesson that I needed to eat continuously as

I traveled. While a man in his twenties might need an hour to recover, at my age recovery from this level of tiredness would encompass the remainder of the day and the night. Too late to undo the mistake, I brought out the day food and ate anyway.

When I continued 20 minutes later, I moved like an old man who badly needed to stop. I found what I was looking for along the northern shore 30 minutes later. Patches of ice had melted on the shoreline, giving me access to the lake water. Still a mile short of the great walls and peaks, at noon I dropped the load and set up camp.

Later, inside the tent, I again compared this first day to the Belly River canyon trip. Today I had traveled eight miles in six and a half hours, while in February, it took four days to get this far with a similar load. No matter, my confidence about what lay ahead stayed low, particularly about what was beyond the lake. I also contemplated the damage I did today by not eating, which was going to have an adverse affect on tomorrow's travel. On the upside, for the first four miles tomorrow, the excellent travel on the lake ice would continue. I crawled into the sleeping bag and was asleep by 4 P.M.

March 23: Another Death on the Lake

I was up at 3 A.M. Although I had been in bed for 11 hours, a painful left hip and right knee had continued to interrupt my rest. I had had surgery on the knee twice, with most of the cartilage removed during the last operation in January 1980. While both knees were arthritic from past injuries, the right knee was in the worst shape. An orthopedic surgeon had informed me several years earlier that he would own my knees if I ever stopped doing whatever I was doing to keep them working.

Worried, I wondered if I ought to turn back. Still in front of me was the harsher snowpack beyond the lake and the 2,000-foot climb to the edge of the approach. Was I finished? In the end, although I decided to continue up Bowman canyon, it was one more sign that the end was in sight for these types of trips.

By 5:30 A.M., the gear was out of the tent and ready to be packed. The pain in my right knee had increased. I thought again about turning around and going home. If I did, I figured that would be the equivalent to my signing off, that I would be finished with such arduous winter trips. Just over one hour later, in the increasing light of dawn I hefted the load and began walking east, toward the high country. After a few minutes, the pain in the knee subsided while the sciatic pain became almost nonexistent.

I had been traveling for three-quarters of an hour when I spotted a dark object near the middle of the lake a third of a mile ahead. I wondered if it was another carcass. A few minutes later, I saw movement. Within a short time, I knew it was no deer, coyote, or wolf. As I continued to close the gap, I was finally able to discern that it was a large, long-necked, dark bird. Clearly much larger than a duck, it was probably a goose. Not wanting to alarm the bird, I hugged the north shore as I continued. Although I never came within 500 feet of it, the bird attempted to fly away a couple of times, but landed within moments, obviously injured.

My heart went out to the goose. While its flock continued north, the bird was going to die alone out here on the ice. Given another couple of months, the goose would have had a huge body of water to protect it from the landlocked carnivores. I figured that hidden in the trees along the shoreline, there was probably at least one set of eyes staring at the hapless bird. Today, I theorized, was probably its last day alive, and though I realized it was a part of the cycle of life, I was still bothered. There was too much about the bird's state that reminded me of my own. Both of us were alone and debilitated. The bird was already in a dangerous neighborhood; I was headed in that direction.

With the end of the lake in sight, I was two and a half miles and one and a half hours beyond the goose. Behind me in a light easterly breeze, I noticed for the first time several objects rolling over the snowpack toward me. It struck me that I had been watching them for quite some time without paying any attention. I did now. Mystified, I stared at the odd, dark rolling balls as they caught up and then passed by me in their slow march to the lake's upper end. Suddenly I realized what I was seeing. Aghast, my heart leapt into my throat. *Oh God, those are balls of goose down!* The bird I had felt the temporary kinship with was dead.

In a world of steep cliffs and peaks, with canyon floors and walls covered by trees, all smothered beneath a deep snowpack or in ice, I had brushed by one living creature today, and within an hour and a half, it was just me again. Tears welled up as I started to walk again, this time in the company of the rolling balls, which were moving slightly faster than my pace. The goose was no longer afraid of me. His ghost in the form of those balls of down accompanied me for a few minutes before moving on.

Then I got angry. I did not give a damn that this "bird-meets-carnivore" event had been happening on this lake for more than 10,000 years. Cycle of life my ass, some cowardly coyote or wolf had waited until I was out of sight, then ran out there and killed that bird. Rationally I knew they had to eat, and the injured goose would not have survived anyway, but right then I felt as if I had lost a friend. With my feelings still in turmoil, half an hour later I arrived at the upper campground of Bowman Lake.

The thick clouds from the day before and this morning had slowly been breaking up. Shortly before I arrived at the campground, the sky had nearly cleared. Eastward, most of the peaks still had a shroud of clouds around them, while to the west the sky was almost cloud free. On the south shore, the clouded veils on the summits of 9,891-foot Rainbow Peak and 8,777-foot Square Peak were fast dissipating. The backcountry of Glacier National Park was turning into a pristine and precious jewel.

I stopped for an hour at the forested campground and even used the toilet, knowing this would be the last one available for the next three or four days. By the time I picked the backpack up and continued, the sun was on the canyon floor and softening the snowpack.

The trail inside the thick forest beyond the lake was easily discernible in the three-foot-deep snowpack. The fronts of my snowshoes were also breaking through the crust at every step. In a sun-saturated opening, I could still see the lake through the trees when I halted, dropped the backpack, and sat down again. The heat from the sun's rays was blissful and encouraged me to linger. Pulling out the English muffins and peanut butter, I slugged down two halves. After 45 minutes, I continued up the canyon. Now the entire snowshoe was punching through the snowpack at every step, a clear sign that I needed to stop for the day.

Less than a mile beyond the campground, I turned right into the trees and began looking for a location to put camp. Somewhere in that direction was Bowman Creek and hopefully open water for my camp. I took the backpack off in an opening that I thought was part of Bowman Creek's floodplain. For 40 minutes, I searched fruitlessly for open water before I quit and set up camp.

The hot sun had turned the surface of the snowpack into slush, thereby preventing my continuing up the canyon, but with an advantage in my waterless camp. Using a scant amount of fuel, but still going a little too far with it, within an hour I melted enough snow to fill two 96-ounce bladders of water.

This morning the right knee had almost turned me around. Through the day and now in camp, the knee still hurt, but I no longer believed it would stop me. Yesterday I had predicted that today would bring fewer miles.

True enough, I had traveled half an hour longer and put only five miles behind me. With a plan for an early rising, I fell asleep in the early evening.

March 24: A Terrifying View

I now had in my possession an indoor-outdoor thermometer with a wire leading outside. The reading was 14.6 F. There would be a hard crust for today's travel. To take full advantage of it though, I would have needed to get up at midnight. I crawled out of the sleeping bag at 4:10 A.M., and was now doubtful that my plan to ascend at least half of the 2,000 feet to the bench on Brown Pass today would happen. I figured the soonest I would get out of camp would be 7:30 A.M., which would give me three or four hours of travel time before the sun softened the snowpack.

I left shortly after 8 A.M. and immediately began a 250-foot ascent on the south-facing wall that took me to a bend less than one mile ahead. With the exception of a few high-altitude clouds, the sky was clear. There was no sunlight on the canyon floor yet, but it was coming. In the open areas, the crust held my weight. Unfortunately, most of the trail was inside a thick forest where the front of the snowshoes and the toes of my boots broke through with almost every step. I tired quickly. After 40 minutes, I took a 10-minute break with another 100 feet remaining in the ascent. An hour after I left camp, I arrived at the small summit and descended back to the canyon floor. I figured this was just a taste of what the climb was going to be like two miles ahead.

The snowpack's depth had also increased as I traveled farther up the canyon. Unlike many less-defined wilderness trails, the wide course of the trail here was easily discernible even in the deeper snowpack. In addition, there were large snow bumps on either side of an easily defined ditch, which was the trail, albeit three to six feet below. Unfortunately, my snowshoes were too wide to travel on the stronger crust inside the ditch. Therefore, I strolled from mound to mound, often from one side of the ditch over to the other.

In spite of the late start, and though the sun was filtering through the tree branches by 9 A.M., the crust held my weight enough to continue through the morning—a good thing, with the troublesome sciatic nerve. I still took numerous breaks.

At 10:30 A.M., with 8,790-foot Thunderbird Mountain now on my right, I began to anticipate a first view of the approach to Hole in the Wall. I entered a large open area near the confluence of Pocket and Bowman

Creeks at 11 A.M., and saw it for the first time. The view of the snow-covered mountain and steep angle of the approach was a shock. As expected, the entire width was an avalanche chute, except it looked worse than my imagination had conjured it to be. The ravine I called the elbow was particularly frightening. It was like a 1,400-foot funnel with a mouth on the summit that was 300 to 600 feet wide—a death trap! Every avalanche up there would be crammed into that narrow, near cliff-angled ravine. Even a small slide from the 8,000-foot summit might be non-survivable by the time it hit the summer trail at 6,600 feet. Although a fog bank from Brown Pass covered part of the approach, I could see enough, and instantly agreed with the park rangers. Hole in the Wall was inaccessible in the winter!

God almighty! What the hell have I gotten myself into?

Then I recalled there would be no attempt during this trip. I was here only to check the viability of the traverse. I had also learned that a distant view was untrustworthy. The final decision would happen from the edge of the approach. I dropped the backpack and spent over an hour walking around the open area. While there, I decided the climb was out for today. My hip and knee were hurting again, and I was tired.

The snowpack still held my weight in the open area. Soon after I continued up the trail, I reentered the forest at the base of Thunderbird Mountain and immediately started to break through the snowpack. On the left and through the trees, I could see the clearing where hidden beneath the snowpack was Bowman Creek. I turned a hard left and was soon in the opening again.

Avalanche Terrain

An hour and a half later, I had traveled less than one mile when I reemerged from a stand of cottonwood trees. On my right was the open water of Bowman Creek 13 feet below me. On the other side of the stream was a level spot in the snowpack that appeared to be perfect for a camp. Staring back across the stream a few minutes later, I saw that I was directly beneath 8,528-foot Boulder Peak. Perhaps I was wrong about placing the camp here. I pulled the topographic map out. The map showed that I was at the low end of an avalanche chute one-third of a mile wide.

As if to verify that I needed to move, a few minutes later I heard a grinding roar. Looking up, I easily spotted the avalanche as it tumbled off the cliffs 3,000 feet above me. That explained the absence of large trees on the upstream side of the cottonwoods. Prior avalanches coming off the peak 4,000 feet above had even reached across the eastern side of the stream and swept a portion of it clean.

I left the backpack behind and re-crossed the stream to climb a small rise on the west side of Bowman Creek. Across the large, open avalanche zone, I saw a possible spot for a camp less than 1,000 feet away. I retrieved the backpack, and just before 3 P.M. set up camp, still near the base of Boulder Peak, but on the east side of the stream in a scattering of small cottonwood and Douglas-fir trees.

Before I arrived in camp, the clouds had begun to thicken. Although the barometric pressure was dropping, a storm was yet to be a forgone conclusion. Nevertheless, in the winter, I always prepared every camp for a storm. Three hours later, as the barometric pressure continued to drop, I changed my mind and decided a storm probably was coming.

Earlier, looking up at the approach to Hole in the Wall, I had spotted what appeared to be a field of ice below the summer trail's approximate location. Although fog prevented an unobstructed view, I was almost certain there were at least two sheets of ice on the traverse. It also appeared that until there was an actual need for them, I would be unable to discern absolutely whether ice screws would be necessary. For that reason I would have to carry a full complement of them, which meant more weight. With a future load that already had the possibility of overwhelming me, how would I carry more?

My sciatic nerve continued to be troublesome, as was the small of my back and right knee. It was easy to conclude that I was physically unready to make tomorrow's climb with the nearly 90-pound load. I decided to leave the camp in place and day hike up to the approach the next day. I was asleep shortly after 6 P.M.

9 • the brown pass bench

March 25: The Day Hike

Through the night, besides the normal pain in the hip and knee, I was unable to lie on either shoulder for long before the respective hand went numb. To make matters worse, the "flat" I put my tent on turned out to be a slight slope, which had me continuously sliding off the pads. It was a restless night; I laid awake from 1 A.M. to 3 A.M., then crawled out of bed at 6 A.M.

As I prepared for the climb, I questioned the wisdom of going anywhere without the tent, stove, and sleeping bag. An ascent without all my gear in the winter was a cardinal sin. If I had to spend the night up high, there would be little or no forgiveness.

Just before 10:30 A.M., with a load of approximately 50 pounds, I began the climb. In 20 minutes, I ascended 200 feet inside the thick forest and figured I had crossed over the trail 40 feet below. I was on the steep northwest face of Thunderbird Mountain, pushing through at least one foot of powder snow. Except for my concern about what would happen if I got hurt, I was glad I had packed a small load. After another 100 feet and 10 minutes, I spotted a gap in the trees, a telltale sign of the summer trail.

A few minutes later the tracks of two wolves merged with the trail. Why were they up here? The deer and elk were still in their winter range in the lower elevations. If they were on their way to Waterton River canyon, why would they abandon Bowman canyon? From Polebridge where the creek drained into the North Fork Flathead River up to Bowman Lake, there was plenty of moose, elk, and white-tailed deer.

As I climbed, the powder worsened. In an hour and a half, I had ascended only 550 feet and traveled less than three-quarters of a mile. Frustrated, I hollered that I had had enough. Through the trees on the left

51

and below me, I could see a ravine paralleling the trail. Beyond it was a treeless white south face, and hopefully a solid crust. I arrived on the edge of the ravine 10 minutes later.

Except for the wind picking up, the south-facing snowpack was all I hoped it would be. The teeth of my snowshoes dug into the crust without breaking through. The steep angle of the climb continued to be tough, though. I would travel 10 to 15 minutes and take 5- and 10-minute breaks.

Just after 1 P.M., I stopped for another 10-minute break. At an elevation of approximately 5,575 feet, I was 1,150 feet above my camp and had been traveling almost three hours.

What to do next was questionable. Having never been in the area, I could only approximate where the trail led. According to the topographic map, a series of switchbacks zigzagged north of the ravine around the steep ridgeline 300 feet east of me. With evidence of avalanches on that 45-degree south face, however, following the summer trail could be folly. That left two possibilities. The first was up the ravine with the nameless creek. The second was to the right of the ravine in a scattering of sapling pine trees. Since it appeared to have the lesser angle, I chose the ravine and dropped in. Getting in and out of the ravine was easy, but within five minutes of climbing, that was no longer the case. The walls of the ravine closed in, restricting my direction of travel to up or down.

I was 150 vertical feet in the ravine when the left snowshoe plunged through the snowpack. I swallowed in fear as I stared into a deep hole at a boulder-strewn falls. Until now, I thought the snowpack had been at least eight feet deep above the mostly hidden, fast-running creek. In reality, the stream had substantially eroded the deep snowpack.

I realized I was fortunate in that I had only punched a hole through the crust without dropping into the ravine. A warning, and I had found over the years that out here fortune was nothing more than a nail in a coffin. Relying on luck in this terrain was a great way to die.

The chasm appeared to be too dangerous to continue up, yet the walls on either side were too steep to climb with snowshoes. Meanwhile, the crampons and ice axe lay safe in the tent back at the base camp. Unless I turned around and retraced my tracks down the steep incline, which was a distasteful thought, the alternative was to continue up the ravine.

I speculated that this might be the only time I would break through. Sure, and the open stream 25 feet farther up the ravine with the revealed second falls meant nothing? I glanced again at the wall on my right.

Apparently, I was going to find out during the descent if that other route was the right one. For now, I would continue up the ravine.

Hugging the right side, a few minutes later I arrived at the open water. I moved to the right and, in spite of the large snowshoes, sank knee-deep in the north-face powder. Gaining access to the water, I unclipped my water bottle from its carabiner and filled it without punching another hole. I drank 16 ounces and then refilled.

After putting the bottle away, I surveyed my surroundings again. This section of the climb to Hole in the Wall was supposed to be the easy part. The targeted challenge still lay another 1,000 vertical feet beyond me. Somehow, that seemed wrong. I could feel the ire rising in me as I asked the rhetorical question of why it was so damned hard getting to the tough areas.

A few moments later, I got back to what I was supposed to be doing. To travel in this type of terrain during the winter, I needed to deal with only the task directly in front of me. Distractions were dangerous. I needed to focus on getting up the remainder of the ravine, which I would exit in another 100 feet. Above it was a less hazardous 500 vertical feet to the bench between Brown Pass and the bottom of the eastern approach to Hole in the Wall.

The Cloud bank

It was also beginning to look like I chose the wrong day for the climb. The weather was changing. When I left camp, there had been patches of open sky above me. Now, accompanied by a strengthening wind, a thick cloud bank was dropping off 9,406-foot Chapman Peak toward Brown Pass. Regardless, to make the crossing I needed to get a close look at that approach. With March nearly over and the end of winter less than 60 days away, I was running out of time.

Maybe I ought to turn back and seek the warmth and comfort of the tent and sleeping bag. No one would fault me for backing away from this ravine and the swirling cloud bank up ahead. Right, and I would not? I continued to ascend.

At 1:45 P.M. I exited the ravine onto rolling but still ascending terrain. I was also within a half mile of the area I had scouted almost six months earlier. It came as no surprise that the world of white looked only vaguely similar to last autumn. Yet, as I recalled, much of the area below Brown Pass had been a thick forest of small- to medium-sized pine trees. Now it was a thinned-out forest of hoarfrost-covered saplings and meadows.

I continued the ascent toward the bench in an arc that would eventually bring me to the bottom of the next climb. From there I would begin the final ascent of 400 to 600 feet to the ridgeline that would reveal the eastern approach.

I climbed only a short distance before the consistency of the snowpack changed and I began to break through with each step. I went back to taking numerous breaks. As the afternoon progressed, my travel time decreased while the breaks lengthened.

The weather deteriorated further. The wind increased, interspersed with gusts, while the clouds thickened, intermittently covering the peaks. At 3 P.M., exasperated with the weather and bad snowpack, I stared at where the ridgeline for the approach was supposed to be just a quarter mile away. The upper slope had disappeared inside a cloud. Once up there I would see nothing. I bellowed in protest and declared the final climb was out for today.

My heart was also in my throat with fear. When I came through here the previous autumn, I had realized the entire mountainside from Brown Pass to Hole in the Wall was an avalanche chute. Somehow, today the 45-degree angle looked far greater than I remembered.

Although I had just persuaded myself not to ascend the final pitch, I closed the distance. At 3:45 P.M. I arrived at the bottom of the ascent and shot some pictures of the once-again revealed ridgeline and open sky. Then with my recent surrender cast aside, I began to climb up the left side of the avalanche chute near some small avalanche-damaged trees. I wasn't surprised at my conduct. Making declarations under duress and then abandoning them was a part of my modus operandi.

Turned Back

Having just spent an hour and a half breaking through the snowpack, I finally had a solid crust on the nearly treeless south face. In spite of the relief, reality hit several minutes later when I fully realized the tremendous mistake I had made by leaving the ice axe and crampons behind. What in hell had I been thinking down there?

Looking around, although the angle of this slope was less, I suddenly recalled aloud why I had quit shooting photos almost five years earlier during the steep eastern ascent of Ahern Pass. On that trip, I learned I could not shoot and survive climbing at such a steep angle in a buffeting wind. At a minimum, it had made me want to throw up or, worse, plummet to my death. At least I had had the ice axe and was wearing crampons then, I reflected sardonically.

A thin cloud bank covered the mountainside 15 minutes later, this time with me in it. The wind increased again, and then the snow pellets arrived. The protective gear against those two conditions was inside the backpack. Nor would I be dropping the load to get at them on this slab. Consequently, and in spite of my rigorous exercise, I felt a growing chill beyond the biting hits of the pellets.

Another gust hit me as I photographed the vague slope ahead of me. With nothing to hold me upright, I experienced vertigo. I dropped the camera, leaned into the ski poles, and kept my eyes on the saplings several feet away until it passed.

Then I remembered that the farther I climbed, the farther I would have to descend without crampons and ice axe. I looked at my watch and was surprised to see that I had only climbed 160 feet: so little for the seemingly great distance between the bench and my position. I checked the time, now 4:04 P.M., and realized it was indeed time to head back to camp. If I had brought the crampons and ice axe, I still would have turned around.

This being the fourth day out of seven, a close-up inspection of the approach on this trip was now out of the question, which meant I was faced with making a decision to attempt crossing Glacier while having scant knowledge of what was waiting for me at the approach. The crossing was becoming increasingly unreasonable. Perhaps I should come up here again the next day, and make another attempt. That would make me overdue, this time deliberately, which was no option. Had this been a wilderness and not Glacier National Park, I reflected, I undoubtedly would have taken the extra day.

Discouraged at the failure while simultaneously having my heart in my throat, I turned back. Another part of me was glad for the turnaround. Descending at an angle, within 20 feet I gratefully realized my Atlas snowshoes were going to take better care of me than I thought. I pointed them straight down the avalanche chute and leaned back. The hard crust let the toothy flotation devices grip the snowpack. I was on the bench six minutes later.

In 35 minutes, I arrived on the edge of the ravine. With my heart once again in my throat, I took the untested secondary route, and 10 minutes later was on the flat 233 feet below. I shook my head at the ease of the route through the scattered pine tree saplings and snowdrifts.

Instead of going back into the trees of the north face, I stayed on the south face and entered the trees below the large avalanche-created clearing. I reemerged 50 minutes later on the canyon floor. When I arrived at a large opening, I looked back up at the approach. Once again, it was inside a cloud. To the left was blue sky behind Hole in the Wall and 8,883-foot Mount Custer. Discouraged, I turned and continued toward camp. So much work for so little reward.

Equipment Losses

Tired and hungry, I arrived back at camp near 6:30 P.M. I wasted no time getting into the tent and settling in. I thought the day was over, but more incidents were in store.

Within an hour, I had the stew on the stove, the sleeping bag was covering me to my waist, and my feet were inside dry socks and down booties. There was equipment and clothing bunched beneath my knees to make them comfortable while I sat in the chair. Before me were bags of pistachios and empty shells. That was when I noticed that the sleeping pad/chair was delaminating. A bubble had formed in the pad on the backside of my thighs.

On winter trips, I carry two pads. I had learned early on to double the protection between my body and the snowpack. Additionally, if anything happened to the self-inflating pad, I would still have the other. The extra pad was a folding foam material with mini indentations that reminded me of an egg carton. The self-inflating, three-quarter-length, lightweight pad did double duty as a sleeping pad and chair. Since the autumn of 1993, I had been unwilling to go without a chair in the backcountry, although it appeared that was about to happen.

This was the fourth time one of these lightweight pads had failed. My history with them indicated I should never have brought it out on a winter trip, or for that matter, any trip. Now I would pay the price for ignoring my experience. (As it turns out, the self-inflating, three-quarter-length pads have a shorter life than their bigger sibling does. Replacing the pad at least every other year would probably eliminate the delaminating problem. That, however, does not remove its other vulnerability which is to be more easily punctured.)

A short time later, I was preparing to eat the stew while I held the audio recorder with a nitrile-gloved hand. One moment I had a grip on

After two nights of storms, on February 6 there was nearly two and a half feet of fresh snow atop the snowpack with another foot coming in the next 24 hours.

In the late afternoon of February 6, I am packing the snow on the trail for the fifth time. The following day, with another foot of snowfall, I would plow through this area in an effort to exit the Belly River.

Crossing an unnamed stream in a "controlled fall," I began the exit on February 7, the sixth day.

In the late afternoon of February 8, the last of the storm clouds has dissipated, opening the door for subzero temperatures.

A thin, wind-created crust on the snowpack at Chief Mountain parking lot made the travel more difficult on February 10, prolonging the slog to my van three and a half miles distant another 28 hours.

On March 22, I arrived at Bowman Lake on a scout of the approach to Hole in the Wall with a backpack that weighed over 90 pounds.

March 24: Two and a half miles beyond Bowman Lake my progress is impeded by four- and five-foot-deep snow bumps.

I set up a two-day base camp near the base of 8,528-foot Boulder Peak.

March 25: With 8,790-foot Thunderbird Mountain in the background, the nearly buried forest peeks from the snowpack on the bench between Brown Pass and the approach to Hole in the Wall.

With stinging snow pellets driven by a wind, the first attempt to reconnoiter the approach of Hole in the Wall ended with failure inside these snowdrifts.

March 26: During the exit, upper Bowman canyon with a light blanket of fresh snow.

the recorder and the next the $200 electronic device had dropped into the stew pot. Shocked, I quickly snatched it out of my steaming supper, removed it from the protective leather case, and extracted the batteries. Then, using my mouth and a cotton towel, I cleaned the machine. Finally, I stuck the recorder in my pants pocket in an attempt to dry it.

Astounded at the sudden mishaps, I recalled there had been other incidents today. During the ascent, I had pulled the topographic map from the front pocket of my camera bag. A few moments later, the wind snatched the now-empty freezer bag I kept the map in out of my hands. I watched with regret as the wind blew it out of sight down the ravine. (The following trip I would find and recover this plastic bag from a leafless bush.) Minutes later, I temporarily lost the second bag with my invaluable supply of glucosamine chondroitin MSM tablets. While I was able to retrieve the bag, I knew I had to do something different. My clumsiness came from numb fingers and wearing the nitrile gloves. I could do nothing about the numbness, and I was unwilling to shed the gloves. I had a problem for which I had no answer.

As tired as I was, I was unable to sleep until after 11 P.M. Besides lamenting on not getting to the approach, there was the normal nightly pain. Additionally, my shoulders hurt and I was getting cramps on the backside of both legs above the knees. Coincidentally that same area was where the huge and growing air bubble was located in the pad. I tried to get comfortable, going so far as to take two ibuprofen tablets. My revulsion at taking this type of medication normally held me back, but not tonight.

Again, I pointed a finger at the rapid passage of time that was aging my body. On the other hand, I also believed I was getting in better shape. Some of these aches and pains were sure to lessen eventually. Nevertheless, with each passing year more pain cropped up in different areas of my body, and exercising became less effective.

Two hours after dropping the recorder in the stew, I pulled it out of my pocket, reinstalled the batteries, and turned the device on. The machine worked! It was 10:50 P.M., and I suddenly felt a small victory over today's losses and defeat. In 25 minutes, I was asleep.

10 • the long slog out

March 26: Flight of the Geese

I crawled out of the sleeping bag at 7:15 A.M. My sore body combined with the bad pad had made the night one of the worst of this winter. Furthermore, the late hour meant a bad day ahead. Although it had snowed intermittently throughout the night, at 26 F. outside, the temperature was warm. In one of the tent vestibules, what remained of the stew in the pan was unfrozen. There would be hell to pay traveling in the soft snowpack. Curiously, the knowledge was uninspiring. It would be four and a half hours before I began the trek down the canyon.

While I would continue to use the pad as a chair, uncomfortable but still better than nothing, it was finished as a sleeping pad. It had been over 25 years since I had used anything but pads to insulate myself from the ground or snowpack. Yet, unless I could get to Bowman Lake's upper campground by tonight, where there was a small patch of open ground in the food preparation area, I would have no alternative but to use tree branches beneath the tent and remaining pad.

The first cup of coffee offset the nasty thoughts about the night before and the ruined pad. With the stove turned down to a simmer after the second cup began percolating, I sat back and relaxed. It did not last. My thoughts soon turned to the crossing of the park.

Every winter trip beyond four days in length is something of a gamble with the weather. However, more than on any other part of the trip, the weather had to be stable before I could attempt to traverse the approach to Hole in the Wall. The extended forecast at the beginning of the trip at Belly River would long be obsolete by the time I arrived at Brown Pass. In addition, I now faced attempting the crossing without seeing the approach up close. Finally, the logistics of leaving a resupply cache near Goat Haunt would also be problematic. At this point, beginning the trip with what information I presently had looked more like an act of insanity than a challenge.

Although I had yet to see the approach up close, I understood now that traversing it and accessing Hole in Wall was a stand-alone challenge. The park rangers' statements about Hole in the Wall during the winter appeared to be right so far. Should I abandon the crossing altogether and use the remainder of the winter trips to attempt to access the elevated cirque? As soon as the question arose, I shook it off. For seven months, my focus had been on crossing Glacier. Abandoning that was no option.

The barometric pressure had risen overnight. I crawled out of the tent at 10 A.M. to a calm and mostly cloudy sky. The cliffs and avalanche chutes on Boulder Peak had patches of sunlight on them. Fresh snow on the trees around the camp, with the backdrop of the cliffs, sunlight, and cloud bank shrouded peak, was breathtaking. As the minutes passed, the scene grew more magnificent.

I was ready to go at 11:15 A.M. The clouds had thickened and again covered the peaks. But above me a large hole in the clouds had appeared, filled with deep blue sky. I heard the flock of geese before I saw them. They emerged out of the clouds from the south and into the open sky about 2,000 feet above me. They were half a mile down canyon and had a heading that would take them into the cloud-hidden cliffs at the west end of the Brown Pass bench near the approach. A few moments later, they altered their direction slightly to the east, but continued heading toward the cliffs.

In half a minute, they disappeared into the cloud bank. I could still hear them though, and it sounded like they had altered course again, this time with a 90-degree left turn. While flying over 40 mph, they had somehow seen or sensed those cliffs in the cloud bank. I followed their honking as they now headed west toward Boulder Peak. Just as I thought they were going to smash into the cliffs over there, they changed course again. The ragged V-shaped formation reemerged out of the clouds.

At first I had thought they were lost and unsure where to go. But, their maneuvers had convinced me that they knew exactly what they were doing. They still needed to get it right, though, as they headed southeast for the fog-hidden cliffs of Thunderbird Mountain. As they again disappeared, a second and smaller flock of geese appeared from the south. The first flock turned again and reappeared in the open sky. Realigned, this time they made a beeline straight toward Brown Pass and disappeared into the clouds for the last time. Their honking soon faded into the distance.

"God damn!" I yelled at the clouds. "And we think we're all there is."

I had no doubt those birds had used the peaks for navigation, something I had been doing for decades. Only they had done it in a solid cloud bank, and without a compass, which was a mockery of my shallow abilities. Two of the three times in my life that I had been lost in the backcountry had happened because the clouds had hidden the peaks.

The second flock was flying lower. Nevertheless, within five minutes, it emulated the first flock and soon disappeared toward Olson Creek canyon east of Brown Pass. Shaking my head in delighted wonder, I threw on the backpack and headed down Bowman canyon.

Too Late to Travel

I stopped an hour and a half later and took a lunch break. The clouds had broken up enough that there was nearly an equal amount of sky. In a light snowfall, I shed layers of clothing while at the same time the sun beat down on me. I looked back at the now fog-less approach and Brown Pass bench with disappointment. If I had arrived one day later, I would have had that unrestricted close-up view.

The crust had softened by the time I continued. An hour later, I had traveled another mile when I came to a stop next to the open-running Bowman Creek near the base of the 175-foot ascent at the bend. Earlier I had decided to travel until 3 P.M. before stopping for the night. It being 2:30 P.M., I now decide against it.

Already difficult to travel in, the sloppy snowpack would have made the ascent a trail from hell, which would have ended with me building a waterless camp. I had also spotted a 10-foot Douglas-fir sapling uprooted and lying across the stream. The needles were still green and would insulate my bed from the snowpack tonight. This also meant I would avoid stripping a living tree of any of its branches, while having access to open water. I crossed Bowman Creek and set up camp 50 feet farther in an open area.

I placed a six-inch layer of the branches on the snowpack directly below where the sleeping bag would be located. The last time I used this method was in July 1983. Like watching another left-handed person write, the six-inch layer on the snowpack looked odd and out of place.

The short distance traveled was the result of a late start. With that in mind, I was determined to do better the next day. In spite of only traveling two and a quarter miles today, tomorrow I would attempt to arrive at the low end of Bowman Lake, almost nine miles distant. To do that, I needed to go to sleep early and then get up near midnight. Moreover, it was shaping up to be a clear night. Without consulting my altimeter, I reckoned that the temperature should drop well below freezing and provide me with hard crust to walk on the next day.

In addition to the plan for the next day, I altered my after-the-exit plan. I would return to Helena, replace the self-inflating pad, and adjust some of the other equipment. Last night, my three-season tent had begun to collapse beneath the weight of less than three inches of snow. I would replace it with the stronger but heavier four-season tent. I also had some regrets in failing to bring the larger 70 to 200 mm camera lens. The reason I had exchanged this equipment for the lighter gear was to drop the load to below 100 pounds. Besides the equipment exchanges, after what I saw of the approach, I also had a strong desire to go home, sit down, and take a couple deep breaths.

A possible problem that concerned tomorrow's travel was the warmer temperatures of the last three days. If travel on the ice of Bowman Lake was undoable, it could take three days to get to the low end of the lake. With this new worry nagging at me, I stayed awake until about 8 P.M.

March 27: Storm on the Lake

The day began shortly after midnight. I knew I was going to pay for only getting four hours of sleep, but wanted to avoid the late-start penalty of the day before. The coffeepot was beginning to percolate when I checked the thermometer. The outside reading was 23 F. Although I had no choice but go with this temperature, I had hoped it would be colder. Unbeknownst to me, a cloud cover had come in after dark, preventing yesterday's warmth from escaping. The day's travel began at 4:50 A.M.

It was still getting light at 6:56 A.M. when I arrived on the lake's edge at the upper campground. I had put only two miles behind me. The snowpack had been grueling. The crust was almost strong enough, but with each step I put my weight down twice: once on the crust and once more a moment later below the broken surface. This body-jarring travel was at least as bad as pushing through slush.

Cracks, Slush, Wind, Snow, and Wolf Games

After a small break, I stepped onto the snow-free ice of the lake. My pace immediately picked up. I walked for three minutes before I saw the first crack in the ice. Too late to stop, I stepped on it while my heart jammed into my throat. I came to a stop and looked around. I was in the middle of the bay west of the campground. The shoreline was 300 feet to my right. A couple hundred feet ahead, the ice and cracks were snow-covered. Without knowing what was between the northern shoreline and me, I turned around and began to head back the way I came.

Angling to the left, I traveled 40 feet before I found a second crack, which intersected with the first. I gingerly stepped from one side of the line to the other. Nothing happened, so I angled further to the left. Within a minute, it turned into a wide arc, which brought me back to a westerly heading and angled toward the shoreline on the other side of the bay, where only a few minutes earlier I had refused to go.

My head is handy at pitching vivid scenes of me lying on the bottom of the lake with all my gear still on—forever. Consequently, I really dislike cracks in the ice. I also figured none of those created scenarios would be that inaccurate. If I broke through the ice, I would have to get out of the backpack, the camera vest, and then the chest camera bag. Next, I would remove the snowshoes and the heavy winter mountaineering boots, which meant removing the gators and outer shell pants to get at the three knots on the laces of each boot. I suppose that before I got it all off, enough time would have passed for me to drown two or three times.

Imagination being what it is, most of my fear, invalid as hell, had its source in my head rather than the reality of the environment I was traveling in. As I moved forward, that reality took hold and lowered the fear, even making it almost nil within a short time. (On the next trip, I would make the embarrassing discovery that the ice was a couple of feet thick.)

Once again headed west, no more than 25 feet offshore, a few minutes later, I discovered the real result of three days of warmth. I stepped onto the snowpack beyond the bay. It turned out to be slush. Unlike what I had traveled on the day before, this stuff was like a thin saturated sponge lying on the ice. With intentional damn little experience of traveling on ice, I immediately (and erroneously) thought the water was leaking from below through cracks and a thinning layer of ice.

As I saw it, I had two ways to go. One was on the ice, the other on shore in the rotting snowpack. If I went ashore, it could be two or three days before I arrived at the low end of the lake. The alternative was to stay on the lake and perhaps drown. Although the decision was unsettling, I kept to the ice.

I stayed close to the shore without getting too close. Like a double-edged sword, there were intermittent strips of water along the shoreline, far more than five days earlier, which was a sure sign of thin ice. Meanwhile, farther out was deeper water, cracks in the ice, and a clueless conviction that the ice was thinner there. I concluded I might be safe if I stayed approximately 30 feet offshore.

I had walked less than a minute in the snowpack on the ice when the newest problem cropped up. The wet snow began to ball up in the teeth of my snowshoes. Every 30 to 50 feet I would shake or kick a snowshoe to break the ball loose so I could walk normally again, only to begin the process all over. I finally dropped the backpack, removed the snowshoes, and then walked without them.

I had been on the ice for 25 minutes when I turned around and spotted an animal crossing the lake. At 700 feet away, I immediately identified it as a wolf. The animal also stopped, and the two of us stared at each other. After a minute, I began to move again and so did the wolf. In another minute, I stopped again, and so did it. For the next half hour, each time I stopped so did the wolf, and we commenced to do a little more staring. While I headed west, the wolf was on a southwest heading, crossing to the southern shore. On the other side, it paralleled me for an hour on the ice before disappearing into the forest. Once again, I regretted leaving the 70 to 200 mm lens behind. On the next trip, I vowed I would find a way to carry the extra three and a half pounds.

Although the snow was no longer balling up beneath my feet, my pace was no quicker. After an hour, I stopped again, tired and in need of a break. I also put the weight-distributing snowshoes back on. Traveling again, nothing had changed with the snowshoes and the slush. Once more, the constant kicking wore me out. Finally conceding defeat, I decided to try to live with the growing snowballs and kept walking. To my surprise, the snowballs dropped off on their own.

Until I had arrived on the shoreline at daybreak, I had been unaware of the weather system that had entered the area during the night. After an hour on the ice, with a strengthening breeze on my face, snow began to fall. This was unlike the Christmas picture with snowflakes dropping out of the sky in an "oh so lovely scene" and a sleigh bell song chiming away in the background. These snowflakes were nearly horizontal and did what they could to drive themselves into my face. Failing at that, they pushed themselves into every opening of my clothing. Fortunately, the wind was in flux and only the strongest gusts did any damage.

Exhaustion and Tears

The short night of sleep combined with the harsh two hours to get to the lake had taken a toll. I began to stop more often. The daily pains were also back. I had traveled almost half the length of the lake when I spotted a large fallen tree extending into the lake ice. Leaving the backpack on, I wearily sat on it. The wind had briefly let up, though the snow continued to fall. I leaned forward against the weight of the backpack and closed my eyes. Sometime later, I woke with a shock. I looked at my watch and figured I had been asleep for 20 minutes. The wind's return and consequential chill had awakened me.

Startled that I had fallen asleep while sitting up in the middle of a snowstorm, I got moving. I began to question whether I would make it to the end of the lake today.

The farther I traveled, the slower my pace became. At 10:30 A.M. I passed by the site of my first camp from the trip in. Something about what I saw stirred me. In the middle of the snow ring where the tent had been located, deer and elk tracks had trampled right over the spot where I slept, ate, and relaxed. Apparently, my recent presence laid claim on nothing. I was also tempted to stop and rebuild the camp, but instead plodded on.

Ahead of me no more than a half mile, I saw another black object in the middle of the lake. At that distance, I was unable to identify what it was. Another bird? The elk and deer tracks were more numerous as I continued farther west. Perhaps what I was looking at was a deer lying on the snowpack. Several minutes later, the animal stood up. A coyote, it had been lying with its rear to the wind. The animal loped farther out on the ice. For another 45 minutes, I watched the coyote as I continued farther west. It appeared to be interested in staying on the lake and near the middle. Was this culprit the one who chomped the goose? Perhaps it was waiting for more manna from heaven.

The last 30 minutes of my walk turned into a shuffle. I arrived at the lower campground of Bowman Lake soon after noon. Near the boat launch area, I dropped the backpack on a snowless patch of ground beneath a large

Douglas-fir. Then I sat on the backpack, never wanting to move again. I knew I had to though. My muscles would start to stiffen, and I needed to set up the camp before that happened.

I scouted around and found a better site on the other side of the boat launch beneath another tree. Once I had relocated the backpack, I grabbed the 32-ounce water bottle and the three water bladders. Then I shuffled the quarter mile to the open water at the lake outlet. The return took at least double the time. When I finally dropped the bladders, 40 minutes later, my arms and the small of my back were on fire with pain. Unable to stop, I wondered how my back was going to do with all that leaning over as I erected the tent and then threw the gear inside.

This camp was substantially different from the previous nights, last night in particular. For starters, there was no snow beneath the tent. Nor was there snow around its sides, a mistake. The wind that had accompanied me throughout the day kept the interior of the tent chilled. Although I realized this, I was too tired to relocate the camp onto the nearby snowpack so I could shovel snow around the base of the tent. Moreover, unlike the night before, in this campground there would be no tree branches to use for extra insulation against the snowpack.

For the first time on this trip, unusual for any winter trip, I mistrusted the water I retrieved. The water filter system I have does not accompany me on winter trips. Although it had been several months since any boats and people had been in the water, the sign that talked about how large the motor could be on a boat was more than just a little disconcerting. Better safe than sorry, I boiled the water before drinking it.

Once the gear was inside the tent, I hurriedly settled in. An hour later, the previous night's short sleep combined with the harshness of the day finally slammed into me. I had just put a spoonful of the steaming stew into my mouth when I broke into tears. Though I was alone, I was embarrassed at my sudden and brief emotional tirade.

By 3:30 P.M., I was buried in the sleeping bag and falling asleep.

11 • polebridge

March 28: Numb Hands

I slept soundly and was up by 12:30 A.M. One of the first things I did was check the outside temperature, which read 32 F. Alarmed at the warm reading, I knew I had to get on the trail as quickly as possible. I had little doubt I would be breaking through the crust on the road. Even with the packed trail created by the cross-country skiers, the six miles back to Polebridge might take six or more hours to complete.

Although I never quite stopped worrying about what lay up ahead, I eventually fell back on the hard-won knowledge that every day had its own experience. Yes, it was fair that yesterday's travel, particularly that first two hours, was a forecast of what might come today; however, I had learned it was not a forgone conclusion. I planned to leave the campground by 6 A.M. and arrive at Polebridge in four hours.

Yesterday the numbness in my hands had worsened. After 17 years of using ski poles, I had been told by an orthopedic surgeon that my improper use of them had caused the problem. Regardless, I still needed the poles. My ankles were chronically weak from numerous sprains, and my knees were worse yet.

In June 1975, I tore both menisci in my right knee. I had two operations, which removed most of the cartilage. In January 1995, I had a cross-country skiing accident. Besides the broken bones, I also tore the ACL in my left knee, which remains unrepaired. As a result, the left knee cartilage wore out prematurely. There were now bone spurs in both knees, particularly in the right, with the associated arthritis. In short, I thought I needed more legs, thus the ski poles. I also used them back home on training hikes up and down Mount Helena.

The orthopedist explained that the straps on the poles put improper pressure on a portion of my wrist, which in turn damaged the nerves in my hand. Great! The year 2011 was when the nerves finally said, "You abusive bastard! We quit!"

Short of not using the poles, I had no answer for solving the problem. Since I was unprepared to do that, the best I could do was rest often. Mostly though, I would have to live with numb hands during the trips.

I left the camp in the darkness at 5:41 A.M. Getting off the road, I took a shortcut through the trees away from the boat launch area, another mistake. For several days, I had been in the backcountry, and the entire time I knew exactly where I was located. Now in a campground with beautiful toilets, picnic tables, helpful signs, and head lantern on, I wandered around lost for five minutes. With growing frustration, I retraced my tracks and tried it again, this time successfully.

Against the warmer temperatures, I had hoped the cross-country ski trail would hold my weight, and it did, mostly. Any variation away from the grooved trail, however, meant I would immediately posthole.

The rotting snowpack forced me to take numerous breaks, yet I still made good time. In one and three-quarter hours, I emerged out of the trees and into the burn area. Although worn out, I was halfway back to the vehicle, and the toughest part of the day was behind me. Between the miniature climbs and breaking through the crust inside the forest, the muscles, ligaments, and tendons, from the small of my back to the soles of my feet, were ready to stop for the day. I kept going.

At 9 A.M., I spotted the Polebridge Ranger Station buildings and my white van. I arrived at the vehicle 20 minutes later. I breathed a sigh of relief. If someone had said I had to go back in immediately, I might have responded with a scream. While great to go in, the exit was just as good.

12 • the greatest obstacle

Planning for a Quick Turnaround

I drove south toward Whitefish for 30 minutes before I started planning my return. At my friends' home near Bigfork, I discovered I had failed to bring the USB cable for the computer and components. I could have driven to Kalispell and picked one up, but that would have taken at least an hour. Instead, I used the hour as driving time toward Helena.

During the three-hour drive, my thoughts returned to the feasibility of accomplishing the park-wide crossing. While concerned about the north face of Stoney Indian Pass, I was more worried about the resupply before continuing west from Goat Haunt. My biggest concern remained the approach to Hole in the Wall and beyond. Once again, I thought about abandoning the crossing and putting all my efforts into a circuit from Polebridge. My ego instantly admonished me with the reminder from 48 hours earlier. I backed off.

With a strong crust to walk on, this trip had been vastly different from the Belly River trip in February. I had traveled 40 miles and ascended 3,500 feet in 7 days compared to 19 miles and 2,000 feet ascended in 10 days. While my body continued to be in pain, I was now almost certain it would handle the crossing. Could I carry more than 100 pounds? I would have to.

Nor would I be home for long, perhaps four or five days. I was running out of time. Winter would be over in another month and a half. Already the effect of the rotting snowpack was making travel difficult in the lower elevations. Although I planned for a quick turnaround, the weather forecast would also have a say as to when I would return. I needed a window that minimized avalanche activity while providing the vital crust.

Back in Helena, the photos were inconclusive. I was unable to see any details of ice fields. Since I was unsure, four ice screws would still be part of the gear—more weight.

Back to the East Side and Canada

The bad weather continued with more storms lining up and rolling through. It appeared I had been fortunate in the timing of the seven-day trip. On March 31, three days after I exited the park, the NOAA website posted an Urgent Winter Weather Advisory, which included up to 20 inches of snow and plenty of wind—a blizzard in the high country. I delayed leaving until Monday, April 4.

In the darkness of early Monday morning, I saw the forecast and delayed leaving yet another 24 hours. On Tuesday at 2 A.M., I stared at another discouraging winter weather message. Nevertheless, with up to 11 inches of snowfall in the higher elevations and wind gusts to 40 mph, this one was less potent. At the same time, the extended forecast gave me the green light I sought. At the Belly River trailhead for April 7, there was a predicted accumulation of one inch of snow with slightly improved conditions in the days after that. It would have to do. I left Helena at approximately 4 A.M., once again headed to Hudson Bay Ranger Station and, later that day, Waterton Townsite in Canada, where I had a two-night hotel reservation.

My latest revised plan called for the unlawful crossing of a closed international border, twice, which was unsettling. Additionally, since I had no idea what the terrain and the snowpack along Upper Waterton Lake was like, the plan was even more vague. Nevertheless, with Hole in the Wall in the mix, I knew of no other way to undertake the trip. On Wednesday morning, I would day hike eight miles south back into Glacier with a cache and hang it on the bear pole at Goat Haunt Campground. Early Thursday morning I would leave the hotel and Canada, return to the winter trailhead at Belly River, and begin the crossing.

Taking Someone Else's Advice

Soon after arriving at Waterton Townsite, my plan unraveled. I put the gear in the motel room. Then I grabbed the snowshoes and went for a walk on the ice of Waterton Lake. On shore, the snow was approximately three feet deep and wet. The storm was abating, driven by the wind sweeping across the snowpack on the lake. Between the deep snow and ice was slush.

On the left, less than 100 feet away, Waterton Lake was ice-free. I traveled onto the lake less than 50 feet before caution turned me back.

Back on shore, I stared across the bay on the right at the forested and steep mountainside, which ended at the lake's edge. I was unsure how much snow had fallen on this day, probably less than one foot, but clearly I was going to have trouble using the summer trail over there. This was all wrong. Besides possible avalanches, I was incapable of a round-trip of 18 miles in these conditions. To deliver the resupply, I would need to spend as much as two nights getting to Goat Haunt and back again. Moreover, I had failed to bring supplies for that contingency.

What I needed was to talk to someone about the trail into Glacier, preferably a Waterton Park employee. I got in my vehicle and slowly made my way back toward the hotel. A few minutes later in a residential area, I saw a young man and woman walking along the street. As it turned out, they were summer employees for the park service. They took me to their residence a short distance away and provided a map of the park and as much information as they had. They also gave me the name and phone number of the park ranger in charge of, among other things, avalanche rescues and recoveries. I figured he would have information about the trail to Goat Haunt. We talked that evening.

His name was Brent Kozachenko, and he had been an employee of Waterton Lakes National Park for many years. Like the Glacier National Park rangers, once he heard what my intentions were he immediately began to discourage me. He keyed in on some items that already had my attention.

Brent's first statement concerned the extreme avalanche conditions. I already had that one and said as much. What I lacked was the location of the chutes, how many, and their length. He mentioned one in particular. Then he focused on my crossing an international border. He started by talking about an individual who had crossed the border, which recently ended up in a magazine, something else I knew about. Finally, Brent talked about the motion sensors. He told me that a few years back during a particularly cold winter, a group of skiers had crossed the border on the lake ice and within a couple minutes had a helicopter hovering over them. I wanted nothing to do with that kind of publicity. Curiously, he made no mention of the volunteers who crossed over during the first part of February for the wolverine studies.

On to Polebridge and the Circuit

It was at this point that I abandoned the plan to cross the park. After hanging up the phone, I sat on the bed and wondered what I would do now. With the approach to Hole in the Wall now front and center, I was unsure of the timing for beginning the circuit. What was the weather like over there? Should I go back to Helena first? I went to bed with the questions unanswered and mystified at what my next step should be.

The following day I got up early, only there was no longer a set plan. The hotel had a winter rate of two nights for the cost of one, and I had just used one. Therefore, I drank coffee, ate badly, watched television, and finished a book on the disastrous Scott expedition to the South Pole nearly 100 years before. Reading about their experiences, similar to some of my own, I felt a kinship to Scott and his men. I was also in awe that they got as far as they did before freezing to death. In relationship to my ongoing trips and perhaps a heads up, I was acutely aware that they worked long and hard only to fail. By the time I was finished with the book, I knew I would be returning to the west side of the park the following morning and eventually Polebridge.

I was on the road before 6 A.M. the next day. I would spend the night with a friend in Columbia Falls and hoped to be on the road to Polebridge by midnight. After nearly eight months, the trips into Glacier National Park during the winter of 2011 had finally become clear. No longer encumbered by the problem of resupply at Goat Haunt, I felt like I had been set free. In light of what was directly in front of me, it was a badly misplaced feeling.

13 • Bowman Canyon

April 8: A Heavy Load

During the night, the temperature dropped to nearly 20 F. It was a good temperature for creating a hard crust, but only if I got up early enough to take advantage of the early morning chill. I had planned to get up at midnight and be on the trail by 4:30 A.M., but did not arise until 2 A.M. I threw the backpack on at 6:30 A.M.

With a backcountry permit for 13 days in hand, I was going back in with a load that was 15 pounds heavier than the trip 19 days earlier. Besides the additional climbing gear, food, and fuel, there were other weighty gear exchanges. The self-inflating camp chair and sleeping pad had an increased weight of almost two pounds, the 70 to 200 mm lens in place of the 28 to 70 mm lens was another three pounds, and the four-season tent added two pounds. Unlike food and fuel, which diminished as a trip wore on, these extra seven pounds would be constant throughout the trip.

With the snowshoes on, I heaved the large backpack onto my bent left knee. The clumsiness of the snowshoes combined with the additional weight of the load meant I had to be more careful with throwing the backpack's weight around. Experience had taught me to treat a load of this size with respect. I could easily lose my balance as I hefted the backpack. If I did while wearing the snowshoes, there would be no fancy footwork as I attempted to stay upright. I had learned to push the backpack away and let it drop to the snowpack, and then start over. I also had the complication of wearing a large camera bag on my chest. Regardless of the size of the backpack, the camera bag got in the way every time I picked up the load.

Because of the difficulty getting the backpack on, once on the trail I went to great lengths to leave it there. Before taking a break, I would search for a log, boulder, or embankment to sit on. Unfortunately, most of these "chairs" were beneath a heavy snowpack. For that reason, I took numerous short standing breaks. Although rare, the inevitable larger breaks usually included removing the backpack.

As I began the slow walk up the road to Bowman Lake in the growing light of dawn, the sky was clear and the air crisp. Sunrise came 30 minutes later. Unbothered, with the increasing warmth I reckoned it would be another two hours before the snowpack began to deteriorate. In the distance, I could still see some clouds from the last storm hanging on the peaks along the Continental Divide. The magnificence of Glacier National Park's peaks beckoned me to get out of the rolling hills of the North Fork Flathead River Valley. As heavy as the load was, I did what I could to oblige them.

I arrived at the lake's edge five and a half hours later. This was far better than I had expected. I was also tired. I dropped the backpack, yanked out the folding pad, and with the sun warming me, napped for half an hour beneath a snow-free tree next to the boat launch. I would have slept longer except the sun disappeared behind a cloud. The chill instantly woke me.

The permit itinerary had me spending the night farther along the lake, which meant more travel. Still tired, I was tempted to stay at the campground. Yet, with little idea of what the trip would bring, experience said to expect delays along the route. Therefore, if I had the energy, I needed to travel as far as possible each day. I stepped onto the beautiful scene of the snow-covered lake at 2 P.M. I stopped for the day almost one and a half miles and an hour later. In spite of the distance traveled and the amount of weight I carried, I was still dissatisfied.

In the trees, I found a patch of bare ground 25 feet from the lakeshore surrounded by timber fall and scattered tree limbs lying about. Removing some of the branches, I created a small opening and set up a non-winter camp. I ate a cold supper and was asleep before 6 P.M.

I should have been more careful where I put the camp, or perhaps worked more on the spot where it was located, and after a tough day, I paid for it through the night. There was an indentation beneath me too great for the pads to fill. The camp was also on a slight slope that had me rolling left toward the foot of the tent. To make matters worse, I had eaten only two mouthfuls of peanuts and drank no water during the eight hours of travel. While the lack of food was going to affect me in the next day's travel, the affects of dehydration were more immediate. At 11 P.M., I woke up with leg cramps and the beginning of a headache.

April 9: A Frightful Awakening

At 2:15 A.M., I woke with my heart jumping into my throat, convinced a grizzly bear was smashing through the bushes and deadfall, and headed my direction. A few moments later, I realized the sound was something else. For starters, it was coming from the direction of the lake. I heard it again, a cracking sound, and a few moments later, again from a different area farther away. That was when I figured out that the ominous sound was the lake ice shifting and cracking.

With reluctance, I crawled out of the bag and soon had the coffeepot percolating. As I listened to the grinding sound of the ice, I speculated whether I would have to travel on the snowpack along the lake's edge today. Then I saw the thermometer reading of 19 F.

It was still getting light at 6:23 A.M. when I meandered through the bushes and the saplings down to the lake with the backpack on. Arriving on the ice, I put the snowshoes on and continued traveling east. Because of the weak ice and open water along much of the shoreline, I stayed at least 25 feet offshore. I considered walking in the snowpack on the shore. But with a temperature in the high teens and a blue sky, in spite of my trepidation, travel conditions on the lake ice were excellent and beautiful. A combination of a bad night of sleep and the load, however, prevented me from taking full advantage of it. An hour after I left camp, I stopped for 15 minutes and then stopped again half an hour later. The second time I spotted a small 10-foot-wide beach with a large fallen tree, which I promptly sat on after removing the backpack. Several minutes later, I drew water from an opening next to the beach, hefted the load, and continued, only to stop again in less than 15 minutes, where I dropped the backpack onto the ice and sat once more.

Along the shoreline 30 feet away, there was a 15-foot by 4-foot strip of open water between the shore and ice. Except for that and my exhaustion, the travel conditions on the lake were far better than the previous trip, yet my pace was half my prior rate. The sun was still behind 9,891-foot Rainbow Peak, although that would soon change. Already the west end of the lake was swathed in sunlight.

I finally found an inspiration to get moving 10 minutes later. After almost two hours on the ice, I had calmed down substantially where the grinding sounds of the ice were concerned. Then one took place directly beneath me, immediately followed by a small thump. The open water 30 feet away jiggled and I felt the backpack drop. It was only an inch, but more than enough for my chest to constrict with fear and plenty enough to get me moving.

I continued stopping for small breaks but kept the backpack on until 10 A.M. I was a quarter mile short of the upper campground. The sun was just edging its way over Rainbow Peak's north-face cliffs 5,900 feet above me, creating sparkles from the frost on the snowpack.

Several minutes later, I pulled out the day food and a fresh change of socks. Once I was through eating, the sun warmed me into a sleepy trance. At 11:30 A.M., I spotted ripples in the open water near shore again. That got me moving.

Before I left, I decided I would spend the night at the campground. Being tired was the main reason to stop. I was also certain the warmer temperatures had weakened the snowpack beyond the lake.

Next to the shore at the campground was open water approximately four feet wide. Beyond the campground, the quarter-mile remainder of the lake was open water. Still 50 feet out, I stopped and looked for ice to come ashore on. Seeing none, I headed straight for the campground.

I was 15 feet from the open water when the ice broke beneath me. With some experience dropping through ice, I had learned to focus on staying upright as I sank. A few seconds later, the snowshoes landed on the rocky bottom with the water only up to my knees. Knowing that within a minute I would feel water seeping into my boots, I moved immediately. It was a clumsy action. Unable to move quickly with the snowshoes, in slow motion I smashed through the ice and was on shore inside half a minute with my feet still dry.

I dropped the backpack on the rocky shore and sat on an island of pebbles. I had traveled almost five miles in six hours. The biggest reason for the slow pace was the load combined with my negligence to eat the day before. The bad night of sleep was a lesser reason. Tomorrow would be different. I had continued to eat and drink throughout the morning, and tonight I hoped to have a long night of sleep on level ground. By 1 P.M., camp was set up in the snow-free food prep area, while my gear dried in the sun.

Yesterday the barometric pressure had begun to drop. Today a breeze had come up, and the few clouds of this morning had become more numerous. I was unsure when the weather would arrive, but it was coming. The four-day-old forecast called for a mixed bag by tomorrow. Far more important, the clouds and wind could mean that tonight's low temperature would be too warm. Tomorrow might find me walking through the snowpack rather than on it.

I crawled into the sleeping bag at 5 P.M., regretting what I had done to myself during the first day of travel. Rehydrating and eating sanely seemed out of reach for me.

14 • a string of storms

April 10: A Short and Harsh Day

I was up by 1:15 A.M. Except for a low breeze in the branches of the trees, I woke up to quiet, but too much warmth. I glanced at the thermometer, which read 36 F. That was 18 and 20 F. warmer, respectively, than the previous two mornings. Regardless, I had to travel as far as I could today. I got after the stove and coffeepot. As the second pot percolated, I realized it might take another two days to arrive at the initial climb. Even if the backpack weight had been as light as on the last trip, I was certain a walk in hell would be in store for today.

I began the morning trek half an hour sooner than the day before. That meant an additional half hour of darkness, this time inside the forest. I had a hunch grizzly bears were smart enough to know that the best time to travel on snowpack was in the early morning darkness when there was a crust. Since there was no one else in the area for me to bounce this keen observation off, I agreed with me that it was true. My head lantern would reflect off the eyes of any animal that happened to be staring at me, whether it was herbivore, omnivore, or carnivore. As far as that went, I trusted the light of the head lantern to alert me far more than my eyes and ears in full daylight.

Approximately 300 feet beyond the western edge of the campground, I stopped to replenish the water bottle at a small stream. Without giving it a second thought, I dropped down the four-foot-deep snow wall to the stream, filled the bottle, took a drink, and filled it again. The trouble began when it was time to climb out of there. Even without the backpack, it would have been difficult getting out of the miniature crevice with the large snowshoes. What took half a minute to drop into I needed three minutes to extract myself from. Back on top, I stared in exasperation at the stream below and doubted whether the pint of water had been worth the effort. After a few moments, I conceded that if I had been paying attention this incident would never have happened. Traveling alone and being inattentive were excellent ingredients for getting into a butt load of trouble.

Before long I was postholing through the snowpack, breaking through the crust with each step and dropping six inches. I would take 20 to 50 steps and stop for a break. At first, the breaks were a minute or less in length, but as I went farther up the canyon, they grew longer and began to include sitting on snow-free logs. The only reasonable way I could continue to travel was to walk on the tracks I had made two weeks earlier. I still broke through, but less often and not as deeply.

By 8:15 A.M., I was at the end of a 100-foot ascent and briefly thought I was at the summit of the bend in the canyon. In two and a half hours, I had traveled only a mile and a half, and was still a third of a mile short of the summit. An hour later, I reached the small summit, began the descent, and arrived on the canyon floor 20 minutes later. I was no longer traveling alone. The fresh tracks of a wolverine followed my old tracks. The animal seemed to have somewhere to go, while intermittently being sidetracked before returning to the trail and continuing. I followed the tracks for the remainder of the day.

After nearly four hours of travel on a rotting snowpack, I was done in. At a small spring a short distance beyond the descent, I dropped the backpack and began to walk up the canyon. A few minutes later, I approached the location on Bowman Creek where I had placed the camp with the pine bough padding during the last trip. The snowless sand and gravel bar on the other side of the creek was enticing. As I continued up the canyon and the posthole travel worsened, my mind kept going back to the gravel bar. After several hundred feet, I gave up, retrieved the backpack, and headed for the snow-free area.

In the last two months, I was sure I had experienced tougher days. Nevertheless, in this type of snowpack, perhaps I should have stayed put at the previous camp. Then it occurred to me that waiting for a cold night in April at Bowman Lake's elevation of 4,030 feet might make for a long delay. April was already a third gone, and I had no idea when the next cold night would take place. With each passing day, the chances of a deep chill during the night lessened as warmer nights continued to make gains. After a short rest, I became grateful to have gotten anything at all for the day, even if it was only two miles.

A few minutes before noon the temperature dropped 10 degrees in an hour, to 39 F., while the barometer began to rise. My hope for a cold night ahead rose with the barometric pressure, but fell when it began to rain and then sleet. The moisture continued intermittently for the remainder of the day and into the night.

With the short distance covered today, the trip's itinerary was now obsolete. The soonest I would begin the approach would be the sixth day, and I was even uncertain about that. If tomorrow's travel became a repeat of today, it would be the seventh day before I began.

April 11: The First Storm

Although I woke up throughout the night, by 1 A.M. I had gotten enough rest thanks to the nap of the day before. Each time I awoke, I checked the altimeter, which showed the barometric pressure continuing to rise. At one point during the evening, the altimeter showed I had lost 100 feet since arriving at camp. Later in the evening, the barometric pressure began to fall again. By the time I got up, the altimeter read approximately the same as when I arrived the morning before, except there was no longer just intermittent rainfall.

The sound of the steady rain hitting the tent was disheartening. Although I still planned to continue up the canyon today, a growing part of me was already muttering about going nowhere. I also doubted that it was rain and sleet in the higher elevations. If I was wrong, some nasty avalanches could be in the making for today. The temperature dropped to 35 F. and the rain turned to sleet. My doubts continued to grow about the day's travel.

Already one day behind, the thought of staying another day was too much. At 3 A.M., I began to pack. An hour and a half later, the rain and snow had once again become intermittent. The barometric pressure began to drop again. Soon the intermittent sleet again became a steady rainfall. The fight continued as to whether to break camp and head up the canyon or stay put. Suddenly tired, I unclipped the chair, laid down, and slept for an hour and a half.

At 9:30 A.M., with the barometric pressure still falling, I wondered if I would be able to move by the next day. If I delayed traveling until the sixth day, a quick check of what was in front of me for travel time said I would be on the edge of running out of supplies when I finished the circuit.

I decided that I needed to make this my last delay, until I realized how ridiculous that thought was. I was still in the low country, while the trip's main challenges would begin 2,000 feet above me.

Unwilling to stay put any longer, I decided to go inspect the snowpack. I pulled on my boots and stepped into the rain. The snowpack was soggy enough that I would have trouble without a load. Above me, a layer of heavy clouds was hiding everything 500 feet above the canyon floor. More discouraged than ever, I crawled back into the tent.

An hour later, I stuck my head outside. The clouds had lifted enough for me to see fresh snow on the trees on the mountain flanks 500 feet above camp. Encouraged, I surmised that the eventual avalanches might only be mild. By noon, the rain had let up enough that I decided to scout the trail. Without a load, it took an hour to walk the one and a quarter miles in the soggy snowpack to the open area where Bowman and Pocket Creeks converged. The cloud mass had thinned enough for me to vaguely see the approach to Hole in the Wall. I waited 20 minutes before the conditions improved enough to photograph the approach with the 70 to 200 mm camera lens. The entire traverse 2,200 feet above me was impassable, while the elbow unsurprisingly took the prize. The rock cave on the other side of the elbow was invisible, buried in snow. Inside the ravine itself, spindrift snow spilled nonstop. For at least the next few days, any attempt to access Hole in the Wall would be deadly.

Similar to 18 days before when I first saw the approach, I forced myself to realize that I needed to do today's work, which only included a scout and packing a trail up to this location. My job for the remainder of the day was to shoot a few more photos and head back to camp.

Back at camp, before I dropped into the tent, the sun briefly popped out on a small area of the canyon floor and then was gone. I was still damn glad to see it, like an omen of things to come, maybe soon.

As I prepared the stew in the early evening, I noticed with a surprise that the skin on my fingers was splitting as if I was still in extreme cold. I applied the barrier wax and put on the nitrile gloves.

I crawled into the sleeping bag at 6 P.M., heartened to see the barometric pressure was beginning to rise. The change, however, was probably too late for the temperature to get cold tonight. I hoped for the chill anyway.

Half an hour later, I was still awake when I heard a sudden roar. I thought I was listening to an avalanche, and then realized it was the wind. I was staring at the altimeter a few moments later when the elevation suddenly dropped 30 feet. Would the temperature drop after all? I glanced at the outside temperature reading, which read 34 F. Yeah, maybe.

April 12: A Mistake in the Route

I got over six hours of sleep but was still tired when I arose at 1 A.M. I figured I could make up for it at the next camp. While the temperature was a warm 32 F., there was still time for more cold to saturate the canyon floor. The cloudless condition outside was right for greater cold. All I could see was the Milky Way galaxy, and a whole lot of black.

Wrong again, the temperature was 30 F. when I threw on the backpack. At 6 A.M., it was still dark as I began to trek up the canyon. The one-mile packed trail from the previous day gave me a good start. With the trail's end, though, came the end of easy travel. To have a strong enough crust to travel on would have required a temperature drop to 23 F. or lower for several hours. Since the overnight temperature got nowhere near that, what I had was a crust that broke beneath every step. I had traveled in these conditions 48 hours earlier. Based on that experience, I could count on half a mile per hour travel. I also became concerned about how much energy I would have in reserve for the ascent.

One hour later, rather than the two I expected, I entered the winter meadow, which marked the base of the climb. A pleasant surprise, I was nevertheless tired from the bad snowpack and a too heavy load. I dropped the backpack and took a 25-minute break before I headed down to Bowman Creek with the water bottle and an empty bladder. I retrieved a quart and a pint for the climb, realizing that would probably be the last time I would have running water for several days.

Although the snowpack was solid in the meadow, the visible route of the summer trail headed back into the less solid snow inside the trees. I left the backpack and scouted the trail for one hour. I walked on a solid crust the entire time, but there was an extra 100-pound test on the way.

Two hours after my initial entrance in the meadow, I hefted the backpack and began the ascent. With a nearly cloudless sky, I figured I would pay a hefty price later when the sun arrived in this area. I would have been wrong on this account but for a mistake.

When I stopped 20 minutes later, I was more than ready for another break. The crust had held my weight, but there was no getting around the toll of carrying the heavy load. A quick calculation showed I still had

2,000 feet to ascend before I arrived at the edge of the approach. I concluded I would be unable to get there today, but still needed to take a big bite out of that large number.

In a repeat of the trip in March, I planned to cross to the south face at the base of the cliff north of my position. During the last trip, I ascended to 5,100 feet before I crossed the ravine and onto the bare surface. Now at an elevation of 4,600 feet, I saw no reason to keep climbing on the uncertain snowpack of the north face. Ravaged for 20 minutes by the huge load, I had a lousy 200 feet ascended to show for the effort. I made the decision to drop into the ravine and ascend in it to the open area. I dropped 60 vertical feet down the 50-degree slope. Once in the ravine, I got a good look at what I had just done. The trees were still in front of me, and so was the climb. I had just lost a hard-earned 60 feet, which I would now have to reascend.

In another half hour, I halted again for 10 minutes. I was still in the trees, and the opening I was looking for remained hidden somewhere in front of me. Wiped out, I was ready to stop for the day, except short of digging a flat, there was no place to set up a camp. I continued to climb. At 12:30 P.M., I finally emerged into the open area. The good idea of dropping into the ravine had cost an exhausting extra hour.

The sun was on me when I dropped the load at the same location I had used three weeks earlier. The flowing stream, most of it still buried beneath the snowpack, was 25 feet to my right. Since I was unwilling to use the shovel, the stream stayed inaccessible 6 feet below the snowpack. After an hour's rest, I began the climb on the south face, still inside the ravine. The snowshoes slipped in the now slushy snowpack and I fell. Not a serious event, I removed the backpack, stood up, threw the backpack back on, and continued up the mountain.

Within a few minutes, I discovered the altimeter had ceased functioning. In the several years I had owned this type of watch-altimeter-heart monitor, it occasionally quit working. When I fell in the ravine, with the watch strapped to the partially buried camera bag, snow had gotten inside the sensor area and incapacitated the device. Although exasperated with the loss, experience said it would be functioning again in half a day. Tracking barometric pressure through the altimeter was a critical aid in predicting the weather. On television, I had seen this brand of watch on the wrist of numerous people climbing Mount Everest. Yet it repeatedly was unable to handle the rigors of the winter environment in Montana and Idaho's backcountry.

In the next hour and a half, I climbed approximately 400 feet before halting for the day. The camp was about 100 feet above the day's targeted elevation among some scattered Douglas-fir saplings. Equally welcome was the realization that I was no longer exhausted. The south face had made all the difference in my ability to travel.

I built camp in an hour and retired. As tough as the first six hours had been, the final three were almost opposites. For the day, I had traveled three miles and climbed 1,100 feet. Today had been the toughest of the trip, and yet only a prep for what lay ahead. I also intended to capitalize on the better travel conditions at this higher altitude the next morning with an early rising.

April 13: Frozen Delay

The next morning at 3 A.M., I was greeted by a temperature of 24 F. There was also a wind, which at my initial rising did me no favors. With some swift and desperate kicks, I crawled out of the sleeping bag for a trip outdoors. The chill and the wind combined for a memorable and quick visit.

I had set the tent up the day before with the southwest wind hitting the low end of the tent. The strengthening breeze changed directions numerous times throughout the night and now approached from the northeast, slamming into the head of the tent. As a result, the temperature inside the tent was only three degrees warmer than outside. Like 24 hours earlier, the nighttime sky was clear of clouds. Obviously, a change was coming, but without the altimeter, I was unable to predict what the wind was bringing—continued clear skies, or a storm. With the change in the wind direction, though, I had a suspicion. That same wind direction had brought bad weather three weeks earlier.

Over coffee and breakfast, I contemplated two nagging problems. First, apparently I was wearing the nitrile gloves too much. The skin on my hands was beginning to peel. I reapplied the hand salve and decided I would remove the gloves once the day's travel began. The second problem was the watch's still inoperative altimeter. In the darkness, I howled, "Perhaps if I stuck it in a fucking vault box that will keep it safe."

I had been packing the gear for an hour when I noticed at 6 A.M. the altimeter was functioning again. Glad to see that, I was also unaware that I had just misread the reading. I thought the watch indicated that the barometric pressure was rising.

I decided the next camp would be at the base of the climb to the ridgeline where the traverse began. Still uncertain if the traverse was possible, I would ascend the avalanche chute and get the close look I had missed a few weeks earlier. I also thought I would only need a few hours to get to the next camp. The plan went to hell as soon as I crawled out of the tent shortly after 6 A.M.

Through the years, I had built numerous camps in wet snowpack, which froze overnight. With that in mind, I took what I thought were enough precautions the day before for this possibility. However, I missed something. I had placed the tent on the wet snowpack during the heat of the day. The tent sank into the snowpack, which froze overnight. I carefully chopped, hacked, and chipped through the ice and snow for two hours. When I finally threw the backpack on at 10 A.M., I was no longer fresh, and was angry at how I could have overlooked something so obvious the day before. A few minutes of readjusting the tie-downs and stakes the evening before would have saved those two lost hours.

I ascended the first 400 feet in one hour and 15 minutes. Unlike the trip in March, I avoided the ravine and ascended on the right side of it. Although I was carrying a much heavier load, I was clearly in much better shape than that old man two months earlier in Belly River. Yet the weight combined with the climb was still costly. I had to take numerous breaks to recoup lost energy. The breaks accounted for nearly half the travel time. Twice I removed the backpack, the second time for 35 minutes while I ate lunch. When I arrived at the base of the climb on the Brown Pass bench at 6,268 feet, which marked the ascent to the approach, four hours had elapsed.

I built the camp 50 feet away from the leading edge of the avalanche whose chute I would be climbing the next morning. Scattered around the camp were Douglas-fir saplings up to 15 feet tall. Several were between the camp and the chute, with a few leaning over from it. Without snow, this would have been a forest of up to 20-year-old trees.

Half an hour earlier, I had also discovered my mistake about the barometric pressure. It was dropping. Ten miles to the east, an ominous cloud bank stretching over the horizon smothered 10,466-foot Mount Cleveland, the park's highest peak. Since the wind was blowing from that direction, I didn't need the altimeter to know what was coming.

An hour later, the freshly built camp was ready for occupancy. I sat down and ate another lunch. By the time I was finished, the plan to climb to the ridgeline had almost disappeared inside the clouds now thickening above camp. In spite of the imminent storm, I still wanted to make the climb. With no idea how long the storm would last, this afternoon might be my only opportunity to get a clear view of the approach. Before the entire load went up, I needed to check the feasibility of traversing the slope to Hole in the Wall. Regardless of what I deemed as a need, the wind and quickly thickening clouds made a strong argument against going up.

I made the right decision on suspending the reconnaissance. At 4 P.M., it began to snow on Chapman Peak one mile east of camp and on the northern ridgeline that overshadowed the camp. The snow arrived in a nonstop wind at 6:30 P.M. Had I gone up, I would have been caught in the snowstorm.

I altered the plan for the next day. I would split the load and ferry the first half when I went up to get a look at the approach. If the traverse was feasible and tonight's snow was light, tomorrow I would try to get at least halfway across the approach.

The previous storm appeared to have dropped about two feet of snow. If that happened tonight, I would go nowhere tomorrow, which caused more concern. Tomorrow was the day I was supposed to arrive at Hole in the Wall. In addition to already being more than one day behind, another one-day delay would have me close to running out of food by the end of the trip. With a load this large, I was able to bring only three extra days of supplies. On the other hand, more time off sounded pretty good. My shoulders hurt, and my hands were numb. The sciatic nerve in my left hip, the small of my back, and my swollen knees were also in pain.

I was in the sleeping bag by 7 P.M. and soon asleep.

April 14: The Second Storm

Outside, the temperature was 19 F. while the tent interior was above freezing. In an ongoing wind, the snow accumulated up the yellow sides of the tent, which provided insulation and a warmer interior. By the time I crawled out of the sleeping bag, the snow was halfway to the roof. Part of the affect of this cocoon-like atmosphere was 12 hours inside the sleeping bag. I arose after 7 A.M. Half an hour later, I was sipping one of the finest cups of coffee I had ever had in the backcountry. The pot had perked an extra five minutes, and that 12 hours of sleep had added to my comfortable disposition.

For the next two hours, the snow and wind continued, interspersed with gusts. Unlike the day before, this morning's wind came almost exclusively from the west. I watched the altimeter climb and drop depending on the direction of the wind.

Soon after crawling out of the bag, I knew I would again have to redo the trip's schedule. There would be no attempt to get across the approach for at least 24 hours. It was also a near certainty I would be unable to ascend safely to the approach. Nevertheless, it remained my plan to climb up there sometime today.

Clearly, on this 7th day out of 13, trouble was brewing. Roughly 10 days of food remained. Would Carleen call the park service? It was impossible for her to know that I was safe. I was also certain she would be watching the weather forecast.

At 9 A.M., I crawled out of the tent and got my first real look at what had happened in the 15 hours since I had entered the tent. None of my tracks remained from the afternoon before. I had used the two-foot-long snow pickets to anchor the tent. The fresh snow had buried two while the two others were barely visible on the west side of the tent. The ice axe, used as another anchor, had also disappeared. The wind was blowing the snow nearly horizontal, restricting my view to approximately 300 feet. The beast had bared its fangs.

Until last night, I regretted that I had brought the heavier four-season tent. But the lighter tent I used during the March trip would have collapsed with this punishment. Back inside the tent, I was grateful for this small bubble of civilization.

The storm continued through the morning. At 11 A.M., the barometric pressure had risen back to almost the same level as when I arrived here. I went to work organizing the climbing gear. I prepared the new 100-foot rope and arranged the ice screws for easy access, although my doubts were growing about needing them. With the new waist harness on, I worked building a chest harness for over an hour and a half before I thought I had it right. The amount of time it took discouraged me, and I wondered if I would even bother with the upper harness once I began the approach. My lackluster enthusiasm concerning the chest harness would eventually bear near-tragic consequences.

I finally admitted aloud my foolishness. I was getting ready to do something alone for which I had no experience. With the exception of the ice axe and crampons, the remaining technical gear was foreign to me. While

I had worked out what each item was for, I still had a justifiably enormous fear of what I was about to embark upon with zero experience.

With more than a hint of anger, I admitted into the recorder what I was doing. "Okay, I just spent the last three hours or so—I don't know how long it's been—hours working on setting all this gear up, and I'm acting like a fucking pro here. How typical, so lame of me. I just hope I survive me today and tomorrow."

What I said was only partially true. I had abundant experience climbing in dire winter conditions. More than the climbing gear, my brain was my most important tool. I knew, for example, that today I would be stepping into a strong avalanche situation for which a rope, harness, and snow pickets were useless.

A Failed Ascent

Shortly after 2 P.M., I packed an approximate 50-pound load with the climbing gear and some day-hike essentials. Still uncertain why I was going forward with this, I got into my outer gear. In three hours, the barometric pressure was unchanged. The wind gusts continued from the west with the heavy snow speeding by like white bullets. Moreover, with the temperature at 25 F., all the snowfall of the last 22 hours was an accumulating powder on a crust. I continued with the preparations anyway.

At 3 P.M., I began to ascend the slope 250 feet north of camp. The fear subsided with each step. On the flat below the chute, the fresh snow was all I had thought it would be—powder and at least two feet deep. Once I began the ascent, I caught a break. The wind had blown the crust clean. Unwilling to travel in the chute, I ascended near the wounded saplings on the left side of the chute. Consequently, I was plowing through the deep powder on the sheltered side of the scattered trees.

The nearly clear slope came with an additional price. The wind, interspersed with strong gusts, slammed into the backpack and me, threatening to knock me over. The wind-driven snow crawled through every opening of the outer gear and onto my skin. Like weeks earlier on this mountainside, I barely stayed warm during the numerous stops.

Wearing the sunglasses rather than the goggles, I had trouble seeing. Those cute snowflakes driven by a 15 to 30 mph wind turned into an ongoing barrage of biting stings on my face. Some got around the sunglasses, stinging and bringing tears to my eyes. Back at camp, I had known this was a lousy idea. Yet here I was on the side of the mountain, full of regrets, but continuing the ascent.

The angle of the mountainside increased, and the snowshoes began to slide backwards. With each step forward, I slid back half a stride. I finally realized I needed to stop somewhere and put the crampons on. The fear continued to grow as I pushed toward a rock outcropping. I finally halted on the high side of a small Douglas-fir sapling, 20 feet short of the outcrop. To get around it I would have to cross the avalanche chute. The only way I would go out there, though, was with the crampons.

I dropped the backpack and removed the bag holding the climbing gear. Searching around the now almost empty backpack and then the bag, I soon discovered that, like on the March climb, I had once again left the crampons in camp. I would go no farther today. In the face of the storm, I was more delighted to have forgotten the crampons than I should have been. Carelessness had created a legitimate reason to descend out of what I now saw as a mistaken ascent.

As if on cue with this latest revelation, the wind began to let up. Within a minute, I could see Brown Pass a mile to the east and Bowman Lake five miles southwest of me. My course was unaltered by the change. I would venture no farther up the 45-degree slope without crampons. For all of that, fate probably lay in wait for me to continue the push upwards just so it could hammer me with another storm or an avalanche.

Knowing I would return the following day, I left the climbing bag inside the branches of the small tree and began the descent. I was back at camp in eight minutes. Moments before I entered the tent, the wind and the heavy snowfall returned. I smirked with the thought that fate had slipped up and missed that I had descended. A sobering thought, I abruptly recalled my location. With more wind and snowfall, the danger of an avalanche would increase, perhaps enough to reach through the small trees that separated the avalanche chute and this camp.

Inside the tent, I immediately adjusted all of the gear around the chair. Then with a clenched left fist on the tent floor, I tried to lift myself onto the chair. The snow beneath the floor was still powder. It collapsed beneath the weight of my fist. The wrist bent and pain shot through the joint. After a few minutes, I decided I only strained the wrist. I was unable to bend it, however, without a lot of pain.

Using a seven-foot length of one-inch webbing, I wrapped the wrist

April 9: From the frozen surface of Bowman Lake, the snowfields of upper Bowman canyon held much promise.

The thinning ice on Bowman Lake finally gave way, 15 feet off the shore at upper Bowman Lake campground.

April 12: The ramparts of upper Bowman canyon, from left to right, 8,528-foot Boulder Peak, 8,883-foot Mount Custer, Hole in the Wall and the approach at roughly 6,300 feet, and 9,406-foot Chapman Peak.

The steep climb out of Bowman canyon ended on this small flat before continuing
the ascent to the bench west of Brown Pass.

April 14, late afternoon: Three weeks after the first failure to reconnoiter the approach, the second attempt ended in failure during the first day of a five-day snowstorm.

April 15: After an all-night storm, the snow briefly let up in the mid-afternoon. Encouraged, I prepared for another ascent attempt. Ready to leave, I realized the danger of my camp's close proximity to the avalanche chute and instead relocated the camp.

April 16: The approach to Hole in the Wall. Just minutes later, the ninth day of the trip, I began the exit back to Polebridge.

April 18: The view from inside the tent. Unable to descend off the Brown Pass bench, I waited nearly two days on the lip for the snowpack to stabilize.

April 19: A cold sunrise, the morning I was able to descend off the Brown Pass bench.

The first rays of sunlight are breaking through the fog and clouds around 8,790 foot Thunderbird Mountain. At 7°F, it is the coldest and the last morning on the Brown Pass bench.

before wrapping the webbing with duct tape. The color of my fingers remained unchanged, which was a good indication that I had not cut off the circulation. I could also still move my wrist, but only slightly.

Once settled in, the solemnity concerning the storm began to dissipate. Soon after, I began to plan the next day. With the climbing gear halfway up the mountainside, tomorrow I would ascend back up with a nearly empty backpack. For a few moments, I entertained the thought of moving all the remaining gear up to the ridgeline and return for the climbing gear. Then I recalled that I needed to look at the approach first and deem whether it was passable, something I was unwilling to do without the climbing gear. My only certainty was that, if the wind and snowfall continued the following day, I would go nowhere.

Hell, I thought with growing frustration, maybe I was only fooling myself. With all the powder that had fallen in the last 24 hours combined with what was presently falling, the snow would have to warm up so it could adhere to the already existing crust. It was possible I would be unable to attempt the climb to the approach, to say nothing of the remainder of the trip.

Before 6 P.M., I heard what I thought was the roar of a jet. Less than a half minute later, the noise abruptly stopped. The avalanches had begun. Several minutes later, I heard a second roar. Unable to see beyond 500 feet, I stayed in the tent. Increasingly, I doubted I would be able to make the climb safely, much less step out on the approach. I also had no doubt that in the elbow there was now a constant flow of spindrift cascading to the canyon floor. With the knowledge that my plans might be for naught, I nevertheless continued to plan for another attempt the following day. I could always postpone it when tomorrow arrived.

Since early morning the barometric pressure had gradually risen, generating wind all day and into the evening. As it alternated directions through the day between easterly and westerly headings, I became convinced that high and low barometric pressures were in a battle for this area along the Continental Divide. Most of the time, the wind came from the west. Although the snow fell heavily into the evening, I concluded that the next day would bring blue sky and warmth. On that premise, I stayed hopeful I would make the ascent tomorrow. I fell asleep a short time later.

Several times through the night I woke to the roar of avalanches. At 9 P.M. the wind stopped. An hour later, I woke up again to more wind shaking the tent. At midnight, I woke with a start. Except for some deep plopping sounds, it was dead quiet.

God almighty, a grizzly is approaching the camp!

Gripping the can of pepper spray, I lay quiet in the sleeping bag. The distinct though intermittent sounds continued while my mind raced around trying to figure out what else would make that sound. Could it be snow falling off tree branches? Yeah? And what about all that wind that had been out there earlier keeping the branches snow free?

In less than a minute, I had had enough. There was only one way to find out where the sound originated. I crawled out of the sleeping bag, opened the two doors, and peered out with the LED head lantern on high. As I looked for grizzly bear tracks or beady and hungry eyes, I barely noticed the beauty of the pine trees, their branches smothered in snow, punctuating the placid surface of the snowpack. In the weighty quiet that comes immediately after a snowfall, all I saw was the smooth surface of a fresh snowpack up to the sides of the tent. In the distance, I heard a few more plops. Several seconds later, one of the nearby tree branches released a pile of snow that landed on the snow below with a plop.

I breathed with relief then got embarrassed. Like so many other ill-felt moments, I decided no one needed to know about this latest bear visit. It approached the silliness of an incident in 1994 when I somehow mistook an approaching grizzly bear as a porcupine. On occasion, Carleen would still work me over with that one.

I crawled back into the sleeping bag and soon fell back to sleep. When I woke at 3 A.M., a blizzard was shaking the tent. The barometric pressure had dropped again. Both inside and outside of the tent, the temperature hovered around the freezing mark. I attributed that to the terrific wind. Secure inside the tent and snug in the sleeping bag, the protected feeling lulled me back to sleep in spite of the racket of the flapping tent.

April 15: Getting Out of Harm's Way

When I arose shortly after 6 A.M., the blizzard continued. I recalled my erroneous weather forecast from the day before. Yep, I was some kind of a weatherman. As dawn's light increased, the evidence of the deep snowpack began to show itself on the tent. The snow was two feet deep on the western wall while the downwind side was closer to three. An hour later the wind let up, and I partially opened the vestibule door to see if the snow had lessened. My timing was almost perfect. Through the heavy snowfall, I saw the swirling wind coming through the small trees 100 feet away straight for the camp while everything behind it had already disappeared in a whiteout. I barely got the door zippered when the wind hit the tent.

I sat back in the chair dejectedly. Yesterday I had forecast open sky and planned a climb to the edge of the approach for today. I looked around for something to blame, and landed on the extended forecast. There was nothing like this in the NOAA forecast. They got it wrong too! A couple seconds later, I realized that this was the eighth day. Their forecast only extended out seven days. I felt the gap widen between the orderly and predictable world of civilization and me.

That damn watch better not quit on me again, not in this. With the increased vulnerability and fear, my oath was more of a plea.

By 8:30 A.M., the wind was no longer as strong nor was the snow falling as hard. While discouraged, I wondered if the day's plan was yet possible. I had already packed the kitchen and was preparing other items to be packed. A few minutes later, I abjectly declared there would be no attempt at getting to Hole in the Wall. There probably was no longer enough food and fuel remaining. It was time to end this trip as a failed attempt, and exit to Polebridge. I would resupply and wait for a forecast for improved conditions, and then return for the fourth and, undoubtedly, the final attempt.

I was resolute, however, that I would go nowhere until I got a look at the approach. If it was undoable even in good snow conditions, there would be no need for another trip. If I could get up there today, I would begin the exit tomorrow morning. For now though, I waited to see what the weather would do for the remainder of the day. The wind and snow continued into the morning with almost no change in the barometric pressure. Sitting in the tent with nothing but the maps to read, I entertained myself with repeated inventories of the food and fantasy reworks of the trip.

It was unnecessary to open the vestibule at 9:30 A.M. to know it was still snowing. The wind had died again, but I could hear the whispered landings on the tent of a thousand snowflakes per minute. The wind returned 20 minutes later and, in a shocker, so did the sun! I opened the vestibule and stared at the wonder of a sunny winter wonderland, the sunlight reflecting off the falling crystals. Out came the camera with the 70 to 200 mm lens attached—along with instant fogging on the lens and camera body. Disgusted, I placed the camera in a plastic bag and the camera bag. A short time later, the sun disappeared behind the clouds.

My negligence of allowing moisture to collect on the camera gear was happening elsewhere. Each time I unsealed a cold fuel bottle, a small amount of moisture coated the interior. Eventually enough moisture collected at the bottom of the bottle to clog the stove. It was a safety factor with possibly dire results. Like the camera gear, the solution was to avoid sudden warmth with the cold container.

By 10:30 A.M., the wind had dropped to a breeze. The snowfall was light enough for me to see the lower elevation of the ridgeline that hid the approach. While I became more restless to attempt the climb, the altimeter indicated that this was nothing more than an interlude. At noon, I could see the cliffs that overlooked the approach with open sky behind. In spite of the small weather change, with at least 18 inches of snow having fallen overnight and through the morning, it remained unsafe to go up. When I decided to make the attempt anyway, the translucent sunlight was spreading across the bench despite a light snowfall.

I normally carried the audio recorder in one of the photo vest pockets. Today it would remain in the tent. I knew what I proposed to do was wrong and that there was a chance I would die. It therefore seemed appropriate to leave the recorder in the tent so Carleen would know what my final plan had been.

I packed the gear and was ready to go at 1:30 P.M. As I inspected the avalanche chute I was going to climb again, I noticed something that made me pause. At the rock ledge just above where I had cached the climbing gear was a wall of snow that crossed the avalanche chute. Was that snowdrift there yesterday? Could it have built up over the last 24 hours, a mere 250 feet above this bench? If that was the case, what was lying on the 1,500 feet of avalanche chute above that spot?

I had been uncomfortable with the close proximity of the camp to the chute since the snowfall began 48 hours earlier. Since then, some three feet of snow had fallen, while only a few small trees stood between the camp and the avalanche chute. In a moment of clarity, I abruptly abandoned today's climb, turned west, and went looking for a safer campsite. I found what I was looking for 300 feet away, and for the next two hours moved the camp. Meanwhile, with a partly cloudy sky, the day got warmer. As badly as I wanted to go up, I was now unwilling to take the chance. The heavy clouds in the distance and the continued low barometric pressure indicated more bad weather was imminent.

In the tent, I berated myself for being too afraid to make the climb. I laid out accusations about how the camp had been fine where it was and that I only used the danger of an avalanche as a way to stay off the mountain. I berated myself again for missing my chance at an unrestricted view of the approach. Behind all this self-castigation was the knowledge that in two hours my one-foot-deep trail between the two camps had almost disappeared under the drifting snow. While I finally conceded that postponing the climb was the right thing to do, the thought of spending 72 hours in this area without getting up there for an inspection was maddening. Yet what other alternative did I have, short of growing a pair of fools between my legs?

By 6 P.M., the barometric pressure was sinking more. Watching the altimeter gain feet was enraging. How much more of this was I going to have to take? My idleness and the sunshine briefly got the better of me, and I backed away from the decision to make an exit to Polebridge. A part of me realized my thinking was askew. Nevertheless, with a permit due to expire in five days, I proceeded to reexamine finishing the circuit. Tomorrow I might find that the west face approach was a blown-clean crust, I argued. I might even camp at Hole in the Wall tomorrow night. If all went perfectly after today, I could exit at Polebridge with one day of food and fuel remaining.

Sure, the remainder of the trip was going to be wonderful just as soon as I got to the approach. As soon as I uttered my thoughts aloud, I knew this hunkered-down tent dream had skittered off the side of rational. Nevertheless, I held onto it as a thread of hope. Otherwise, my alternative inside the tent was a state of hopelessness.

On the upside for the day, the wrist brace had worked flawlessly throughout the afternoon. When I crawled inside the sleeping bag just before 7 P.M., there was still a mixture of open sky and clouds overhead, although the barometric pressure stayed low.

15 • the approach

April 16: Storm Be Damned

I woke briefly at 1 A.M. to the same sounds of the night before. In a dead calm, snow was dropping off the tree branches. For the tree branches to drop loads of accumulated snow, it must have snowed for hours. After waking for the final time at 2:45 A.M., I stayed inside the bag for another half hour. At 22 F., the temperature outside had been the same throughout the night.

The illusion of the previous evening continued. Without a wind, I might be able to ascend. Then I saw that the barometric pressure had dropped some more through the night. No matter, today I had to attempt the approach or begin the exit. Either way, I was desperate to get that close-up view of the approach.

To ascend went against my experience, which said stay off the mountainside. Getting back to the climbing gear located 250 feet above me looked ominous, much less going beyond that point. Even if I were able to ascend to the ridgeline, would a cloud bank prevent me from seeing anything?

I thought about the exit. Was it possible to get off this bench? There was over 1,700 feet between the Bowman canyon floor and this camp. Was I stuck up here?

At 6 A.M., the temperature had risen to 25 F., while the barometric pressure had fallen some more. The kitchen was packed and my morning hygiene completed. I removed the brace and was relieved to see that the wrist had nearly recovered. There was less snowfall and it was calm. Through the partially open vestibule door, I could see the cliffs above the ridgeline. My hope for making the climb went up a couple notches. Back to thinking there was still a remote chance I would be able to continue on to Hole in the Wall today, I kept packing.

At 6:30 A.M., a combination of snowflakes and pellets hit the tent. I again examined the likelihood of what would happen today—an exit. It could take two days to arrive at Bowman Lake's upper campground and possibly another five to arrive at Polebridge. Near the canyon floor, there would be the nightmarish travel in rotting snow, probably the full distance to the lake. Nor would my problems with the spring melt be over once I arrived there. I would be unable to walk on the remainder of the lake ice. The trail, however, would probably be snow free along the lake's edge.

For the next trip, there was only a nine-day supply of food and fuel in the vehicle, several days short of what I would need. I would also need an extended forecast, one that favored me a little more. The thought of traveling six days through rotting snowpack to get back up here only to run into more of this weather was sickening. The tears began to flow and I howled the rhetorical question, "Why is it so fucking hard?"

The outburst lasted only a few moments.

The Approach Revealed

I broke camp and placed the gear that would remain behind beneath the collapsed tent. With the wind's return, to keep the tent from being blown away, I shoveled chunks of snow onto the light fabric.

I was ready to go at 8:40 A.M. With the backpack on and staring at the equipment on the snowpack, I commented that I hoped I would see the gear again. Through the falling snow, I could vaguely see the ridgeline and the avalanche chute. The scene looked horrible, and the fear of what I was about to do overwhelmed me; I began to cry again. This time it was more than a whimper. With tears blinding me, I bellowed in protest. I did not want to go up there, but the thought of leaving without getting to the edge of the approach was unbearable. The sobbing ended only after I started moving toward the vacant white slot on the mountainside. Once I focused on the ascent, much of the fear turned to resolve.

Unlike the two previous climbs up the chute, today I prepared for the wind and snow. I was wearing the balaclava and ski goggles, with the crampons inside the backpack. Once the snowshoes were unable to get a grip in the deep powder of the slope, I would replace them with the crampons. If I were unable to get through the fresh snow with the crampons on, I would have no option but to turn back.

A light snow and a steady 15 mph wind accompanied me out of camp. As I entered the level area where numerous avalanches had pushed themselves into the scattered saplings, I encountered deeper powder. I pushed through, again continuing to stay on the left side of the avalanche chute. The snowdrifts on the lee side of the trees were deeper and more difficult to get through. Two days earlier, it took 19 minutes to ascend to the location where I left the climbing bag. Today I needed 30 minutes.

After packing the climbing gear, I altered my route. I had planned to go left, into the scattered trees below the rock outcropping, circle around it, and continue the climb. Once I arrived in the area, compared to the avalanche chute, that direction appeared to be far more dangerous. The snow over there seemed ready to slide down a more steeply angled mountainside, which was directly above the cliffs that overshadowed Bowman canyon. If I started sliding in this powder, I could go over the cliff. In addition, the huge snowdrift I had spotted from camp extended only partway across the avalanche chute. I would take a chance and switchback around the drift on the other side of the chute. The downside to the avalanche chute route was the 1,500 feet above me uninterrupted by scattered trees.

When I threw the backpack back on, which had increased to over 50 pounds, I now had a fair load to carry. I climbed another 160 feet in 20 minutes before the first real trouble began. I was almost back to the western side of the chute on a swept-clean crust. Approximately 30 feet from the edge, I reentered six to eight inches of powder. Pushing on, I was 10 feet from the edge of the chute, marked by an avalanche-damaged sapling, when I found out that the warmth of the afternoon before had turned the crust into slippery slush. The overnight snow had covered the softened snowpack, protecting it from the cold. When I stepped onto it with the left snowshoe, my left leg immediately slid down the slope.

Using the ski pole on my left hand and ice axe on my right, I stopped the sudden slide. With my heart in my throat, I used the teeth of the snowshoe to kick away the powder and slush down to the more solid snowpack. A quick look around showed I was in trouble. I was approximately 430 feet above the bench, and it appeared I was going no farther. The sapling suddenly looked far away. I started kicking a trail to the tree. I slid a few more times, but within a minute was safe on the high side of the tree. I dropped the backpack and leaned it against the badly beaten, two-inch-thick sapling.

At this point, I believed I had two alternatives: slide off the mountain with the snowshoes or posthole with the crampons. Wearing the crampons

30 minutes later, I instead decided to continue the attempt toward the ridgeline. I took my first hesitant step away from the tree. The crampon sank four inches, stopped, and got a firm grip. Several steps later, I pushed through a snowdrift without a problem, my hesitation all but gone.

Compared to my previous pace, I sped toward the ridgeline, almost unmindful of the snowfall and low-hanging clouds threatening to hide everything. I was now somewhere above the hidden summer trail and had been in scattered trees since exiting the avalanche chute. I was also encouraged by the slightly gentler angle of the slope. The breeze and the snow were continuous. Wearing the ski goggles and balaclava, my heading was northwest, straight into the weather.

For 15 minutes, I plowed through at least one foot of snow. The still-falling snow and clouds restricted my view most of the time, but I knew I was getting close. Then the cloud bank lifted above the cliffs that overlooked the approach. Before I could get the camera into position, they had disappeared once again. Although I snarled something, it was a happy noise. I figured I was less than five minutes from the hidden view of the approach. About 100 feet away were a couple of large, dead trees. With mounting excitement, I headed in their direction. Several minutes later, I arrived between the trees and onto a much steeper 50-degree slope.

With the cloud bank and snow restricting the view, I nevertheless could see the first 250 feet of the approach, and it was a God almighty heart-wrenching sight! Although the angle of the slope I stood on was steep, in the scattered trees I was relatively safe. A few feet beyond them, the angle of the mountainside increased another 5 degrees. The powder was midway up my thighs and the crampons were no longer able to penetrate to the crust. I had no doubt that if I stepped onto the empty slope less than 15 feet away, I would start an avalanche. If I somehow survived the slide, the cliff below would take me.

A Doable Trip But Not Today

The heavy snowfall that had stranded me for days on the bench 500 feet below was much deeper on this traverse, which meant that even if I had the necessary supplies I still would have been unable to go any farther. Nor was I disappointed. With numerous unknowns suddenly known, I felt relief. Once a crust formed on this huge, but smooth and seemingly tranquil slope, without a doubt, I could see myself out there. While I would begin the exit to civilization today, I would be back.

Then I wondered how I was going to get that past Carleen. She had taken a much stronger stance against these trips at the end of the March trip. When I had told her of my intent to come back on this trip, I could see her rising concern and anger. Now I proposed to go back after being gone two or three weeks and tell her, "one more trip." I had no answer for how I would broach this with her.

Simultaneously, both of us were concerned about how much time, effort, and money had already gone into the trips. By the time I got back to the vehicle, counting the eight-day scouting trip at the end of September, I would have spent approximately 40 days in the backcountry of the park for this endeavor. Yet what a waste it would be to exit now without returning and attempting to access Hole in the Wall.

I spent two hours on the ridgeline and even descended 100 feet in a half-hearted and unsuccessful attempt to find the summer trail. Mostly I inspected possible places from which to begin the traverse. I descended slowly in the deep snow of the rounded ridgeline seeking safe vantage points in attempts to get better photos of the approach. I came upon an eight-inch-thick limber pine tree about 20 minutes later and took some photos on its upper side before I skirted around the tree. Already dropping nearly three feet through the powder, my right leg suddenly kept going down. On solid footing, the left leg dropped no further. I fell backward, and was suddenly up to my chest in the snow.

Acting like a flotation device, the backpack saved me from going all the way under. A few minutes later, I was out of the hole. Thereafter I gave a wide berth to the downside of the larger trees. Oddly, I was never afraid, and when I got back on my feet, I let out a delighted laugh, pulled out the camera, and took a series of shots from the new vantage point of freshly packed snow.

Throughout the time I was on the ridgeline, the wind and snow never stopped. The clouds on the slope, however, rose temporarily, and the snowfall became lighter. I finally shot some photographs that showed more than a vague scene of the approach.

As I prepared to make my way back down the mountain and to the former camp, I put away the ice axe and brought out the second ski pole. I figured the poles would be more effective on the powdery descent. The one area of concern was the avalanche chute. If needed, I could always pull the axe back out.

The nonstop snow and wind had filled most of the tracks I made earlier. No longer climbing, I moved quickly and was soon around the bend and on the south-facing slope. One small open area I entered gave me a few interesting moments when the entire expanse of fresh powder suddenly broke loose and headed down the mountain. As the snow slid and tumbled down the slope, I immediately argued that it was no avalanche. Avalanches were much larger than this puny thing. Nevertheless, I proceeded at a much slower pace. A few minutes later, it happened again. Neither slide was large enough to knock me down, but they certainly brought to my attention the danger I was in.

In the three days I had been on the Brown Pass bench, there had been no nearby avalanches, which now gave cause for concern. Too much snow had fallen, and these small slides in the scattered trees were a good reason to become alarmed. I was on Chapman Peak's steep ridge that leads west for the one-mile length of the bench. With the entire mountainside an avalanche chute, it was only a matter of time before it slid. It occurred to me that to make a return I would need to survive this trip first.

The slope took two hours to ascend, but only 45 minutes to descend.

Back at the camp, I hurriedly packed the remaining gear. An hour later, at 2 P.M., with the snowshoes back on, I headed east. Although the snow had almost stopped, the wind had picked up and was gusting. Fortunately, it would be at my back until I made the right turn and dropped toward the base of Thunderbird Mountain.

After my morning experience, as I began to trek eastward I looked forward to the rolling knolls of the bench. I traveled 50 feet before I realized that my hope for the rest of the day had pinned itself to another illusion. The powder was deep, and I sank nearly 2 feet with every step. Experience said to drop the backpack and build a trail; however, I angrily balked and continued to plow through the snowpack.

Half an hour later and now exhausted, I triumphantly thought I had found another solution. The wind appeared to be keeping the open south-face slopes clear of the fresh-fallen snow. No more powder for me; I took the first step on a 30-foot ascent. Instead of digging into a crust, the teeth of the left snowshoe encountered slush. A moment later, I was lying in the snowpack, and the day's travel had just changed.

I removed the backpack and slowly got back to my feet. There would be no exit of the bench today. A gentle slope had just toppled me, while several hundred feet ahead was a series of much steeper slopes. I would be unable to descend them in these conditions.

I needed to make a camp; the only question was where. My options were limited. I could turn around and go back into the small trees, or I could continue eastward and build a camp inside the larger trees near the pass.

I had left the old area for more than one reason. Besides the increasing vulnerability to avalanches, I also needed to use as much of the day as possible to close the distance to Polebridge. Most of all, but with the least value, was my desire to feel I had accomplished something rather than holing up in the same area for a fourth night.

To the east a third of a mile, the larger trees would provide better protection from a sliding mountainside. Deciding on them, I traveled for another 45 minutes before finding an area I thought was reasonably safe. In that time I fell four times, further validating my need to stop. Shortly before I arrived at the campsite, holes appeared in the clouds showing the sky beyond, creating patches of sunlight on the snowpack.

While providing some shelter from the incessant wind, the large trees around the campsite were also indicative that no avalanche had crashed through the area in at least 50 years. I placed the camp inside the eastern edge of the trees near the bottom of the gentle ravine that appeared to end at the top of Brown Pass. The location also gave an unrestricted view of Chapman Peak. At 1,600 feet away, perhaps during the summer I would have been able to see Brown Pass from the location of the camp, but just now, it was invisible. Either the wind had created a huge snowdrift 500 feet east of my position or an avalanche powered by 3,200 feet of Chapman Peak mountainside had filled the space over there.

The patches of open sky and spotty sunshine disappeared. Three hours later, I was lying awake inside the sleeping bag at 7 P.M. when the snow returned. It began with snow pellets, but within several minutes became straight snowfall. I was neither alarmed nor surprised; the barometric pressure had dropped again. Outside, the temperature was 28 F., while inside it was 12 degrees warmer. I fell asleep half an hour later.

16 • stuck on brown pass

April 17: Fortress Mentality and Half Rations

After nine nights alone, a part of me had begun to adjust. I slept a solid eight hours, all the while knowing that a winter storm continued throughout the night. At 3:40 A.M., the interior of the tent was warm, while outside the temperature was less than 18 F. I arose and after hitting the vestibule several times to knock the snow off, I partially opened it and got a first look at what had happened in eight hours. Although a lot of snow had fallen in the last four days, I was still impressed. The snow was halfway up the door, while the snowfall continued to be heavy. The view was upsetting. In the early morning hour, I somehow forgot that this was a winter trip. With the tent vented and me now in a funk, I got the percolator going.

An hour later, I started the second cup of coffee. My depressed mood was unchanged. I missed home, Carleen, the dogs, and the security of civilization.

It occurred to me that if the snow was dumping inside Bowman canyon the way it was up here, even with a seven-day supply of day food remaining, I might get hungry. While I realized the unlikelihood of that happening, I still put myself on smaller rations.

The new snowfall was heightening the already dangerous avalanche conditions. Although the day before, I had paid scant attention to the roars on the surrounding peaks, my complacency did not include thinking I was safe. This morning my fear was back in force. There was no safe spot up here. Yesterday I had walked through several recent avalanches to get to the relative safety of this area. Although the trees here were large, this close to Brown Pass also meant I was near the most dangerous area of the bench, the one-third-mile swath below Chapman Peak.

At 5 A.M., I dug the snow away from the vestibule again. Without a doubt, this was the heaviest snowfall of the trip. I reflected back on the original route when it was supposed to have been a crossing of the park. At best, the trip would have ended with me exiting down Bowman canyon. For that matter, I doubt I could have gotten over Stoney Indian Pass in these conditions. If I had, and had stayed on schedule with the crossing, I would have arrived at Lake Frances yesterday. My supplies and the weather conditions would have dictated that I exit either to Waterton Townsite or down Bowman canyon. I also doubted an ascent was possible from Thunderbird Creek to Brown Pass on this day.

In another hour, it became evident that before I crawled out of the tent I would once again have to clear away the vestibule. To conserve fuel, I decided to use the stove only to melt snow for drinking water. There would be no more stew cooked until I was moving again. I was almost certain I would stay at this location for another 48 hours. Unfortunately, every hour that passed, the avalanche danger increased.

By 9 A.M., the outside temperature had risen to 20 F., while the barometric pressure continued an almost imperceptible movement upward. A breeze came up, and the snowfall almost ceased half an hour later. Suddenly through the clouds and light snow, Thunderbird Mountain briefly emerged.

In another 15 minutes, the heavy snowfall had returned when I heard the familiar cawing from a flock of ravens or crows headed east. Their numerous calls out to each other were much like the geese. Nor were they letting the wind and snow stop them, and they were traveling together. Already depressed, the companionship of the birds with each other and the realization that they were able to move quickly in this stuff darkened my already down mood.

Why were they traveling in a storm anyway? With them being scavengers, the answer seemed simple enough. There was a carcass out there, or something that soon would be.

That got me to thinking in a different direction. Maybe they knew something about the storm that I had missed, and maybe they were anticipating the arrival of an avalanche and a soon served-up meal. Since there was nothing up here but the bears coming out of hibernation and me, perhaps it was time to reconsider my location. As I listened to the birds fade to the east, I wondered what normal people thought about when they were in situations like this. Then I remembered that normal people stayed home.

At 10:30 A.M., sunlight touched the tent. The heat instantly changed the small world of the tent interior from a fortress under siege into a warm and confident environment. I felt the urge to get moving. With the still low barometric pressure, however, I resisted the temptation. More bad weather was in the works.

I gloomily settled back into the fortress mentality. A few minutes later, I landed on a thought about the last time I had been on this bench less than a month before. I had made a round-trip day hike from the base camp in Bowman canyon: God, what a difference between the two trips!

Camp Relocation

I was also hungry, but felt unable to eat until I knew when I would move again. I would wait until this afternoon, or I could start packing and go have a look at that descent a third of a mile from here. No, I should stay put until the barometer indicated the storm was going to pass.

Several minutes before 11 A.M., sunlight burst upon Boulder Peak and Pass. The urge to move spiked. After all, while unable to go all the way down to Bowman canyon, I could get to the edge of the drop and build a camp there. I had seen no evidence of previous avalanches the two times I had passed through the area. Traveling down there sure beat the hell out of sitting here. Not knowing what shape the steep face was in, I began to pack.

Soon after I made the decision to move, although the snowfall had almost stopped, the sun once again disappeared. I kept packing. Nearly an hour passed before I had the gear packed inside the tent. I declared I would be ready to go in another 45 minutes. Once again I forgot how much slower it was to pack under these conditions. Inside another heavy snowfall, I hefted the load at 1 P.M.

The entire time I was in the camp I had known I was near Chapman Peak's huge avalanche chute. Once I began to move down the slight slope into the indentation that marked the beginning of the ravine, I got a fresh perspective of how close. There was evidence that avalanches had crashed through the area less than 100 feet from the camp. Suddenly I was glad to be moving.

As I plowed through the powder, I looked for any hint of the summer campground location but saw nothing. Since I had never been there in the summer, I had no idea where the camp was located. With the heavy snowfall now wind driven, I emerged out of the trees 500 feet west of the former camp. (Later examination of the photographs taken from my just-vacated camp would show a pole for hanging food poking out one foot above the snowpack, no more than 200 feet southwest of my camp. An earlier avalanche that slid off Chapman Peak had already partly destroyed the campground. The camp was located in a thick and fully mature forest on the south side of the ravine.)

In the meadow, the depth of the powder was far worse than the day before. The snowshoes dropped two and a half feet with every step. Fortunately, descending made it possible to continue. Within minutes, though, I discovered there was still wet snowpack beneath the powder when I slid and fell twice. There would be no getting off the bench for at least the next 24 to 48 hours. Although I had expected this before leaving the last camp, the verification was depressing.

The strength of the snowfall wavered, making it possible for me to see between 200 and 500 feet. Half an hour after leaving camp, I arrived at the edge of the steep slope 400 feet lower. Near the edge of the cliffs and ravine, I leveled out an area between some scattered saplings with the shovel and built the next camp. I was in the tent by 3:30 P.M. Since I would be doing no cooking or percolating coffee the following morning, I had no need to assemble the stove. I also had over one gallon of water from the old camp, which would cover my needs for at least 24 hours.

The half rations for lunch had been two handfuls of peanuts and three quarters of a dehydrated banana. I repeated this for supper. Although by following this plan I was getting insufficient amounts to eat, I would have food for over seven days. I considered it a reasonable plan, which in turn gave me a sense of purpose and hope as the 10th day ended.

The temperature at 6 P.M. was 18 F., with more wind and heavy snowfall. Inside the tent, the temperature was a comfortable 40 F. as I crawled into the sleeping bag. That was when I made a couple of discoveries: my feet were higher than my head, and I needed to go to the toilet. I rotated the sleeping bag and gear, and placed my head at the other end of the tent. I ignored the other need and soon fell asleep.

Sometime during the night, I rolled over and then woke with a start. A visit outside would wait no longer. Regretting my inaction of many hours earlier, I scrambled for the toilet bag and down booties. Outside, the wind, snow, and the coldest temperature of the trip, 11 F., welcomed me.

Back inside the sleeping bag, I could feel the chill whenever I lay on my side. Normally the bag and bivy sack would have kept me warm in this colder temperature. It being the tenth night, however, the fill power of the down bag had deteriorated substantially.

April 18: Delayed on the Lip

I woke at 8 A.M., but an hour passed before I finally crawled out of the sleeping bag. In a reversal of the decision of the day before, my inspiration was to get a hot cup of coffee and warm up. I realized this meant I could run out of fuel before the trip ended. Better, though, to use the fuel in the cold than save it for the warmer temperatures down below.

I did something different with the stove by setting it up in the tent rather than on the snow inside the vestibule. The result was a vastly warmer tent, but with the increased danger of carbon monoxide poisoning or burning up the tent. On this morning the venting system of the tent combined with the wind outside easily removed the gaseous poison.

I doubted I would be able to travel today. Through the night, the wind had created a thin, weak crust that was unable to hold the weight of a frozen ant. I was also unconvinced last night's cold had penetrated the deep powder enough to freeze the wet snowpack below. If I was right, any attempt to continue today might prove fatal. Moreover, if I used the crampons rather than the snowshoes, the deep powder would stop me one step beyond the edge of this campsite.

All right, what about heading toward Goat Haunt and crossing the border to Waterton Townsite? Was it possible to descend Brown Pass? If I went that direction and was hurt or killed, no one would know that I had traveled east. Based on my experience of yesterday and the day before, any attempt to descend Brown Pass could also be fatal and my body never recovered. I backed away from the thought. Except for an emergency, my route would remain unchanged.

This being the 11th day, I was concerned about the 13-day permit. Would the park personnel at Polebridge be watching for my exit? I knew Carleen would do nothing until at least the 14th day. Nevertheless, if the park service sent a helicopter out after the 13th day, it would mangle this trip.

I had received a citation in 2006 for being overdue. A winter storm on Ahern Pass had delayed me. In the five trips I took through that winter, my wife called twice, the first time in March. The citing officer informed me that I needed to be more "liberal" about the amount of time I would be in the backcountry. Yet contrary to that statement, park personnel insisted on knowing where my camp would be located each day. With thousands of daily backcountry visitors during the summer, I saw the need for this rule. During a lengthy winter trip, however, this insistence on knowing "where and when" I would camp often fell somewhere between difficult to impossible to comply with, coupled with being outright dangerous. I came away with a citation, convinced that some park employees were unaware that disobedience of the laws of nature could have a much graver penalty than violated manmade laws.

If I attempted to keep myself from going overdue, I might die 300 feet from here. I was alone, and the decision of what to do rested solely with me; I chose continued caution.

Later in the morning, I recalled the scattered saplings on the 300-foot descent below my present camp and wondered if they would keep the avalanches from occurring. To get over there I could use the snowshoes and at some point during the descent replace them with the crampons. A part of me thought that was utterly insane, while another wanted to scout the area.

When I was ready to go two and a half hours later, the clouds had thinned enough for the sun to emerge partially. The outside temperature had risen to 36 F. With today's warmer temperatures, there might be a partial crust to walk on tomorrow morning.

At 1 P.M., I descended 120 feet before being compelled to put the crampons on. I also discovered that if the backpack had been ready to go, I could have descended. Now too late in the day, I headed back to camp, disgusted by my overly cautious decision.

In spite of a packed trail, I needed double the time to return to camp, arriving at 2:30 P.M. Once inside the tent, I prepared for an early sleep. Although the barometer showed only a small change, I still had a hunch that tonight there would be an open sky, which meant a lot of cold, perfect for hardening the snowpack. For now, in the wind and sunshine, it was snowing.

There would be no stew until I arrived at the lake, which meant the next hot meal was likely 48 hours away. That was too bad because I had grown weary of the nuts and fruit. At least I would have creek water in tomorrow's camp. Compared to stream water, snowmelt in a pan had a bland taste, particularly where coffee was concerned.

Although I doubted I would arrive at Bowman Lake tomorrow, I would do everything I could to get there. If I did, besides the stew, there would be the possibility of arriving at Polebridge 48 hours later. Should that happen, then depending on the weather, I would begin the next trip on approximately April 29. Determined to get up early enough to follow through with this latest revised plan, I was inside the sleeping bag before 6 P.M.

Yes, the plan; it struck me that my sudden optimism was the result of more foolish thinking. Regardless of my experiences of the last week, I planned to travel almost six miles tomorrow. This increased confidence came as the result of descending 120 out of 300 feet of the initial descent.

Unable to sleep, I listened to the tent fabric flap in the wind. At 7 P.M., with the temperature rapidly dropping, now in a foul mood, I realized that without a wet snowpack earlier in the day, no crust would form tonight. This newsflash came with the additional information that three days to exit was ridiculous, and that I should continue to plan on seven.

Yeah? Well I already did, but I can still hope for three days, so shut up.

I was still awake at 7:30 P.M. and the temperature outside had now dropped below 18 F.

All that sleep I got the night before must be the reason I'm still awake.

Meanwhile the barometric pressure continued to rise. An hour later, I was shocked that it was still daylight outside.

When did the days get this long?

For 15 years, I had been an obsessive daily observer of when sunrise and sunset took place.

Damn, too many days of getting to bed early so I can get up early did this.

For nearly seven weeks, the heartening event of spring's later sunsets had been taking place. Now the next event, the beginning of the longest days of the year, was a mere 17 days away.

Good grief, I'm missing everything!

Not quite. Pushed by the wind, the outside temperature had just dropped to 7 F. I fell asleep after 10:30 P.M.

17 • descent to bowman canyon

April 19: The Coldest Morning

I woke up and knew I had overslept. The watch showed 4 A.M. To get any kind of distance today on the canyon floor I had to get down there while it was still cold. At this late hour, the soonest I would leave camp would be 8 A.M. With two hours to descend, I would arrive on the canyon floor by midmorning. Nevertheless, the burning cold on my face told me I should be in no hurry to escape the toasty warm sleeping bag. Several minutes later, I unzipped the bag and hurriedly got into my outer clothing. In half an hour, my mitten-covered hands wrapped themselves around a hot but small amount of coffee. Staring at the small cup with some consternation, I resolved the next cup would be a full mug of percolated java. Time be damned, I would just have to make it to Bowman Creek later.

At 5 A.M., the temperature in the tent was 35 F. while outside it was less than 8 F., and I was sipping the second mug in a normal morning setting. The lantern was off, and I wallowed in the best time of the day. I was also increasing my difficulties for farther down the trail by leaving the stove running. If it took seven days for me to get back to Polebridge, I would probably run out of fuel. Just then, I did not care. To hell with living like there was an emergency. Yet I was cognizant that my actions might be creating that emergency on the other end of the trip.

Nor was I in full darkness. A full moon, or the better part of one, was out there. While Thunderbird Mountain robbed the camp of direct moonlight, the snow-covered surrounding peaks reflected the light into camp.

I love moonlit nights in the snowpack. One can easily travel without a head lantern in those conditions. There is something magic and unexplainable about traveling in that low light. Nor is it a secret. Skiers have full-moon skiing parties. This condition is particularly delightful above the forested canyon floors. On the other hand, where Glacier National Park was concerned, I would always travel with a head lantern on to light the eyes of a wandering and hungry bruin.

Several minutes after turning the stove off, I zippered all my clothing fully up. Even though I was sipping a hot cup of coffee, I could still feel the cold running up my back. Additionally, I needed to go outside and visit the toilet. I returned cold, turned the stove back on, and let it run until shortly after 6 A.M. After that, I stayed warm by packing. Once again, I ran into the uncooperative stiffness of cold gear as I packed. I exited the tent at 7 A.M.

The weather had definitely changed. Although there were still clouds hovering around many of the peaks, much of what was over my head was a pure deep blue sky, the type that arrives after a storm. The sun was on Thunderbird Mountain and touching the clouds around the other peaks.

The temperature was still in the single digits when I left camp at 8:30 A.M. I was on the edge of the descent six minutes later when the sun first touched me from behind the clouds and peaks. The fresh snow at my feet sparkled, while Chapman, Thunderbird, Boulder, Peabody, and Numa Peaks stood out in a majestic winter setting. I came to a halt and took in the scene until my toes started hurting with the cold. As I moved on, it struck me that if I was going to die in the next few minutes, this was a glorious place for it to happen.

There was no crust to walk on, but the danger was far less than I thought it would be. Based on my scout from the day before, I planned to wear the snowshoes until I was near yesterday's turnaround and then switch to crampons. That never happened. The slippery surface beneath the powder no longer existed. Nevertheless, the combination of the heavy backpack and the powder was still a challenge as I slowly descended through the small trees. I fell only a few times, and removed the backpack but once to stand. Half an hour later, I breathed a sigh of relief at the bottom of the 300-foot descent.

Like three weeks earlier, I stayed on the south face and dropped into the trees. The snowpack in the forest was more powder, but all downhill. I was near the bottom at 10 A.M. when I took a half-hour break. I ought to have been happy with arriving near the canyon floor, but the condition of the snow dampened the party mood. There was at least two feet of fresh snow inside the trees, and the route was no longer a strong descent.

Every step I took broke through as soon as I put my full weight onto the snowshoe. When I arrived in the opening where the summer trail was located, I was ready to make camp. Bowman Creek was 300 feet away, which meant water for camp, but the campground at the lake four miles away was still the key for a hot meal. I traveled 250 feet across the opening, dropped the backpack, and took another break. In that short distance, I discovered that the crust was no longer breaking beneath the snowshoes. I plunged ahead 30 minutes later.

The next time I removed the backpack for another break I had entered the opening where Pocket and Bowman Creeks converged. Because of a badly packed load, the backpack was top-heavy, and the shoulder straps were cutting into me. At the same time, the sciatic nerve was testing my resolve to continue. I ate more food and shed some clothing. I also moved the 70 to 200 mm lens from the backpack onto the camera in its chest pack, hoping to ease the load and the painful strain of the shoulder straps.

No Lake, No Stew

An hour after I left the open area, I arrived at the gravel bar where I had spent the third and fourth nights on the trip in. With the snowshoes off, I stood on dirt, sand, and gravel for the first time in over a week. The sensation was as if I was suddenly on another trip. Since I had left here, much had happened, yet there was little to show for it.

I was convinced I was on my last legs. Once again, I contemplated stopping for the remainder of the day. There was still that stew to be considered though, and I was determined to have a hot supper. I had to try for the lake. In half an hour, I was ready to begin the small ascent. In the last half mile to the lake, typically the worst of the day, it took 45 minutes to travel through the numerous islands of rotting snowpack, plunging through with every step. There was also intermittent open trail, hard on the snowshoes but a tremendous relief for my exhausted body. Eventually the snow gave way to bare ground. With the snowshoes in hand, just over two hours beyond the gravel bar, I arrived at the upper campground on Bowman Lake. The shock of having only rocks and dirt to walk on was greater than what I had experienced a few hours earlier on the gravel bar.

I saw evidence that the snow and cold I experienced had dropped down to this altitude. Snow still lay on the tree branches facing north. Icicles had also formed where water splashed off the rocks and onto the lower tree branches above the fast-running Numa Creek.

After a small break, I built camp and laid out gear to dry. Once done, I walked over to the rocky west-face shore where I had broken through the ice 10 days earlier. In what had become a mostly cloudy sky, the sun emerged from behind a cloud and warmed me. Looking west, I could see the ice line on the lake now several hundred feet away. There was also a chill in the air. Still damp from sweating on the trail, when the sun went behind the clouds again, I was immediately cold and had to move. I had a hunch that the short sleep combined with the need for food also played a role.

Back in the tent, I got the well-earned stew going while the heat from the stove filled the tent interior. Still unable to shed the chill, once the stew was cooked, I wasted no time getting the hot and delicious food down my throat. Afterward I was still cold. With the interior of the tent at 43 F., it was obvious the problem was inside me. In my exhausted state, I failed to think this through. Once I realized that, I should have removed the damp shirt, heated some water, and sipped it down. Being alone, it was on me to get it right. Instead, I let the open and thawed ground disarm my normal cautious conduct on the snowpack.

I crawled into the sleeping bag and was asleep shortly after 6:30 P.M. Through the night, whenever I lay on my side, I would feel the chill on my back. Lying flat on the pads was the only way I stayed warm. I had little doubt that the deep chill I felt when I went into the bag was part of the reason for the failure of the sleeping system. A sleeping bag would only retain the heat my body manufactured.

18 • leaving bowman canyon

April 20: The Guide

I got out of the sleeping bag before 3 A.M. and was sipping the first cup of coffee within 30 minutes. Soon after and finally warm, I considered the coolness in the sleeping bag for the last three nights. There was nearly two weeks of accumulated moisture inside the down of the sleeping bag, only partially remedied by leaving the bag in the sun yesterday. The addition of the fleece blanket would have been useful. I concluded that thereafter the fleece would be with me on the longer trips during April.

I also addressed the damage the top-heavy backpack was doing to my shoulders and the sciatic nerve. As much as possible, I needed to place the heaviest materials I possessed up against my spine and balanced in the center. This was easier said than done, and the heavier the load the more difficult it was to balance. The best I would be able to do was adjust the backpack as I traveled, which I had been unsuccessful doing yesterday.

With the area around the campground nearly snow and ice free, the previous evening I had devised a preliminary plan to scout the trail without the load, and see how far this condition lasted. This morning, uncertain how far I would get without them, I added the snowshoes to the reconnaissance.

If I ran into much snowpack today, with the present outside temperature of 26 F., the snow would be rotting. That could prevent my arrival at the low end of the lake today. Therefore, I allowed for two days, but hoped to get to the foot of the lake by day's end.

After 4:30 A.M., I was inside the tent packing the gear when it suddenly occurred to me that I had lost a day.

Goddamn! When did that happen? Maybe it is only last night that I am unable to remember.

What was certain, the previous days had rolled in on top of each other, while today's date, April 20, meant I was one day overdue with at least two more days of travel still in front of me. (This was another miscalculation. If I had examined the backcountry permit itinerary stashed in my backpack, I would have seen I was due to return to Polebridge on April 20.) Carleen would wait until at least tomorrow before calling the park service. Would they wait to hear from her or take it upon themselves to initiate a search today? Though I was unsure about either of these items, I was certain that I would do nothing hasty in an effort to exit sooner. I was still determined to travel only in a safe manner.

Beneath a cloudy sky, I left the campground before 7 A.M. with the camera bag and snowshoes. Except for the exterior gear such as the ice axe and snow shovel, the backpack was loaded. One mile and 20 minutes later, I dropped the snowshoes on the side of the still snow-free trail and returned for the backpack. By the time I returned with the load, attached the snowshoes, and took a small break, the time was 8:45 A.M.

Frustrated by the wasted time, I headed down the trail. Within a few minutes, I realized the backpack was unbalanced. Attached to the exterior of a full load for the first time in 10 days, the snowshoes combined with the snow shovel and large lens threw the load off balance. I adjusted the backpack and traveled for another 40 minutes. By then I was tired, sore, and frustrated.

"Sure would be nice if these shoulder harnesses would quit cutting into my shoulders," I thought. "It would be even nicer to get the pack balanced and off that left hip."

Then, full knowing the hopelessness of that ever happening, "Nicest of all is if I had wings," I dripped.

With increasing pain in the left hip, the next four hours became another walk in hell. My stops to readjust the backpack were successful only for the extent of time that the load was off my back. Eventually the breaks became lengthier than the walking.

I was back in the rolling hills and approximately two miles from the low end of the lake at 1:45 P.M. when I halted. In front of me was a small ascent 200 feet in length and covered in snow. For the last two miles, I had been encountering increasingly larger patches of snow, which I had been able to get around or punch through without the use of snowshoes. This one however, stretched out of sight. I speculated there might be more dirt trail hidden on the other side of the rise. Wanting to avoid dropping the load,

I took a chance and began to ascend toward the small knoll. Exhausted, I nevertheless thought I could handle the short distance. Four minutes and 30 feet later, I dropped the backpack and brought out the snowshoes. The snowpack was horrific. The snowshoes were unable to prevent postholing. In spite of my close proximity to the low end of the lake, I was on the verge of looking for a camp spot.

Just beyond the knoll, two white-tailed deer were standing in less than a foot of snow on the trail. The closest deer stared at me for half a minute before he nonchalantly went back to browsing on the tender willow tips and Douglas-fir pine needles above his head. As I moved closer, he finally leaped over the mounds of snow on the right side of the trail and soon disappeared. The second deer continued toward me and then stopped where the other deer had jumped off the trail. After half a minute, he turned around and bounced back down the trail. Within 100 feet he dropped off the left side of the trail toward the lake another 200 feet away. Amazed at their ability to get through the rotting snowpack, I stopped where the last deer had left the trail and stared through the trees to see if I could spot him, which I did. He was on the lake ice!

Did the deer panic, and in an effort to escape, run onto the deteriorating ice? Not keen about bringing it harm, I stayed quiet and continued along the trail while I watched to see if he would stay on the lake or come back on the trail. After five minutes, he disappeared around a small bend along the shoreline. The damned animal was either going to be killed or he knew more about that ice than I.

If I failed to reach the lower end of the lake today, I would need an extra day to exit the park. Yet, the possible consequences of that must not trump safe travel. Anyway, how much did that deer weigh, 150 pounds? If the ice were as thin as I made it out to be, surely those small hooves slamming onto it while he jogged and bounced would have broken through. Was I wrong about the ice thickness? Maybe I ought to go down and have a look.

Actually, my intent was more than an inspection. Once I thought of following the deer, I knew I was going to do everything I could to do just that, abandoning safe travel for a gamble. The pain in my body, my exhausted state, the rotting snowpack, and the growing risk of being "rescued" by the park service pushed me over the edge and down the ridge to the lake ice 40 feet below.

There was open water along much of the lake's edge. In the thick brush, deadfall, and trees along the shore, I needed another few minutes before

I found a spot where the ice and the shoreline connected. I got a good grip on a thick tree limb that hung out over the lake and took a cautious step onto the ice less than two feet off the shore. I broke through, and most of my right leg below the knee dropped to the rocky bottom. I used the limb to pull myself out of the water and then pushed through the brush looking for another spot. The deer got out there and so would I. Another 40 feet up the lake; I spotted two fallen trees lying in the lake, ice frozen around them. I used them as a bridge onto the thicker ice farther from the shore.

With only a cursory thought about how I would get off the ice later, I slowly walked out onto the ice beyond the fallen trees. About 30 feet offshore, I stopped and looked up. The deer had joined two others 1,000 feet away. I figured there was now approximately 400 pounds of venison over there.

I moved in their direction and they sprang into action. Jogging, jumping, and walking, they headed west. Several minutes later two more deer joined the small herd, giving me further evidence of the strength in the ice. While reassured, I remained watchful, which was an empty gesture. If I broke through the ice, there would be little or no chance of survival.

After several minutes on the ice, a mystery covered in cautious relief developed. When I had removed the snowshoes from the backpack back on the trail, the shoulder straps quit chafing me. The sciatic nerve pain continued though, until I started walking on the snow-covered ice, where the pain almost disappeared.

The deer continued to guide me over the ice toward Bowman Lake Campground. I figured that when they headed for shore I would also. Yet when the herd turned north a third of a mile short of the campground, I hesitated, and then changed my mind. My exhaustion was overwhelming. I was walking two minutes and resting for five. If I continued to follow the deer, the distance to the campground would double to almost one mile, all of it in the snowpack. I threw out any remaining caution and continued west on the ice. I came ashore at the campground 20 minutes later, awash with relief, although the last hundred feet I plunged through slush that had the feel of lake water.

An Old Man's Shuffle

I dropped the load on the snow-free ground beneath the Douglas-fir tree near the boat launch sign. After I set up camp, I slowly shuffled toward the creek 1,400 feet away. I walked on the ice, although I had seen evidence where I came ashore of the imminent ice breakup. I traveled 500 feet before the ice collapsed beneath me. I was able to pull myself out with the other leg before the foot sank to the shallow bottom. Thereafter I plowed through the rotting snowpack on shore.

Later that afternoon, some of my strength returned and the exhaustion eased. I even began to feel some pride in what I had accomplished in the last two days. While there was no doubt that my age had a marked effect on my travel, there was also a huge difference in my endurance compared to two and a half months before in the Belly River canyon.

Throughout the last 24 hours, the barometric pressure had continued to drop as another storm approached. Except for getting down that six-mile road to Polebridge tomorrow morning, I did not much care. The events of the next day would have to wait for me to step into them.

In a repeat of the last camp at this location, I boiled the water before drinking it. Several months without people and boats were insufficient for me to believe that the water was drinkable. Decomposition of things left behind could go on for a long time. In my lifetime I had gotten sick numerous times by drinking bad water, twice with Giardia (beaver fever). The last thing I needed was to be lying up here unable to move while unloading at both ends.

After cooking and eating the stew, I made some final notes concerning the day and any adjustments for the next day's travel and beyond. It was painfully obvious that no amount of walking with a load or loss of body weight was going to ease my sciatic nerve issue. If the problem stemmed from a lower back injury in 1994, coupled with improper posture and weak core muscles, I resolved to get back to a regular routine of strengthening those muscles. In the meantime, the inflamed nerve would likely delay my planned return one week from now. Weather and the sciatic nerve would be the final deciders, but I now figured it would be two weeks before I returned. As I sat inside the tent, I had a second and familiar reason to postpone my return in one week. The thought of returning was repulsive. I was more than a cupful of ready for some civilized pampering.

As I closed the vestibule door for the final time that evening, sunshine broke through the trees. It was the last vestiges of yesterday's weather; the next storm might arrive tonight. Unlike the last storm and all of its preceding buddies though, this one would have no avalanche terrain to get after me with. On the other hand, those clouds also brought in warmer temperatures, which in turn could soften the snowpack more than it already was. I was asleep shortly after 7 P.M.

April 21: A Painful Trudge Out

I was up in five hours and aware what today meant. I was going to do everything I could to be home with Carleen and the dogs before the end of the day. Although my intent was clear, many experiences from this trip said to expect disappointment, while the last two days gave some small reason for optimism. As I got the day underway with the ritualistic two cups of coffee, I continued to review the trip as a means to plan the next. I also noticed that I was no longer so revolted with the thought of coming back to the park in short order.

The temperature dropped to 28 F., almost enough to harden yesterday's soft snowpack, unless no snowpack remained on the road. By 3:40 A.M., I was packing the gear. I left the lake's edge and began the final six miles to Polebridge at 5:50 A.M.

. Not 500 feet beyond camp, attempting to stay on the almost invisible cross-country ski tracks, a snowshoe punched through the crust. A moment later, the other foot plunged into the hole with it. With a firm grip on the ski poles and my arms stretched out, I tried to keep myself upright, to no avail. The fronts of the snowshoes were in the hole, while the back of them pointed at the dark sky. In spite of the camera bag on my chest, I did a face-plant. Hollering my frustration, I removed the backpack and regained my feet.

Five minutes later, I continued, my progress now slower and more cautious. I broke through the crust every 5 to 15 feet until I began the shallow ascent on a curve 2,000 feet beyond the campground. Beneath the trees, I spotted dirt, rocks, and ice, while the other side of the road was rotting snowpack, two and three feet deep.

When I arrived at the highest point on the road, one and one-quarter miles from the lake's edge, almost one and a half hours had elapsed. Dawn had recently broken on an overcast sky. I also had company. I had spotted a fox in the semi-darkness 20 minutes earlier, crossing the road behind me. The small animal had crossed again a few minutes ago, this time in front of me less than 150 feet away. That was the last time I saw him, though for the next couple hours he would let me know he was still around with his barks. Loneliness could be an undesirable partner during my winter trips. Like the deer from the day before, the fox was a welcome presence. Somehow having him around encouraged me to push harder in spite of the dilapidated snowpack. I took fewer breaks, and each time I prepared to stop, I walked an extra 100 feet first.

Shortly after dawn, a light snow began to fall, interspersed with heavy spring squalls. In the daylight, the trees and even the burnt forest turned into a temporary winter wonderland while the snowpack on the road continued its torturous ways with me.

By 8:30 A.M., I had traveled three miles and the sciatic nerve pain was back. Like the day before, the length of the breaks I took eventually became longer than the travel time. The short night of sleep also had an effect. With each passing hour, I became more discouraged while the pain increased, and yet I still had enough vim to snarl and cuss my way down the road. At one point, I howled that this was the last winter trip forever.

I needed another hour and a half to travel less than two miles, which included a 350-foot drop to the edge of Bowman Creek. Back to bare ground, I removed the snowshoes at the bottom of the drop. Unsure if I would need them again, I hand carried the devices. Less than 45 minutes later, I arrived at Polebridge. In spite of the relief of finally arriving on the edge of civilization, I nastily noted that I had needed almost two hours more than the March trip exit.

Planning the Next Trip

An hour later, I had been driving for only a short time when I pulled out the recorder and began to make plans for the next trip. I stayed with the decision to wait two weeks, weather permitting. Besides weather and the sciatic nerve, I wanted to let the rotting snow melt at the lower end of Bowman Lake. I would carry 13 days of food and fuel plus several extra days of peanuts and fruit. Numerous items would stay behind. The 28 to 70 mm lens would once again replace the 70 to 200 mm lens to save weight. I would also replace the full-sized self-inflating pad and chair. Finally, there was the four-season tent. Without it on this trip, I would have had some serious problems with the snowfall for five of the nights. Consequently, my decision to bring the lighter tent on the next trip was disquieting.

The sciatic nerve was a cloud over scheduling the final trip. There was a window for making the circuit. While winter continued in the high country, spring weather on the canyon floors was crawling up the sides of the mountains. Spring was the most dangerous season in the backcountry.

If I got the timing wrong, becoming stranded, or worse, were two possibilities. Rotting snowpack and spring flooding in the low elevations, and more winter storms with horrific spring avalanches in the higher elevations, combined to make a two-edged sword. Because each year had its own flavor, there could be no set date. If a warm spring suddenly appeared, there would be no final attempt this year. What's more, if the heat came on suddenly with me in the high country, I would be unable to move, even as the spring avalanches gathered strength around me.

Exhausted, I seesawed between feeling that this trip had been a failure or a complete success. Hope finally relit inside the darkness of my mood as I realized that this trip, like the others, had well prepared me for what was to come. What I could not know was whether it would be enough. In less than three weeks, I would begin the process of finding out.

19 • a bad beginning

By May 1, the sciatic nerve pain had eased up. With more storms in the forecast though, I delayed the trip to May 5. On May 3, with yet more bad weather forecast, I pushed the date back to Friday, May 6. On that same day, the NOAA predicted at least one more month of cool and wet weather. Rain and wet snow on a snowpack that approached 200 percent above average was bad news. Another day passed, and I pushed my departure date back again. The weather for the weekend and Monday called for yet more storming. The same forecast also showed a mixed bag of slightly improving weather beginning Tuesday, May 10. I finally had the starting date, although it would now be well inside the most dangerous of the four seasons.

May 10: Delayed at Apgar

I left Helena at 6 A.M., already one hour behind. As I headed west, Highway 12 paralleled a deep and muddy Tenmile Creek. MacDonald Pass, at 6,325 feet 15 miles west of Helena, was blanketed with one and a half feet of fresh snow from yesterday's storm. On the other side of the pass and now west of the Continental Divide, the Little Blackfoot River looked like the big brother of Tenmile Creek. If the streams in Glacier National Park were similar, there would be no trip. Should the NOAA forecast for May turn out to be wrong, and a heat wave arrived while I was in the high country, besides the massive spring avalanches, there would be roiling waters like this. Spring runoff could prevent forward progress and simultaneously keep me from backtracking to safety.

Unlike the previous trips, I had packed hard copies of the extended forecast for Bowman canyon floor and the 6,800-foot elevation around Hole in the Wall. Both predicted an increased chance of rain showers in

48 hours. Not a good forecast, but better that than the snowstorms of the past two weeks.

The normal travel time from Helena to Polebridge was five hours, which included a stop at Apgar's backcountry permit office. Closed through the winter and reopened on May 1, I would obtain the backcountry permit there. I figured 20 minutes in the office and an hour to drive to the trailhead.

Because I went overdue on the first and third trips, I had earlier called the park and found out that they generally initiated rescues only after a loved one or a friend called. With that information in hand, I told Carleen I would be gone for at least 14 days and to delay calling the park service until the 16th day. While I thought 12 days would be sufficient, there was no need to take a chance of her again calling the park if I was only one day overdue.

At the backcountry office, the actions and attitudes had changed in the last month among the park employees. They were gearing up for the summer visitors. Some of the summer personnel were on the job, and the rules of conduct for non-winter backcountry travel were now in place. I was unaware of the changes until I arrived.

Behind the counter, a bearded young man took the information of where I was going and when. Having forgotten to bring a copy of the itinerary, I tried to recall from memory what I had outlined 10 days earlier. We agreed on the itinerary for the permit, but he did not yet print a copy. The park employee then made it clear that I would carry a bear canister, something required for undesignated campgrounds, and it would be the largest they had. I commented that three weeks earlier I had been in the same area without a canister, that perhaps he should call his boss to verify that. A few minutes later, he informed me that beginning on May 1 the summer rules applied. I said nothing further.

With the office only recently reopened, there was no large canister in the building. What he had available would carry only a fraction of my supplies. Since I was already carrying more than a 100-pound load, I let him know that I was fine with a smaller container. Nevertheless, the employee made another phone call in his search for their largest canister. While I waited, I reexamined the timing and locations of the camps throughout the trip. The itinerary was smaller than the one I had laid out back at the office a week and a half earlier. I addressed this to the park employee and he redid the permit. In spite of the redo, although I would try, I had little confidence I would be able to stick to the permit that now had only an

11-day itinerary. Even in the area I had already traveled twice, I was unable to say with any certainty how far I would be able to travel each day, or predict each night's camp location. Since the park service had always insisted on knowing exactly where I would be at the end of each day, I did what I could to get it right.

At the time, I also failed to notice that the park service's printed itinerary, which would accompany me on the trip, lacked most of the specific information I had given for dates and locations. The description on the itinerary was "NORTH FORK UND CAMPGROUND" for 7 out of the 10 camps. Based on that, I could have stipulated to Glacier the same amount of time as I had given Carleen, which was 16 days, without regard to where I would be at the end of each day. (This was later confirmed to me on August 24, 2011, several minutes after a court hearing where I agreed to pay the $3,671.60 fine.) That there was a breakdown in our communication I have no doubt. To be clear though, the events of the trip and their timing would still have taken place.

With as many people that traveled in the backcountry during the summer, I understood the need to know the "where and when" for everyone staying one or more nights in the backcountry. Indiscriminate camping by thousands of people would soon destroy the wilderness setting, and play hell on the permanent residents. To prevent that from happening, established campgrounds with designated camp spots were essential. The permits made it possible for the park to let in large numbers of people, who would always have a slot in a campground for each night they were in the backcountry. As a bonus, the campgrounds had bear poles to hang food, log chairs to sit on, and my favorite, toilets.

Violation of the permits would negate part of the park's mission, which was to make certain all visitors had a campsite reserved on the scheduled night at the campground. All infractions except perhaps an emergency received a citation, a fine, or both.

During the off-season, however, there were few daily visitors, particularly during the winter. In my experience, Glacier National Park was similar to the wildernesses of western Montana and Idaho, with hikers rarely going beyond day hikes throughout the winter. Since 1996, with over 200 nights spent in the backcountry during the winter, and more than 70 of that number spent inside the park, I had encountered only one group of overnight visitors.

I preferred to stay in the backcountry campgrounds, if for no other reason than to have an outhouse, though there were other reasons. Unfortunately, the campgrounds in the higher elevations ceased to exist during the winter. The park recognized this and issued undesignated campground slots for each day of the permit. Their mindset, however, continued with "where and when," which normally went onto the permit itinerary. That is where trouble developed.

Weather, particularly during the winter of 2011, governed where, when, and if I would go. The longer the trip, the greater the chance that weather would force changes to my itinerary. With each passing day, it became less predictable where my camp would be located. The only accuracy would be the route, including the direction I would take if I turned back, an oft-happened occurrence through the years.

The timing of the route was unpredictable inside the 12 miles between Bowman Lake and the snow-free trail above Upper Kintla Lake. The most questionable area of the trip was the approach to Hole in the Wall. For that leg—less than three-quarters of a mile in length—I gave two days of travel time, with the end of the second day arriving in the cirque. The worst area of this traverse was approximately one-third of a mile in length. I gave this section one day. At the end of that same day, I would dig out the snow-covered cave on the other side of the elbow and spend the night. From Hole in the Wall, I planned on 72 hours to arrive at the Upper Kintla Lake Campground. I figured I would arrive back on the dirt trail just beyond the last avalanche chute below Boulder Pass Campground. Once on the canyon floor, I planned liberally for another four days to arrive at Polebridge 25 miles farther.

I gave the route into and out of Hole in the Wall, a distance of less than three miles, only three days because of the improved condition of the late-season snowpack. Though I kept it to myself, a part of me naïvely believed I would need only half a day to get across the approach, while the remainder was reserved for perchance.

After the large bear canister arrived, the park employee declared it would only carry enough for seven days and I would have to carry two. Having some trouble believing this conversation was happening, I uttered with some irritation, "Yes, it is big enough."

Every pound added to my more than 120-pound load imperiled not only the trip but also my life. Three and a half months later, this conversation would come back up in a courtroom with a claim that I had to be convinced by a temporary office worker to place more than seven days on the itinerary for the trip. I left the Apgar backcountry permit office still irritated.

In spite of that, the sky was a beautiful blue with fluffy white clouds toward the east, and the day was getting hot. I arrived at the Polebridge Ranger Station at noon. I talked briefly to a summer employee as I repacked the load. He informed me there would still be snow on the ground along Bowman Lake and that I would need crampons only at the elbow on the approach. I said nothing.

Two hours after I arrived, I was ready to go. In that time, I had packed the supplies, as many as would fit in the canister, and repacked the backpack twice in an attempt to make the canister work with the rest of the gear. The expedition-sized load remained unbalanced.

The difference on this day compared to the last two trips, besides an afternoon start, was the heat and lack of snow. The combination of the load and warmth was harsh. I felt the effects on the immediate 70-foot ascent beyond the closed gate of the Bowman Lake road. Already tired at the top of the small climb, I noted with disgust that this was the most rested I would be for the remainder of the day.

With the heat draining my energy far more quickly than on previous trips, the distant snowy peaks were like a mirage on a desert, visible and unattainable. Rivulets of water and small streams ran down the ditches paralleling the road, increasing my concern about the larger streams farther on. At 4 P.M., I finally got through the burn area and gratefully entered the shade of the forest. Soon after, I began to encounter small patches of snow, but got around them easily enough. I took more frequent and longer rest breaks.

By 4:30 P.M. I was certain the best I would do for the day was to get to the campground at Bowman Lake. Just after 6 P.M., I arrived at the lake. It had taken four hours and 17 minutes to get there. Months later, I would discover that on March 22 I had used only one more minute on the same route while wearing snowshoes.

Unlike the previous two camps at the campground, I retrieved the camp water from a small creek near the park building. The stream was up and partially cloudy. If I arrived at the approach without a problem, and got through to Boulder Pass Campground, how heavy would the stream flows be in the Kintla Lake canyon?

While some ice remained on the lake, it would take a 40-foot swim to get out to it. Nor did the ice look much thicker than perhaps an inch or two. This trip I would be walking on the trail. After dinner, I hiked a short distance along the lake to see if any snow remained. While there were scattered patches of snow in the campground, I found none in the quarter mile I walked. Twenty days earlier, the upper four miles of the lake were snow free during the exit. Now I was almost certain no snow remained along the north shore of the lake.

At 8:30 P.M., I photographed the interestingly colored icy surface of Bowman Lake. The fast-disappearing ice had a blue and white color with an unfamiliar hue. In the scene, I noticed another sign of the passing of winter. The setting sun was still on the peaks. After the previous trips, particularly in February with the subzero temperatures and a sunset just after 5:30 P.M., this evening seemed odd. Through the years, the advancing sunset week after week had always been a pleasure to experience. Tonight, however, that was replaced by worry. I was running out of time, or maybe already had. The sunlight reflected brightly off the snowpack-covered slopes on the peaks—beautiful, but a sign that the spring avalanches were coming.

It was just after 9 P.M. and still daylight when I crawled into the sleeping bag. I fell asleep to the sound of chirping robins.

May 11: A Hard Day without Snowpack

At 5 A.M., I crawled out of the sleeping bag and into the chill. I thought about those hard copy forecasts inside the map storage bag. This morning's predicted low temperature was supposed to have been no lower than 35 F. The thermometer read 28 F. While this reading favored the trip, would later inaccuracies go the opposite direction?

In the darkness, I listened to the percolating first cup of coffee. Somewhere nearby, the haunting hoots of at least one owl were interspersed with an increasing thumping, the territorial proclamation of a male ruffed grouse. The most peaceful time of the day was upon me. Several minutes later, with the first cup of aroma-laden coffee in my hands, the sounds continued. I sat back in the chair and became glad for my life. While the owl continued to hoot, the quacking of ducks replaced the grouse's sudden silence.

The contentment continued until I realized it was getting light. With some reluctance, I focused on the day ahead. According to the forecast, today was supposed to be another warm and sunny day. I needed to get an early start while the temperature was still cool. It was going to get hot on the north shore of the lake. Except for two pounds, the backpack still weighed all it had when I left the vehicle yesterday. With numerous miniature ascents and descents on a trail rather than the road, today would be tougher. The employee back at Polebridge could be right; I might yet find a rotting snowpack to posthole through.

During April's trip, I had used 66 ounces of fuel in 14 days. Now, with warmer temperatures and carrying 88 ounces, I was still uncertain there was enough. At the same rate of consumption from the last trip, there was an 18-day supply for this trip.

While I would continue to have coffee, to conserve fuel it would be with less water and coffee grounds. I would prepare stew only where running water was available. That meant I would eat cold food for approximately four days, which would provide two or three more camps of hot food on the other side of Boulder Pass. With the amount that I had brought, it was possible I could exit with eight days of stew and a slightly smaller amount of day food still in the backpack. In another interpretation, I would be traveling those steep slopes with approximately 20 pounds of dead weight—unless the trip went to hell, and then that "dead weight" would prove vital.

I began to pack at 6 A.M. My goal was to be on the trail no later than 8 A.M. I left at 8:03 A.M. The monstrous load continued to make the going tough, in spite of the cool early morning temperature, near-level trail, and the lack of snowpack. Within a short time, I began to take breaks. By 12:30 P.M., I was two-thirds of the distance to the upper end of the lake. Before leaving that morning, I had wondered whether I would be able to arrive at the next scheduled camp, beyond the bend two miles past the lake. That was now out of the question. With this damned load, just getting to the lake's upper campground would be tough enough.

Until this trip, I had been unable to see how close to the shore the depth of the lake fell off. In my research, I had learned it was glacier made and over 250 feet deep. With the ice now 40 and 50 feet offshore, I finally saw what I had been walking on. I had stayed between 30 and 75 feet offshore during most of the travel. My hope was that if I broke through, I might survive by being in shallow water. The rocky bottom's disappearance into the greenish-blue depths no more than 20 feet offshore debunked that theory. Had I broken through, I would likely have drowned.

Springtime Avalanches

At 1:30 P.M. and another mile farther, I was taking a break in a thick stand of mature old-growth trees at the base of 9,003-foot Numa Peak, when from behind me came the deep guttural roar of a boulder-moving and tree-shattering avalanche. It continued for nearly two minutes. My attempt to assure myself that I was in a safe place all but collapsed with the memories of shattered trees as big as those around me from previous trips.

The load and the afternoon heat had taken a huge toll. I needed another hour to complete the last half mile to the upper campground. I dropped the load at the same camp as the previous two trips. I had averaged approximately one mile per hour, which I blamed partly on my age, but more on the loathsome size of the load and the heat.

The first thing I did was tear the backpack apart to get at the rubber-soled down booties. The expensive approach boots had amply demonstrated that they were no damn good for walking when the temperature was 50 F. or more. My feet felt like they had just spent the day in a meat grinder, as perhaps they had.

With supper over before 5 P.M., I took a stroll up the canyon. I got as far as the small stream beyond the upper side of the campground before turning back. I had found the snowpack. Since it was only in patches, tomorrow the snowshoes would remain off my feet for a while.

I also spotted fresh grizzly bear tracks leading away from the campground going up the canyon. The bear's direction struck me as peculiar since it was going back into the snowpack.

More avalanches continued to roar. One in particular sent shivers through me when it roared violently on 9,216-foot Mount Peabody. While I was safe for now, tomorrow that would change. In the quiet of the forested campground came the whispered question of whether I should continue the trip. I shrugged it off.

As the result of the late start from Polebridge, I would have to redo the schedule. I was supposed to have camped two miles farther tonight, just beyond the bend, setting up for an ascent halfway up the canyon wall toward Brown Pass tomorrow. If the snowpack was rotting as badly as I thought it was, I doubted I would get any farther than the bottom of the climb out of Bowman canyon tomorrow, although I would try.

The forecast for the next four days through Sunday called for a mostly cloudy sky with 40 percent chance of showers and a high temperature above 60 F. The forecast also predicted a partly sunny day on Monday, the seventh day. At the elevation of 6,829 feet, 200 feet higher than the trail on the approach, the temperature was supposed to drop down to 34 F. on Saturday night and 32 F. on Sunday night. If that were the case, there would be a strong crust on the approach for the sixth and seventh days. That meant I needed to be in position to begin the traverse no later than Sunday morning, the sixth day. On the original itinerary, that was also the day I was supposed to arrive at Hole in the Wall. If I was able to stay with the newly revised schedule, and only needed two days to traverse the approach, then I was presently one day behind.

The new schedule looked chancy. The forecast called for rain in the next 48 hours and thunderstorms on Saturday. With the roars of today's numerous avalanches still strong on my mind, those clouds might keep the sun's heat off the rocky south and southwest slopes I would be traversing.

At 6:16 P.M., another loud roar of an avalanche came from the east. A few minutes later, it struck me hard that I could really die out here, that the only real control I had on those avalanches was to back out. Sure, I would do that. A short time later, I was asleep.

20 • rotting snowpack

May 12: Not Early Enough

I was awake by 1:30 A.M., but waited 20 minutes to start the coffee. The temperature outside was an entirely too warm 32 F. Without question, today I would be on snowpack. How much posthole travel would there be?

Long ago, I had quit questioning why I woke almost every morning with a tune rolling around inside my head. This morning was no exception. Comfortable in the darkness, I started whistling under my breath. My imagination suddenly conjured up a picture of a boy's figure silhouetted in a dark room, eyes staring about at invisible walls, and lips pursed as he attempted to whistle himself calm. The sudden realization of what I was doing, and where, stopped me.

I chuckled at the verbal observation. "Good grief, I'm an old man whistling in the dark!"

My laughter faded as I recalled the beer cans I saw the last time I was here and again yesterday. One was 150 feet away, bear punctured and scrunched, while the others still lay at the bottom of Numa Creek no more than 50 feet from the tent. As I recalled, bears were smart, and like us, had learned behavior, with food normally being their highest motivator. That small 12-ounce can of beer the bear drank last fall was 145 calories. It seemed to me that he might remember that. Could bears be alcoholic? Maybe after a long winter sleep, having a beer for breakfast would sound like a good idea. Wait, I was even more calorie laden, and thus did my whistling end.

The beer in the creek and the illegal fire ring in the food prep area were also supporting evidence of what the park employees too often had to deal with. I could understand why some of the employees had copped an attitude toward visitors, although I was uncomfortable with the sometimes over-the-top conduct.

The temperature was still hovering around 32 F. when I left the campground shortly before 6 A.M. Within 30 minutes, where Bowman canyon was concerned, I concluded I had waited too long. I encountered snowpack soon after getting back on the main trail at the upper end of the campground. In the beginning, there were large areas of open ground and patches of rotting snowpack interspersed with occasional water running down the trail. While I was able to circumvent the snow, as I continued farther up the canyon, increasingly I postholed through larger islands of snow.

Although the sky had begun to fill with clouds, the temperature rose above 40 F. by 8 A.M., turning the weak crust into slush. At one of my numerous breaks, I finally detached the snowshoes from the backpack and hand-carried them. To put the snowshoes on would require me to take the backpack off, remove the snowshoes, and reattach the other exterior gear, so it was better to hand-carry them, although I would still have to remove the backpack to put them on. Since I wanted to avoid that, I began to posthole through small stretches of knee- to mid-thigh-deep snowpack. Although I was unsure at the time, it might have been better to drop the load and temporarily put on the snowshoes.

I eventually did test the snowshoes, only to find that even with the flotation devices, the snowpack was unable to hold my weight. Soon after removing them again, I came upon a 30-foot-wide and 3-foot-deep snowpack with no way to get around it. I was damned if I would put those snowshoes back on for such a short distance, which I would probably posthole through anyway. I plowed ahead, arriving on the other side five minutes later.

Almost three hours passed, and I had yet to summit the 250-foot ascent less than two miles up the trail. Exhausted and discouraged, anger became a handy tool. Behind a bellow of rage came the resolve to continue.

I stopped for a break at the edge of a large and uninterrupted snowpack. I could see the compressed snow of my three-week-old tracks from the April trip. There were also the recent tracks of at least one skier. After a few posthole steps on the tracks in the snowpack, I dropped the backpack again and put the snowshoes back on.

At 9:20 A.M., I began the descent of 150 feet back to the canyon floor. I was two-thirds of the way down when the left snowshoe plunged through the snowpack and toppled me. With a steep incline on the right, I counted myself fortunate that it had been my left rather than right leg. A fall off the trail could have been injurious or fatal. As it was, I found myself sitting on the snowpack with my left leg buried to the knee. To stand up again, I removed the backpack and took a few minutes to dig my leg and snowshoe free. I arrived on the canyon floor 25 minutes later and for a short distance, returned to more intermittent snowpack.

Where a small spring flowed across the trail, an opening in the trees let the sun warm the ground. Another sure bet that spring had arrived on the Bowman canyon floor was the scattered trillium flowers in the opening. Exhausted, I dropped the backpack and took a nap for most of an hour.

With the snowshoes back on, I continued up the canyon at 11:30 A.M. While certain the nap did me well, there was no getting around that I was tired. The snowpack was now continuous and unreliable. I finally dropped the load and headed up the canyon in an attempt to pack the snow. Without the load, I stayed on the surface, but postholed when I returned with the backpack. A frustrating failure, I had expended energy that seemingly was no longer available. Too tired to continue, a quarter mile short of where Pocket Creek converged into Bowman Creek, I began looking for a large enough flat for camp.

Sitting on the backpack during another 45-minute break, I listened to the roar of a nearby avalanche, the second since I started the break. The first had dropped off Boulder Peak, while this one came from the area of Hole in the Wall. If caught in one of those roaring masses, the chance for survival, whether alone or with a group of people, would be slim.

When I arrived at Pocket Creek, I had gone as far as I would for the day. All I needed to do was find a place to set up camp. That was easy enough since there was room to put 200 tents in this open area. I had one more issue to put behind me though. I was not so tired that I would foolishly spend the night on the west side of Bowman Creek. It was still crossable but rising with spring runoff. I might be unable to cross it by tomorrow morning. Besides, starting the day with a creek crossing just before beginning a big climb was a great way to create blisters. Still wearing the snowshoes, I crossed Bowman Creek just below the mouth of Pocket Creek and made camp 250 feet away in the center of a 50-foot-wide floodplain. The day of travel ended at 2:28 P.M.

As exhausted as I was, there was no one but me to build camp. I sluggishly made my way back to the creek and retrieved water. I decided the warmer nighttime temperatures made shoveling snow along the edges of the tent unnecessary. It was also a winter rule broken. I cooked the stew, ate, and prepared for an early bed.

As expected, the third day had been much tougher than the previous two. The transitional zone of the spring to winter season had been harsh. Today I had attempted to get to the upper side of the rotting snowpack. While uncertain I had accomplished that, I had no doubt that once I began the climb one mile away, the condition of the snowpack would improve.

Throughout the day, I heard numerous avalanches, enough to get complacent with them. During the latter part of the day, at the most I would glance in the direction of the roars and continue walking. Nevertheless, they would become a concern in the upcoming days. For now I was reasonably safe, and frankly too exhausted to worry about them or anything else. I was asleep soon after 5 P.M.

21 • onto the approach

May 13: Springtime Travel

At 1 A.M., I was up and relieved to see that the forecast temperature was once again wrong. Never mind that it was cold outside the sleeping bag, a crust had formed on the snowpack. The sky was clear and the temperature was 28 F. The forecast had called for 40 percent chance of showers, mostly cloudy, and a low temperature of 37 F. In spite of the chill, the first 40 minutes after I woke I heard several loud roars of avalanches. Again, I questioned whether I was too late.

I had also awakened with a dehydration headache. While there had been plenty of water sources throughout yesterday's travel, I ignored them. In one interval, I traveled four hours without a drink. Through the years, I had awakened with this headache numerous times. In each case, there was the recollection of going without water for an extended period the day before. I could do nothing about the headache but drink water and redouble my efforts to prevent it from happening again the next night. Today I would also carry an additional partial bladder of water, replacing part of the backpack weight loss of the last three days.

I was on the trail by 4:30 A.M. One and a half hours later, and less than 100 feet from the meadow in the upper canyon where the climb began, the left snowshoe broke through the snowpack, immediately followed by the right. As I fell backwards, I heard a grinding sound followed by a shock of pain in the small of my back and both knees.

For perhaps a minute, I lay unmoving as I let the pain subside. With both snowshoes buried, to get back to my feet I broke loose from the backpack and rolled to my right. This had happened before, although never with both knees and back getting hurt simultaneously. Individually, none felt any worse than the previous incidents. Nevertheless, I wondered if this was where I would turn around and exit.

After three or four minutes, I tested the affected areas of my body by walking around before repeating it while wearing the backpack. In the meadow, I dropped the load again and took a break. Though still uncertain how bad off I was, unless something else developed I would continue.

The meadow was less than one mile from last night's camp. There had been no strength in the crust the entire distance. With each step, I had broken through and dropped another two inches. Although tired and somewhat disheartened at what I had encountered before the fall, I was almost certain the condition of the snowpack was about to improve. I was at the bottom of the 2,000-foot ascent to the approach.

In the early morning light, the view of Hole in the Wall and the approach, except for more revealed rock, looked no less frightening than the previous trips. The real difference was the knowledge that I would be on the approach in 48 hours. The thought drove home my need to stay in the present. Today I was making only a partial ascent.

With the goal for the day to ascend at least 1,000 feet, I threw the backpack on 45 minutes after the fall and began the climb. I was delighted that the crust held my weight from the onset. I moved slowly and took breaks every 15 minutes to half an hour, resting for an equal amount of time. The pain from the fall eased until it was almost imperceptible, and then only in the left knee. I climbed 600 feet in two hours. Shortly after 9 A.M., I emerged out of the trees onto the huge avalanche slope on the north face of Thunderbird Mountain. The travel up to this point had been good enough for me to entertain the idea of continuing beyond my goal for the day, which was only 300 feet higher. Then I stepped into the sunlight and soft snowpack. I returned to the day's original planned goal, with the immediate need to get beyond the avalanche chute.

A Bothersome Friendship

The traveling portion of the day ended just before 11 A.M. in the scattered Douglas-fir trees on the other side of the avalanche chute, while still on the south side of the ravine. The altimeter said I was at 5,568 feet. In the hour and a half since I emerged out of the trees, the crust had turned to slush, confirming the need to stop. Immediately in front of me was the 300-foot climb that would place me near Brown Pass.

After what I had experienced the day before, getting this far was somewhat unexpected. Meanwhile, another part of me was paying attention to the permit. I was supposed to arrive at Upper Kintla Lake Campground in four days, something I now expected would happen in no less than five days.

The extended forecast had called for partly cloudy skies, a 40 percent chance of precipitation, and a chance for thunderstorms. The barometer said otherwise, and the sky was cloudless. I needed to be in bed early because in these conditions, tonight's probable cold would create another strong crust, but only during the morning. With the numerous avalanches that were taking place during the afternoon and evening, after today I was keen on traveling only before noon as much as possible.

There was also no telling when the next front would arrive. The hard copies of the extended forecast had ceased to have any accuracy. Once the clouds arrived though, it was possible that the avalanches would continue through the night and then into the following morning during my traveling time. On the other hand, those same clouds could stop the sun from heating the mountainsides, creating the dreaded springtime avalanches. Again, I questioned whether I had returned too late.

Earlier I had spotted a small falls in the ravine 250 feet away, which required only a short climb. After the camp was set up, I casually put the snowshoes back on, threw the bladders into the backpack, and headed for the stream, leaving the camera, crampons, ski poles, and ice axe behind.

As it turned out, the small opening in the snowpack was a deep hole to an unapproachable falls. Spotting another opening 100 feet farther up, I kept climbing. The angle of the draw combined with the slush soon became too much for the snowshoes. I began to slide backwards almost as much as I went forward. Several minutes later, I arrived at the small opening, where I filled the three bladders and the quart bottle. Then I looked around for an alternative route in the now steeply angled ravine. Seeing none, with some reluctance I turned around. Before I began the descent, my imagination conjured up a picture of me sliding down the ravine and into the 10-foot-deep hole at the falls. To counter that, I removed the snowshoes, used them as ski poles, and posthole traveled down the ravine. The round-trip took one hour.

Back inside the tent, I was disturbed to have gotten into so much trouble so close to camp. That was only supposed to occur while I traveled, not in the safety of camp. While this illusion took a hit at the end of the fourth day, the heavy-hitter delusion smashers were still a few days out.

I brought back far more water than was needed for the camp, with a plan to carry the extra water to the next camp. While the additional weight would be at least another 14 pounds, it also meant less fuel used to melt snow, and I would get one more stew before going to cold rations.

In mid-afternoon, a deer mouse came to visit. Normally I detest the small mammals, but not this enchanting little guy, who got my attention with his fearlessness. I chased him off after catching him chewing on a small cord connected to one of the open vestibules. He was back in a couple of minutes. This time he climbed over the edge of the tent's bathtub floor and into the shelter with me.

Now intrigued, I asked him if he knew he was in danger. He ignored me, so I slammed my fist on the floor just behind his lengthy tail and bounced him about a foot into the air. On his way back down he grabbed a couple paws full of mosquito mesh and wobbled his way off the tent's doorway, then sat on his haunches in the snow for a bit. I knew then that no harm would come from me to that mouse. I would just have to take a chance with the threat of getting hantavirus.

Eventually he made it over to the mineral- and salt-soaked backpack at the other vestibule door. I crawled out of the tent and stuck the backpack in the branches of a six-foot-tall Douglas-fir sapling five feet away. Several minutes later, his persistence paid off, and the mouse managed to climb up to the backpack. I threw the backpack into the tent again, now thinking about the inconvenience of having a backcountry buddy. That was the last time I saw him.

The grizzly bear tracks I followed up the canyon from the campground at Bowman Lake had continued straight for the avalanche area several hundred feet to the northwest. On this side of the ravine, I found a second set of grizzly tracks. They paralleled the base of the small cliffs that were part of Thunderbird Mountain. I became convinced the bruins were in the snowpack looking for winterkill. My conviction of having no need for a bear canister in the high country because the grizzlies were eating green shoots down below disappeared. (These smart bruins may have known that warmth equates to springtime avalanches, with a possible bountiful harvest of goat and other fresh meat delights.)

"Great," I uttered sarcastically. "So am I a living carcass and fair game?" I rechecked the location of the pepper spray.

With the goal of getting up early enough to take advantage of the hard crust, I was in the sleeping bag shortly after 5:30 P.M. The pain in my knees and back combined with fearful thoughts concerning the next few days prevented me from falling asleep right away.

May 14: Pain and Fear

At 1 A.M., the breathtaking beauty of Glacier National Park in the light of the nearly full moon greeted my awakening. If the weather held, the next 96 hours would show a landscape even more beautiful.

There was some question about the weather though. Although the barometric pressure had dropped very little since I arrived at this location, there was a breeze and occasional gusts, and a temperature of 35 F. The hard copy forecast called for a chance of showers and a low temperature of 37 F. Eventually, the temperature outside dropped to 27 F. To create a strong crust though, it would have needed to arrive several hours earlier.

The waterproof nitrile gloves that were nearly vital around the kitchen, snow, and icy water looked ready to come apart. Toward the end of the last trip, I had decided to replace them, but while packing for this trip changed my mind, another probable mistake. Now all I could do was hope they would last through the trip.

I placed the stove on the casualty list. While I wanted to blame the unyielding bear canister, it actually broke as I attempted to assemble it. Although now in two pieces, I would still be able to use the stove.

By carrying the two remaining water bladders to the next camp, the total weight of the backpack was six pounds more than what I started with at the trailhead. If necessary, I would drain a bladder while I traveled.

I left camp at 5:25 A.M., half an hour before sunlight touched the highest peaks. An hour after I began, with the initial steep climb behind me, I had ascended 400 feet when my back began to hurt. Then as I arced left and began to climb the last 300 feet to the main bench, the snowshoes started to break through the snowpack. The sudden additional effort increased the sciatic pain. As I neared 6,250 feet, the elevation where the final climb to the approach began, I began to doubt I would make the ascent today.

There had been numerous avalanches on the south face since the last trip three weeks earlier. None, however, had stretched far into the small trees where I had traveled during the two previous trips.

As I neared the western edge of the bench where I had camped for three nights on the previous trip, I discovered the latest equipment breakage. A strap on the right snowshoe was broken. Although disappointed, I was neither alarmed nor mystified. Three years earlier, the snowshoes had gone through the hellish winter-to-spring transitional zone in three different areas of the Selway-Bitterroot Wilderness. This winter I had also traveled through numerous snowless areas. Prior experience with the Atlas brand snowshoes said they would hold up, although I would have to be more careful when I entered the transitional zone above Upper Kintla Lake. I was also aware that for the next three days, I would wear only crampons until I neared Boulder Pass.

Several minutes later, I arrived at the western campground from the previous trip. The time was 7:36 A.M., and the sun was almost on the bench. The final ascent to the approach was already in sunlight, and the snow on the south face was soft. What stopped me, though, was the flaring pain in my left hip and small of my back.

I was also afraid. Often this emotion was a total liability, stealing my ability to discern the right thing to do. This was one of those times. While the avalanche chute I would ascend 500 feet had slid recently, I was unable to see whether it was ready to slide again. My presence up there this morning might be the final ingredient needed to begin a slide. Alone, my counsel was all that was available, and I had just decided to pause.

I rebuilt the camp at the second location of the previous trip. The recent avalanche had failed to enter the former camps, but did reach within 20 feet of the first camp, 300 feet east of the present camp. It validated the precautionary relocation I had made on April 15.

Just after noon, I put the crampons on and did a partial climb in the avalanche chute. Whatever it would become later in the day, before 1 P.M. the lower area of the chute was stable. In spite of the pain in my back, I regretted stopping that morning. I should have emptied the water bladders and ascended, and then built camp on the edge of the approach. Later in the afternoon, I heard the thundering crashes of boulders rolling down the nearby peaks, but no more avalanches, and my regret increased.

Increasingly the weather had become a different story. Throughout the day, the sky was almost clear, with just a few clouds to the south and east. The wind resumed before noon and continued to increase throughout the remainder of the day. The barometric pressure also began to drop. I packed away the hard copies of the extended forecast. Besides being uselessly inaccurate, they only extended out another 48 hours. The altimeter became my only guide. Between 11 A.M. and 3:30 P.M., the altimeter gained 62 feet. A front was on the way. My regret at building the early camp peaked. In what was now almost a routine, I was asleep by 6 P.M.

May 15: Ascent into a Nightmare

Arising at midnight, I used the flimsy excuse that this may be the last time I drank coffee and so increased the portion of coffee grounds by a third, though with no additional water. I also had a short sleep and figured those extra grounds were a reasonable aid. The day before, I had measured the remaining coffee grounds. Because I was using less, I had a 19-day supply; it was time to reward myself. I was also pleased with the resultant fuel consumption. I had used less fuel than expected. The 22-ounce bottle had fuel remaining, and the two 33-ounce bottles were untouched.

There was no doubt another storm was coming. Without the altimeter, the wind was indicative of the change. Unknown to me was when it would arrive, what it would bring, how big, and for how long. Regardless of the weather, today I would climb to the approach and begin the traverse.

Realizing that once up there I might have to turn back, I wondered if I would be able to exit down Bowman canyon. The creek crossing had been no cakewalk three days earlier, and after another three days of warm weather, the spring runoff would have increased. Was an exit to the east and north via Goat Haunt possible?

For part of the climb this morning, I would have plenty of moonlight to aid the head lantern. I would also wear the crampons and carry the ice axe out of camp. The bulk of the climbing gear would remain unused until I arrived on the ridgeline. At the edge of the approach, I would build a small flat and prepare the gear. Using a spare bag, I would create a two-load ferrying system. I was unwilling to find out if I could safely carry everything in one load. A mistake up there could be fatal. I would attempt to reduce the backpack weight to 80 pounds by carrying approximately 40 pounds in the other bag.

Although I considered most of the traverse reasonable enough to cross, my fear of it was ongoing. The main trepidation concerned the elbow. If there were but one location that would turn me around, it would be there. In this nearly vertical chute, avalanches and falling debris were an almost ongoing event during bad weather, and possibly on warm days. I had already concluded I would have to wait until I got there to decide if, when, and how

I would get through. Since September, I had also allowed for the possible need of that shallow cave 30 feet beyond the elbow, although I was uncertain of the timing.

I had the kitchen and much of the gear packed by 3 A.M. However, there was weariness in me that was only partly derived from the short night of sleep. I crawled back into the sleeping bag for a catnap and fell asleep almost immediately. Shortly before dawn, I woke up immediately alarmed by the late hour, and began packing the remainder of the gear. Still afraid of what was coming today, being active minimized the fear. I left the campsite at 7:15 A.M. as the sunlight crept down the peaks—and the avalanche risk crept higher.

There were clouds in the sky, but plenty of blue that would let the sun eventually heat the peaks, putting me in a race, one with an uncertain outcome. The crust was excellent, a good thing since the avalanche-damaged snowpack was far more daunting with a monstrous load than yesterday, when I carried only the camera bag. I stopped often for 30-second breathers, before I finally took a sitdown break 20 minutes into the climb. In sunlight for at least half the climb, I was back in shadow when I arrived at the edge of the approach. What took 50 minutes to accomplish today had taken two hours in April with a third of today's load.

The view was also vastly different. Without the swirling snow and clouds, with the exception of the elbow I could see the entire mountainside and Hole in the Wall. It only vaguely resembled what I had seen at the end of the previous September. Steep inclines and small cliffs lay buried beneath the deep snowpack, creating a huge placid slope with at least a 50-degree angle. With the cliffs hidden, stepping out there without an anchor, even without a load, would have been a fool's route.

Standing motionless, the fear grew. Turning to face the slope with the shovel in hand, I went to work. I dug the flat into the snowpack in 15 minutes. In another hour, I had set up the technical gear and prepared the two loads, but skipped out on building and wearing a chest harness. The first anchor was an eight-inch-thick Douglas-fir tree. Thereafter there would only be the snow pickets. With the sun now on me, I extended the first leg across the crisp snowpack, dug another flat, and returned to the original flat.

I picked up the first load and then stopped. Although the first 100 feet was ready, until I started the first ferry, the beginning was still in front of me. I stood on the flat below a large dead tree and gave myself a chance to reconsider. There was a reason the park service considered this eastern approach to Hole in the Wall inaccessible. Could I really get across, or was I trying to snag an illusion off the horizon?

For seven and a half months, this approach had been entrenched in my head. When I was in the office looking at the photos taken during the September scout, and considering the crossing of Glacier National Park, this was always the target. In the deep powder of February's trip in the Belly River canyon, and the two trips up here afterward, this slope was always foremost on my mind. My first winter view of it in March shook me as I stood on the floor of Bowman canyon and stared up at this wall. I had declared then that the approach was undoable, but reminded myself I was only on a scouting mission.

Now finally standing on the edge, rope extended onto the great white slope, should I do what some considered a regaining of my sanity, and back out? I could capitulate to the advice of others and exit. Yeah, and none of them had ever been here, or ever would be. To my knowledge, even park service personnel shied away from this location under these conditions. I could feel the ire rising. I stood alone, and although I was keenly aware that the decision could have a great affect on others, it was still mine to make. All the prior trips through the winter had brought me to this spot. Experience said if I were careful, at the least I could get to the elbow.

The fear was huge, but so was the desire to continue. With the smaller load on, I stepped off the flat and dropped the several feet down to the rope connected to the tree, connected the carabiner to the jumar that was already clipped to the rope, and began the traverse. (A jumar is a toothed cam that slides freely along the rope in my direction of travel but jams and holds fast against a fall.) The time was just short of 11 A.M., late for making a start. Including the autumn trip and all the days of the winter trips, however, it had taken 45 days to get to this spot and I would wait no longer.

Halfway to the flat, the first of numerous chunks of ice, large and small, from the rock outcroppings and cliffs 500 feet above the traverse broke loose. Several seconds later, they tumbled across my route 100 feet ahead. While the sun had been on the cliffs for hours, numerous ice-covered angles up there were still untouched by the warming rays. A closer look told me the dropping bombs had only just begun. Failing to bring a helmet may have been a mistake.

A few minutes later, I arrived at the end of the rope and dropped the load. I turned around and retrieved the still heavy backpack. I dropped the load at the extended flat and with a quickdraw (two carabiners attached to a loop of webbing), connected it to the rope, returned to the tree, and disconnected the rope. A part of me declared that I had just disconnected from sanity. Now my only connection to life on the steep slope was a moving island that was composed of a rope, four snow pickets, a climbing harness, crampons, and an ice axe. This equipment instilled in me a sense of freedom similar to the first time I lifted off the ground in a helicopter.

As it turned out, every 100 feet consumed nearly one hour. At the far end of the rope, I would remove the shovel from my shoulder and dig another flat. Each time I did, my arms had less strength to get the job done, which made digging that much more difficult and lengthy. Once again, the breaks were more often and lengthier.

Danger from Above

By noon, the snowpack was no longer crisp. The crampons and boots sank at least two inches into the snow. From above, the falling chunks of snow and ice increased as the sun touched more of the cliffs. In the still-shaded area of the cliffs, I could see large and small icicles, with layers of ice that yesterday had been water running on the rock shelves. After beginning the second leg, I heard a crashing above and behind me. I watched as large and small chunks of ice and snow bounced, slid, and rolled past the area I had abandoned half an hour earlier.

Several minutes later, I delivered the first load to the flat at the end of the second leg. I had just paused for a breather when the largest icefall yet broke loose. The mass originated in a hollow in the cliff that was hundreds of feet above and 150 feet in front of me. I could see a vague disruption in the snowpack over there, where past slides had crashed down the mountainside. At some point, I would have to cross whatever was there. I was equally certain that if I had been in there when the ice and rocks had passed through, I probably would have died.

While I had known at the edge of the approach that it was a mistake to go out so late in the morning, it was only now that I began to feel the weight of the earlier decision. I looked back at the 200 feet I had traveled, but refused to turn back.

Two hours later, at 2:40 P.M., the slope and I were temporarily shaded by increasing clouds. I had just returned from delivering the first load to the 400-foot mark. Standing on the third built flat, I was changing out a memory card in the camera when the largest ice- and rockfall thus far took place on the scarred area now only 70 feet in front of me. The fourth flat with the first delivered load was 30 feet beyond the largest ditch. The rope crossed several ditches with the second and third pickets in their midst. The main ditch was more than three feet deep and five feet wide. When the mass broke loose, I stopped what I was doing and watched it tumble and slide down the steep incline, powerless to stop whatever it would do to the rope and pickets. If I lost the gear, how would I get back to the trees? Several seconds later, the debris hit the rope. I watched as a large slab of ice snagged the lifeline, which broke loose a moment later only to have another slab grab it. This happened four or five times before the mass moved out of range down the mountain. Less than a minute later, I watched the ice, snow, and rocks disappear over the cliff hundreds of feet below.

I breathed a sigh of relief, got into the backpack and began the second ferry. I had already been across this dangerous zone four times, but still had three more to complete. I hoped this latest event would be the last for a while. The cliffs continued to spit ice, snow, and rocks, but nothing like what I had recently witnessed recurred.

By 3:20 P.M., I had retrieved the rope and snow pickets. On the north side of the ditches, the cliff was no longer in a hollow, which was the reason for the large shaded area and the consequent masses of falling ice and rocks. Here the cliff bulged toward the steep slope I was on, which eliminated almost any ice buildup and avalanches.

The First Fall

Throughout the afternoon, my direction had been toward two Douglas-fir saplings, now 100 feet away. I altered my direction now to go below the larger upper tree. There was only one way they were still alive—no avalanches. Although I already felt a small margin of safety from loose ice and rock debris, I was less certain about an avalanche. I needed to keep moving until I got to those trees, where I would finally take a long break. The last time I had stopped for more than a couple of minutes had been four hours earlier.

By coincidence, the rope ended at the tree. I was looking for a spot to thrust the last picket when my right foot broke through the snowpack in an unusual way. With my weight on the left leg, I looked down and into a two-foot-deep black hole. Apparently, I was standing on the wrong side of a small ledge. The snowpack appeared to have melted away from the hidden rocks, creating a hole beneath its surface.

Connected to the rope, I was unalarmed, but would have to alter the route, though only as much as needed. I stepped backward down the mountainside, braced myself, and plunged the picket into the slushy snowpack. Several attempts later, I found a satisfactory spot, unclipped the rope from the jumar and harness, and clipped it to the quickdraw on the snow picket.

Satisfied, though suspicious of the area where the hole was, I took the roped snow shovel off my back and prepared to dig the next flat. Too close to the rope, I shoved the shovel into the snowpack and took another couple steps backward down the slope. When I put my weight down on the left leg, I found the next ledge or cliff.

There was no chance or opportunity to catch myself. One moment I was standing firmly and the next I was in a freefall backward. My mind immediately slowed time down enough for me to suck in a lungful of air and brace for the impact. Realizing I was unroped, fear shot through my body. In that brief span of time, I questioned how in the hell I was going to reverse myself and bring the ice axe and crampons into play after I landed. I knew I had to, or I was going to slide down the mountain and over the cliff.

I landed on the slope flat on my back with my head pointed down the mountain. I lay quiet as I grasped what had just happened. Dazedly I lay unmoving on the mountain. The flood of relief lasted only long enough for me to fully realize my predicament. My left leg had found another hole, which after trying to kill me now gripped my leg and prevented my slide down the mountainside.

I am unsure how long I lay unmoving, perhaps half a minute before I realized I had to do something. Help was not on the way.

God almighty! Why did I come out here alone? For heaven sakes, I'm not even roped! Is this what it all looks like on the day I die? Not roped! What the hell? If I get out of this, I'm going home.

My right hand had a death grip on the ice axe, while simultaneously a length of parachute cord connected the tool to the harness. I switched it over to my left hand and shoved the axe into the snowpack near my waist. With the axe breaking loose, I sat up, but was unable to hold the position for more than four or five seconds. Knowing I would have done better without the weight of the camera on my chest, I decided to remove it, only to discover I was unable to remove the vest, which covered the camera bag straps. Whatever happened, the camera bag would be there through it all.

Using the ice axe again, I attempted to pull myself upright, but was unable to get a strong enough angle in the snowpack of the now 60-degree slope. For several seconds I quit struggling long enough to twist my neck and look down the mountainside beyond my head. A moment of that and I decided no more looks at the upside-down surreal view would be necessary. (Months later, with the snow gone, I discovered that a 20-foot cliff lay directly below my position.)

I tried to sit up without the aid of the ice axe and was successful for several seconds while I inspected the area around my stuck left leg. I lay back down and rested for a bit, and came back up again. I did this several times as I went from inspecting the hole to looking for a safe way to release the leg. For several minutes, I searched and struggled. Through it all, there was a growing conviction that my efforts were going to be for nothing and today had become my day to die. I continued my exertions.

I tried to get my free right leg pointed down the mountain but couldn't manage it, at least not while I was flat on my back. Another option finally came to mind. I rested for a few minutes before I once more sat up. With protesting stomach muscles and the camera thoroughly in my way, I grunted my way forward toward the stuck foot and managed to grab the right boot and crampon, bend the knee and pull the leg downhill toward me.

A few moments later, I had created what gymnasts call a split, except my stomach muscles were now holy hell on fire! My right leg was finally in position to stop a freefall once the left leg was free. With the ice axe in hand, I desperately enlarged the hole, and a few moments later the leg broke free. With stomach muscles screaming, and my body sweating profusely, the leg slipped out of the hole. I gave a final heave forward and to my left, rotating my torso and left leg, while I shoved the ice axe into the snowpack. A few moments later, both legs were together and the toes of the crampons were digging into the slush; the struggle was over.

Still wearing the camera bag, I was unable to lie flat on my belly, but lay I did for a minute while the pain in my stomach muscles subsided. With the adrenal shakes still ebbing, I weakly but carefully stood up.

The trip had just changed. In another lifetime, no more than 15 minutes before, except for the falling debris and danger of avalanches, the traverse had felt like a cakewalk. That attitude and the complacency created by it had disappeared. A few minutes later, I climbed up to the rope several feet away and attached the jumar to it. While I felt a small increase of security,

I doubted I would get back what I had before the fall. The horror of what almost happened and could happen again would stay with me on and off for the remainder of the trip.

The First Camp

I was also through traveling today. Tomorrow there would be a new route, an exit of Glacier National Park. The park personnel and armchair quarterbacks were right. The approach to Hole in the Wall was undoable, at least by me.

I moved away from the tree and traveled along the length of the rope, looking for a location to dig out a camp below the bulging portion of the cliffs. I traveled 25 feet before I thought that I was far enough away from the cliff-like terrain around the trees. The first test dig turned out to be the only one. I dug out the final and largest flat for the day.

The lesson about staying connected to the rope at all times had been harsh. As I dug out the flat, the rope and jumar were in the way, but no complaint escaped my lips.

I dug a six-foot-deep flat by 4:20 P.M. Where the pads and sleeping bag would be located was eight feet long while the gear area was six feet. There was also a one-foot buffer where neither the loose gear nor I ventured. On the other side of the edge was the slope that had almost taken me.

Generally, as I grew more tired I looked for shortcuts. After digging the flat, one such time- and effort-saver popped up, and then like a hovering hummingbird, was gone. I thought of leaving the rope in place, since that would be the direction and the route for the next day. The still raw memory of the fall slashed out and brought me to my senses. Staying alive depended on the rope and pickets. Extended, they were vulnerable to avalanches.

Six trips later, all the gear was in camp. In the process, I had to make one more visit to the area where I had fallen. Anchored by two pickets back at the camp, I carefully made my way out to the trees and back again without incident. Before breaking down the loads and building the camp, I set the rope and snow pickets in the buffer area as further protection.

Staying with what was left of the plan, I ate a cold supper. Having barely eaten anything through the day, I should have been ravenous, but my appetite was nonexistent. I force-fed myself with pistachios, peanuts, and fruit, but ate only a small amount before nausea stopped me.

Once the queasiness passed, outside of the sunburn on my neck and face, I felt fine physically. My mental state was another case. While I was calm, I saw nothing to be reassured about from my lofty perch on the slab. I had completed only 500 out of 1,600 feet of the technical portion on the approach. Somewhere out there, perhaps 1,000 feet away, the worst part of the approach still waited.

God almighty, I almost died today and the worst is still up ahead.

But tomorrow morning I was probably going to exit. I planned to retrace the route that brought me here. I frowned at the thought of having to cross those ditches again, but better to follow a stomped snowpack and ready-made flats than to continue into the unknown. If I did go ahead though, I would change the route. To approach those two trees and continue beyond them was out of the question. Maybe I could build a switchback from this location down to the approximate location of the summer trail—except I was going home.

The Avalanche

Near 6 P.M., I was beginning to gather my wits concerning the day, the precarious camp, and the next day, when hell came for a visit. I was sitting in the camp chair within the concave that was the sleeping area when I heard a cracking sound like the firing of a high-powered rifle—an avalanche, and close by! Beneath me, the snowpack began to shake. The guttural and grinding roar was behind and above me!

God almighty!

Like two and a half hours earlier when I fell, time slowed down. Some fool said to stand up and shoot some pictures. A saner voice said to curl up and make myself as small as possible inside the dugout area against the wall of snowpack.

I sure hope to God I'm right about this cliff. Oh God, what an awful way to find out.

Several seconds later, the snowpack now shaking horribly like a helicopter in a hard turn, the massive roar arrived at my elevation, and I found out why the ditches 100 feet away were numerous and deep. That other guy spoke up again and said that if I were a photographer I would stand up and shoot pictures.

There was no way I could tell if any of the debris would make it over here. Better to keep my head down. Over the roar, I yelled, "Then I am no photographer."

The cut snowbank on my left prevented me from seeing most of what passed. What little I did see was a mixture of boulders, roots, filthy ice, and raging muddy water. After the mass was below me, I rose up six inches and watched the massive mess spill over the cliffs below the slope. I let out a sigh of relief and reiterated the need to get the hell out of here. All I had to do to make that happen was stay alive through the night.

Throughout the day, the wind had been steady except when it was gusting. The barometric pressure continued to fall. Now in the evening, to the west I could see a mass of clouds. Tomorrow the weather would change. If it came as rain on the already-wet snowpack, I figured my chances for surviving were going to take another drop. For this evening though, I had no choice but to watch the looming weather.

As my bad location continued to deteriorate, I lamented on the decision this morning of entering the approach regardless of the late hour. I had known that it was too late to begin the traverse, and yet had cast aside caution almost without a pause. Now I was in the process of finding out if this was nothing more than a whirlpool of events that would end with my demise. What a fool I was. I realized that, whether it rained or snowed, I was uncertain what I would do the following day. Before sleep overtook me, I replayed the terrifying fall. I had no words to describe how it felt to be alone as I had lain upside down on the steep pitch and struggled to live.

22 • the coming storm

May 16: The Increasing Peril

I woke up throughout the night. I was alive but under the threat of dying. At 1 A.M., I awoke with a panicked thought.

Get the fuck out of here. You're going to die!

I set the chair up, sat in it, and started packing. Overhead there was only the darkness brought on by an overcast sky. Before now, each time I woke, the moon had been bright on the snow. Now in the lantern light, I saw the beginning specks of a mist. Like tiny messengers, they informed me that my situation had just deteriorated more.

I had prepared for this event the evening before by placing the shell of the tent near the foot of the sleeping bag and bivy sack. In the now calm air, I spread the waterproof material over the equipment and sleeping bag and then lay back down. Pools of water began to grow on the fly. I soon came up with the idea of attempting to erect the tent shell. The flat was too small to erect the tent, but with plenty of anchors, I could set up the shell while it hung over the edge.

Several minutes later, with the shell erected and over my head, I felt comforted. The familiar olive drab color was soothing. Suddenly it was time for a cup of coffee. In the process of setting up the broken stove, I tore the thumb off the right nitrile glove. I had been expecting this for a few days, and ignored it. Within a few minutes, the temperature rose to a comfortable 50 F. inside the shell.

With the first cup of coffee in hand, I felt better than I had any right to. The familiarity of the tent with the sense of comfort it brought deepened with the roaring stove, perking coffee, and sips of the scalding liquid. Knowing it was temporary, I nevertheless sat back and enjoyed the lull.

At 3 A.M. I went back over the plan of exiting along the trail I had built yesterday. My thoughts were disrupted by a familiar but distant crack. In the darkness, the roar of a far-off avalanche became my reveille.

Jesus Christ! Ain't doing any good here now, time to pack up.

It would be 26 hours before I would record another entry into the audio log.

Descend and Continue

The cramped space of the narrow flat slowed me. By the time I was ready to break the shell down it was getting daylight. The rain was intermittent and had stopped again when I removed the shell, providing my first look at the day. The scene took me back decades. Monsoon season was upon me again, except here there was no green Vietnamese jungle. Not to be outdone, the deep snowpack was slushy and at least as inhospitable as the red, slimy mud of Southeast Asia. Each had its own way to terrorize.

During the monsoon season in Vietnam, we used helicopters to supply some mountaintop artillery firebases. For five to six months, we were their lifeline. Today, on the dizzying flanks of Chapman Peak, my lifeline was a 100-foot rope, four snow pickets, a pair of crampons, and an ice axe. Yesterday afternoon in the wet snowpack, it became difficult to get a good anchor with the 24-inch pickets. This morning in the rain and the warmth, travel would continue to be difficult and dangerous. Unlike yesterday, though, I had a partially packed trail that included flats every 100 feet. That gave some margin of safety and ease for the day's travel. Or maybe not.

My eyes wandered downslope to where I thought the summer trail ran. If I could get down there and hold a level traverse on the route of the summer trail, I reasoned, I should be able to avoid any cliffs beneath the snowpack at least as far as the elbow. With the cloud cover, there would be no sun to heat the mountain and hurtle more ice and rocks at me.

There is a two-word explanation meant to bring hope to those who are suffering: "time heals." While that might be true under some circumstances, it damn sure is a fallacy in others. Time can also make a person forget what ought to be remembered. As I lay upside down a day earlier, I had resolved that if I survived the fall I would go home. This morning, a mere 15 hours later, the terror of that incident had faded. The resolve to exit disappeared, replaced by the belief that I could descend 40 feet and continue to Hole in the Wall.

Shortly after 6 A.M., I left the now familiar flat and roped southwest down the slope. The snowpack was exactly what I thought it would be; I dropped six inches with every step. Anxious to stay away from the ditches, I still traveled 80 feet before I dug the first flat. I packed the snow down further as I ascended back for the first ferry.

The rain returned soon after I began the second leg, this time with a northerly breeze. Undeterred, for the next five and a half hours I pushed north across an area that had previously slid. Within the first hour, I began to tire and soon started to stumble in the soft snowpack, particularly with the heavier main load. For fear of losing it down the mountainside, each time I went down with the backpack I kept it on as I regained my feet. To accomplish that, I moved my feet into a position where they faced down the slope, then I rolled over and got on my knees. Finally, using the jumar on the rope, I pulled myself upright. With each fall, it would take longer to regain my feet. Mostly I would lay there for a bit before going through the effort of standing up. Eventually I began to take shorter steps to build a more firmly packed trail, which greatly reduced the postholing and falling.

The cold, wet day made it impossible for me to stop for any lengthy breaks. I realized that I should stop to eat or at least drink some water, but I kept putting it off, wanting to complete one more ferry or leg of the traverse. The cooler temperatures encouraged me to keep moving. I walked no faster than before, but I traveled nonstop.

A Complainer in the Storm

I was careful and consistent in my work through the morning, but exhaustion got the best of me during the last two legs. I started to make mistakes. There were intervals of two and three seconds when I was unclipped from the rope. Horrified at each instance, I cried out a few times in self-reproach. Each time, I immediately reconnected to the rope. I knew, however, that it was only a matter of time before a moment of being unroped would coincide with a fall. By 9:30 A.M., the wind-driven rain had turned to wet snow. I needed to stop, but doing so on the huge, naked slope would be unsafe. Forced to continue, my condition deteriorated.

My leather gloves were soon soaked, drooping uselessly on my hands. I finally brought out the combination mitten-fingerless gloves, but found I couldn't properly grip the ice axe with a mittened hand. I had no alternative but to use the fingerless glove with whichever hand was gripping the ice axe.

Soaked within minutes, both hands were soon solid with cold, particularly the right where part of the nitrile glove was missing. My carpal tunnel syndrome helped numb the pain, but I worried about frostbite, which would doom me. At each flat, I stopped and placed my hands in my armpits for warmth.

As the fog swirled around me, I heard the bawling roars of a grizzly bear not more than a quarter mile north in Hole in the Wall. Exhausted, I paused to listen, wondering what the bear was complaining about. My own critical circumstances urged me onward. Yes, the bear had problems. So did I.

In Trouble

Shortly after 11 A.M., the weather picked up the pace as it headed toward hell. I shoved the fourth anchor into the snowpack, tested it, and clipped the rope to the picket with a quickdraw. Then I clipped the jumar to the rope and was safe again. Not 25 feet away was the edge of the snow cornice marking the entrance into the elbow. I was unable to see any of the elbow itself, just the trees on the ridge across the ravine some 300 feet away. Regardless of how I gained entry into the elbow, it would have to wait for another day. The condition of the snowpack combined with the weather and my exhausted state had stopped me for the remainder of the day.

I trudged 50 feet back up the rope to a rock overhang I hoped to use as shelter for the night's camp. I started to dig the snow out from a rock ledge beneath the overhang, but the tiredness in my body was awful. My arm and shoulder muscles felt like boneless putty. I quickly realized the overhang was unusable—water was dripping off every surface. I decided to build camp at the far end of the rope, but I still needed to dig a flat and ferry the equipment. I was exhausted, yet less than an hour later I had dug a flat and ferried all of the gear to it; travel for the day was finished.

I pondered what to do next, but soon discovered that sitting around and thinking about it was dangerous. I was damp to the skin from sweat, rain, sleet, and snow. Only my heavy activity throughout the morning had kept me warm. Now that I was no longer moving, hypothermia would soon set in.

During a storm in April, I had photographed this area from the canyon floor with the 70 to 200 mm lens. I had watched the unnerving, constant spindrift flow down the huge snowdrift I was now on. No tent would stand up to that barrage. A repeat of last night's camp could be deadly here.

May 10: Sunset at the low end of Bowman Lake was beautiful but came with an ominous warning of the inevitable spring avalanches.

May 15: The sixth day began late with an ascent of the avalanche chute from the Brown Pass bench. Before the day was out, there would be a price to be paid.

At the beginning of the third 100-foot leg, the first serious avalanche occurred in the ditches 50 feet beyond the end of the rope.

May 15, 3:30 P.M.: Unclipped from the rope, I found a hole and fell over backwards. This photo shows me just after recovering almost 20 minutes later, and still unclipped.

The end of the first day out of six on the approach found me in a camp I dug into the slope, with a beautiful but ominous view of Bowman canyon.

May 16: With a winter storm blowing in, I had no alternative but to build a snow cave in a "minor" avalanche chute, which I would not exit for two days.

May 17: Unsure how much longer I would be alive, in the late evening of the second night inside the snow cave I took photos of myself with the moisture-ridden camera.

The doorway with snow blown in around the poncho, and my equipment inside the snow cave.

May 18: Inside the elbow, I built the second flat of the day after I abandoned the first, and then took a well-earned break.

During the break on the flat, this photo shows the route between the first snow cave and 75 feet into the elbow.

In the mid-morning hours, the terrain above my route inside the elbow remained stable. One hour later, that would all change.

After taking nearly a half hour to recover from the second fall, retrieving the heavy backpack remained problematic.

This is the view of the area where I fell; the rope is stretched taunt with the nearly 80-pound backpack below me.

May 20: After two days inside the dugout cave, I pushed on toward Hole in the Wall. With trees now below me, I turned and photographed the entire elbow, where only a few hours earlier I was uncertain I would survive. From the right to the left side of the photo there are four dugout flats. The first flat on the right shows a hole in the snowpack above it and to the left, which is where I fell. The three other flats grouped together are where I rested before I retrieved the backpack from below. The final dig is on the left side of the photo below the cliff where I dug the second cave.

May 21, mid-morning: My crampon-laden footprints descending off the approach from the late afternoon of the day before.

The warm day of sunshine was a life-preserving respite as I dried my water-soaked gear.

May 22, midmorning: During the two-day ascent out of Hole in the Wall, my view midways up the western wall.

With the snowpack too soft to walk in with the backpack, I continued to the top of the wall, bringing these three pieces of gear and the camera.

May 23: The day brought a mix of rain, snow, and sunshine as I retraced my tracks from the day before to the top of the western lip of Hole in the Wall.

With the day's travel over by noon, a reconnoitering to 7,470-foot Boulder Pass without the heavy backpack was undertaken. Two hundred feet short of the pass, 9,944-foot Kinnerly Peak is coming into view.

Aurreal view of a small lake and the valley leading up to 7,470-foot Boulder Pass.

Near Boulder Pass Campground I could see the edge of the snowpack 2,000 feet below in Kintla canyon.

May 25: The trip ends less than one mile from the snow-free trail with an extraction inside this helicopter.

The only other alternative was to build a snow cave and hope it would withstand an assault from whatever had already scarred the slope. With the gouges of previous slides in the snowpack at this location, I nevertheless saw no other option. Except where I had spent the previous night, slides had scarred the entire approach.

At noon, I placed the pickets and rope above and on either side of the flat, moved the gear to the right side, and then started to dig into the base of the five-foot-deep wall of snow. The temperature continued to drop and the wind never let up. The wet snowflakes soon became flying and swirling powder, gradually filling the flat I had worked so hard to create.

Ignoring my exhausted body's protests, I raced to get the snow cave dug before the flat vanished under the new snowfall. After an hour or two, I lost track of time. The measurements for elapsed time narrowed to how deep I had progressed into the snow and how large the space had become. I am uncertain when it happened, but at some point, the environment ceased to be a winter storm, replaced by the quiet of the growing cave. Occasionally I would reemerge through the four-by-four-foot entrance to send the loose snow I had thrown out of the cave tumbling down the mountainside.

I dug five feet into the snowpack and then enlarged the cave at either end sideways by another eight feet with a four-foot ceiling. In the late afternoon or perhaps early evening, I finally decided the hole was large enough. Everything but the pickets, rope, and poncho came in. Before I entered the cave for the final time, I fashioned a door with the poncho.

Inside the cave, desperate to rest, I worked to put a buffer between the snow and my body. While warm from the exertions, I was damp. Once cooled down, I would be in trouble. I soon had the two pads and camp chair set up. My continued exertions in the quiet staved off the chill.

As I broke the loads down, it soon became clear that I had made a grave mistake at the last camp. Most of the gear was soaked, and the critical sleeping bag had numerous wet spots. I reasoned I could work the moisture out of the bag with my body heat. I stuffed the sleeping bag into the bivy sack, and draped it over my legs and midsection.

Once I had the gear properly arranged, I finally shed the layers of damp clothing and crawled into the sleeping bag without eating or drinking any water. I realized it was a bad idea, but I was too tired to care and was soon asleep. Just before nodding off, I looked at the watch for the first time since late morning. It was a few minutes before 6 P.M. Only then I recalled that I had not turned off the logbook inside the timepiece.

23 • the snow cave

May 17: The Horror of Unknowing

Although the temperature stayed a moderate 32 F. through the night, I woke up numerous times damp and cold. I had no doubt I was paying the price for yesterday's lapse in protecting the gear. Throughout the night, I jogged numerous times to get warm. From my knees down, I stayed chilled, particularly my feet. I finally realized they were touching the snow wall and that was the reason they were cold. Sometime during the night, I moved one of the pads so it would cover that portion of the wall, but my feet remained cold.

In spite of the chill, I had long periods of deep sleep, and awakened for the day after 10 hours. According to the altimeter and the wind, which was driving snow around the edges of the doorway and onto the equipment, the storm continued. I sat quietly in the camp chair and felt the growing chill as I waited for the first cup of coffee, which I began sipping by 4:30 A.M. The chill disappeared within five minutes, and for the first time inside the cave, I felt calm.

Each time a gust overrode the steady wind, snow pushed its way around the leaky entrance, a reminder of what was on the other side of the poncho. The wind had continued through the entire night, and I assumed the snowfall had also been steady. In the gathering light around the edges of the doorway, it looked like three feet of fresh snow was lying on what remained of the flat. If that much snow had dropped on the steep slope, travel was out for at least one day. More disturbing was the increased avalanche danger, which could sweep the cave away.

I began to comprehend a little more clearly the grave peril of the location. If even as little as one foot of snow fell last night, any movement by me would put my life in jeopardy. On the other hand, staying put on this slope could also be fatal. Unsure of what to do, at 5:30 A.M. I poured a second cup of coffee and prepared a rare third pot.

One certainty was that I needed food and rehydration. I had no memory of drinking any water after leaving camp yesterday. Although I had never felt thirsty, I had to be dehydrated. I had also eaten nothing throughout the entire day, including last night. Fear had removed more than my appetite. It had shut down other parts of my body, too. Except for urinating, nothing was exiting me.

At 6 A.M., I finished the third cup of coffee and turned the stove off. By now, I was almost certain I would be going nowhere today. I needed to think about this, however, and I needed to do it with the clear head that came with nourishment. I brought out two handfuls of pistachios, the tastiest part of the larder, and began to force them down my throat. Throughout the 15 minutes of de-shelling and eating the nuts, I was nauseous. After finishing the nuts, I continued the punishment with some dehydrated fruit. The food had the expected calming effect, although all I got was a clearer picture of a bad situation.

Even with a hard crust snowpack such as 48 hours earlier, if the elbow were passable at all, it would still have presented a serious challenge. After the warmth of two days, followed by more than 24 hours of rain and snowfall, today it was a madman's route.

I thought about the avalanches I had heard yesterday morning. Avalanches were common enough on all of my winter trips that I paid scant attention to them, but yesterday morning they reawakened me with a shock. Exhausted and justifiably fearful of the steep slope scarred from previous slides, I let the roars of yesterday's avalanches puncture any remaining sense of security. I knew that inside this snow cave, with powder snow blowing around the edges of the doorway, I was a sitting duck. No more than 25 or 30 feet beyond the snow cave was the edge of the ravine, with the elbow another 150 feet beyond. During the April storm, even at a distance I could see that this avalanche chute was a death trap. Now, in the trap myself, I was certain of it.

I thought about my reluctance to protect the gear before leaving camp yesterday morning. I had seen patches of clear sky in the last half hour that I packed. The rain had been intermittent and never more than a mist; if it had been heavier, I would have placed everything inside plastic. Moreover, my final resort to protect the backpack was the poncho, which would cover the entire load. When the need to use the poncho arrived, however, I had pushed on, telling myself that the rain would stop again, which it did—only to be replaced by sleet—and then snow.

Now most of the gear was still damp or soaked, and in an environment where most of it would never dry. The humidity was 74 percent. Only the sleeping bag and maybe the camera would dry because of their close proximity to my body. The remaining equipment would have to wait for the next day of sunshine, and after I was off the approach.

This morning, both hands were numb and blackened by the dye from the soaked U.S. Army-issue gloves. I still was unable to tell whether there was any damage—they moved when I wanted them to.

If I decided to pack up and travel with my clothes and gear still wet, I would be fine until I left the cave, when there would be a lull in activity before I began to travel. That would be when the wet gear would be most dangerous. Also, I could not tell how long the foul weather would last. Avalanche danger would increase with each passing day, while the dwindling food and fuel supplies became an issue. Was I even going to be alive by day's end?

I looked at the altimeter and saw that the pressure had risen, if only a little. That small bump in the barometric pressure meant little would change. To be convincing, the altimeter would have to lose at least 150 feet.

Tired and again beginning to feel the chill, I crawled back into the sleeping bag. With the slight increase in the barometric pressure came more wind and worrisome gusts. Snow continued to blow in around the poncho and onto some of the gear. I was still pondering how to better seal the door when I fell asleep.

I awoke at 5:30 P.M., having slept on and off throughout the entire day. The barometric pressure continued to rise and was now slightly higher than 24 hours earlier. With the doorway pointed at the western sky, I saw the sun pop out in the early evening. Although the snowfall had stopped, the snow was piled four feet high up the poncho, leaving a small eight-inch gap at the top of the doorway. That was enough to see the sunshine and keep me supplied with fresh air.

I considered opening the poncho so I could actually see what was happening out there. The thought lasted only a moment, replaced by my mind's eye showing cascading snow spilling into the cave when I pulled the poncho aside. As vital as it was to see what the weather was doing, keeping my cocoon intact was more important. I would have that look tomorrow at daybreak, after the equipment was packed.

The fear was a constant except when I slept. Sometimes it was worse depending on what I was thinking. As much as I dreaded the elbow, I was more fearful of what might happen at any minute inside this cave. How much snow was actually out there? Was it going to break loose like I had observed in April? For a moment, I reflected on what would have happened if I had attempted the approach in March or April. The fear increased even more as I realized that the slides I had seen then might be happening around me right now. The nausea returned.

God almighty! What have I done? Am I in the last minutes of my life?

I felt the tinges of panic and tried to twist away from the thought that my present position was another way mountaineers died. Two men had recently been killed not far to the south when an avalanche swept them away inside their tent. I tried to convince myself that there was no evidence of recent or strong avalanche activity at this location. Yesterday I had even spotted a few bushes on a rock outcropping that appeared to be about 100 feet above me. I also wondered whether there actually was three feet of fresh snow out there. In the wind, the flat would collect more snow than the smooth, 50-degree slope that surrounded it.

I thought about what I might face from both directions tomorrow. The elbow was a near cliff; going back the way I had come was an avalanche chute. Both directions were unreasonable.

Shortly before 9 P.M., I made a recording for Carleen. I admitted that I might have gone too far this time. I expressed my regret for leaving her to celebrate our 22nd wedding anniversary alone. That was when I broke down and cried as I realized that I might have given her the worst wedding anniversary present ever. Then I knew I had to do everything I could to avoid mistakes tomorrow.

Oh God, there are so many mistakes I can make. Any one of them can take me out.

Out of the many thousands of steps I anticipated taking before day's end tomorrow, one misstep might be all it would take to kill me, if I survived tonight.

24 • the elbow

May 18: The Worst Day of Any Trip

I was up in four hours. With the stove running wide open, the temperature in the cave rose to 50 F. but dropped to 35 F. when I placed it on simmer. I made three weak cups of coffee and shut the stove off.

The coffee cup was a one-quart wide-mouth polyethylene container with a waterproof lid. The jar had a variety of jobs that a coffee cup could never cover. Unfortunately, it lacked a handle and was too large around to hold onto easily. Through the years, I had learned to live with the shortcomings. The almost-unbreakable jar was too useful in camp and as a storage device in the backpack. With both hands numb from carpal tunnel syndrome, however, and with the condition worsening, I was dropping things more often. Like some other developed habits, I had to change from a one-handed to a two-handed coffee drinker. I worried though. Many things could go wrong as I continued to lose the ability to feel. A dropped container of water or fuel in a tent could be devastating. Possibly worse would be dropping any unattached gear while traversing the steep slope. It would likely be lost.

How I would get to the elbow from this camp was still problematic. I had no idea how large the snow cornice was between this snowdrift and the elbow. To find out, I would rope up to a rock outcropping 100 feet above camp for a clear view of the cornice.

As impossible as it seemed to go forward, I still held out hope that I could access Hole in the Wall today. If I could get there, I might be able to dry out the equipment, especially the sleeping bag. My altimeter showed a rising barometric pressure, and the wind had quit. Perhaps the sun would shine today. But I worried about how much snow had fallen overnight. All I had to go on was the almost four feet of snow pushing the poncho doorway inward. As little as one foot of fresh snow on the slope would make travel too risky. Yet with each passing day, this slope became more dangerous. I had to try to get across today. Four days earlier, the last time there had been a lot of blue sky, the mountains of Glacier National Park had roared mightily. The memory made me nauseous.

I gotta get off this wall.

In spite of the mounting fear, I knew that if I panicked, I would probably die. I started packing, this time using plastic bags to protect everything that went into the backpack. The task brought a welcome focus. A tremendous roar broke the silence. I desperately hoped it was an aircraft. The noise ended within seconds.

Jets don't suddenly roar then stop.

As long as I continued packing, I could minimize my fear. When I stopped and forced myself to eat two handfuls of pistachios for breakfast, the fear immediately overwhelmed me, and I once again felt sick to my stomach.

By 5 A.M., I was dressed and wearing the climbing harness. The rest of the gear was still scattered and waiting to be packed. As I looked through the eight-inch opening at the top of the doorway in the early dawn light, I couldn't tell whether the western sky was open or overcast.

At 6:15 A.M., with the gear finally packed, I removed the poncho from the entrance and felt the cold air pour through the enlarged opening. Unable to extend the thermometer's external wire before sealing the doorway two days earlier, until now I had no idea what the outdoor temperature was. What I felt and saw told me two things. Last night had been cold, but today was going to get warm. Through the opening, Boulder Peak was bathed in sunlight with a cloudless blue sky behind!

I brought out the shovel and several minutes later had restored the flat. With the exception of the flat I now stood on, yesterday's wind had kept the mountainside clear of fresh snow. The surface of the snowpack was a hard crust! Could I have traveled yesterday? Had I made another bad call? Then I recalled the nonstop spindrift that would have been in the elbow. I moved carefully as I brought the two loads out of the cave and prepped the climbing gear.

Into the Elbow

Sticking to my plan, I used the rope and snow pickets to climb what turned out to be only 65 feet above camp to the crumbly rock outcrop at the top of the snow cornice. My perch provided an excellent view of the large snowdrift and the cornice. Less than 30 feet from camp was the shallowest angled section of the cornice on the entire 300-foot snowdrift. I had an access into the elbow!

I dropped back down to camp and carefully worked my way over the edge of the snowdrift and into the most dangerous area of the approach, planting snow pickets and extending the rope along my route. At nearly 80 degrees, the angle of the 300-foot-wide area was a measly 10 degrees shy of being a cliff. To access it, I dug out a three-foot portion of the cornice. Then I extended the rope into the elbow 25 feet before placing the third picket near an ice-covered rock outcrop. Seeing where the snowpack had melted away from the rock and remembering what had happened three days earlier, I placed the picket four feet out. I dropped another 15 feet, placed the final picket, and dug the first flat of the day. With only two days of technical experience, I nevertheless sensed there was something about the 25 feet between the third and fourth picket that seemed wrong. Unable to put my finger on what might be wrong, I continued.

Back at the cave, I noticed the tiredness in my body and wondered how that could be. I had just used an entire day to recuperate. Abruptly, I recalled how old I was, coupled with the small amount of food I had eaten. No matter, I had to keep going; most of the day was still in front of me.

At 9:45 A.M. I hefted the smaller of the two loads, made my way to the edge of the cornice, and stopped. While unconcerned about what lay between my present position and the third picket, the descent to the flat still looked wrong. Suddenly unwilling to go down there with the load, I dropped it and relocated the fourth picket and rope farther into the elbow. In so doing, I eliminated the extreme drop and used the remainder of the 100-foot rope.

With the new flat dug by 10:30 A.M., I took a break before I continued ferrying loads. The rope was now so close to the rock outcropping that I was able to take a few steps up to it and peer into the deep and elongated hole. Where I stood was safe, but closer to the third picket the rope now lay over the hole that extended into the snowpack a couple of feet beyond the cliff. I would give that area a wide berth on every ferry.

The Second Fall

Back at the snow cave with the first ferry completed, I noticed how much of the sun was now in Bowman canyon and climbing up the west face of the approach. I figured I had another hour at the most before the sun began to heat the snowpack I was on and the rock walls above me. I was running out of time. I threw on the backpack, made my way over to the snow cornice, and descended to the third picket. I had traveled the route six times this morning, and with each trip my fear eased. Wisely or not, familiarity with the route bred confidence.

With the load on, I scooted backward down the slope, placing my left foot a good three feet from the hole near the cliff. It wasn't far enough from the hole. The snowpack collapsed and my left leg plunged into empty space. I toppled backward down the slope. Still grasping the jumar, I instinctively yanked on it as I tried to keep myself upright, but the device was going the wrong direction. I continued to fall backward. Like three days earlier, fear instantly permeated my entire body.

Oh God, not again!

Although clipped to the rope this time, I had an additional 75 pounds on my back and was on a near-vertical cliff! As I fell, I wondered if the pickets would hold. I landed in the snow on my left side, head pointed downhill and the weight of the backpack pulling me toward the abyss. Somehow, the pickets held.

Just as in the fall three days earlier, my trapped left leg again prevented me from falling any farther. But this time the backpack continued to pull me down the mountain. The combined weight of my body and backpack on a much steeper slope was wrenching my leg against the hole. The pressure on the shin of my leg was intense. How much more would it take before the bones snapped?

With my left hand still grasping the jumar, I crossed my right arm above my belly, thrust the ice axe into the snowpack, and attempted to arrest any further movement down the mountain. In a replay of three days before, I was unable to place the ice axe in a levering position.

God almighty, it's not working! The ice axe is fucking useless!

The jumar and rope were also no help. The one-way device was going the wrong direction, and I had no spare. The rope, on the other hand, worked exactly as it was designed to, stretching under the load. Unable to stop the slow inching down the slope, the painful pressure on my left leg increased.

Minutes passed as I struggled to break free. Unlike the first fall, there would be no sit-ups this time. After several minutes, I finally acknowledged that as long as the backpack stayed attached to me, my situation would only worsen. If I released the backpack, however, I would probably never see it again. How long could I survive without that gear? Hell, what did that matter when I was going to die right here if I held onto the backpack. With each passing minute, the pain in my leg worsened. If I waited too long, the bones would snap. I would likely be dead of exposure within 24 hours.

The backpack had been with me since March 1994, and I had a strong emotional attachment to it. I took a few moments to explain that if I did not release it I was going to die, and that for all we had been through together, I was still the priority.

As I talked to the backpack, I unclipped the sternum strap and then the large waist belt. It immediately loosened, but it went nowhere. Something was entangled. I could barely move, though, and couldn't see what was hanging up, although I suspected it was the left hip belt buckle and waist harness. If I'd had a knife handy, I would have cut myself loose. Without one, I continued to struggle desperately to break free. The fear and frustration grew. Finally, I hollered that now that I was ready to let go of the damned backpack, it was unwilling to reciprocate.

Between numerous rests, I spent the next three or four minutes yanking desperately at the right hip belt in an attempt to wrench the backpack loose. When it finally broke free, with the right buckle in my right hand and my left arm wrapped around the rope, it occurred to me that rather than let go of it, I might be able to pull the web belt up and over me, and wrap it around the rope. To lengthen the belt, I yanked the buckle up the length of the webbing, without noticing that the webbing was twisted. It hung up with seven inches of webbing still loose. Having twisted webbing inside the buckle had happened before. An occasional occurrence, it sure as hell had never happened while I was upside down on an 80-degree slope with a leg screaming that it was about to break.

My scream was more plea than demand. "Not now! Not this place! Do that some other time, but not now."

I took more breaks and worked on straightening the webbing. A few minutes later, I was able to remove the twist and pull the belt and right-hand buckle around the rope. Then I reached for the left buckle and webbing. Several heaves later, with most of the load now on my chest and stomach, I heard a click and knew the buckle was locked around the rope. The backpack that had refused to let go of me was safe on the rope. I let go of it again, and this time the huge load shot down the mountain 20 feet before it slowed and stopped. The rope, pickets, backpack, and I were still there!

The moment the weight of the backpack broke away, the tremendous pressure on my leg stopped. The relief that I was going to live was enormous. I lay still for perhaps a minute and gathered my wits. Finally, using the rope, I sat up and dug my leg out of the hole. A short time later, I regained my feet. Still shaking from the surge of adrenaline, I headed for the flat at the end of the rope 30 feet away to regroup.

After a short break, I descended to the backpack, grabbed the three-foot length quickdraw on the backpack, and clipped it onto the rope. Without a flat there would be no putting the backpack on, so I dragged it across the steep slope until I was 15 feet below the flat. Exhausted, I lacked the strength to pull the backpack up the final distance. I returned to the flat and took another break.

Staring at the backpack, I realized the fall had suggested another way for me to safeguard the load. Thereafter I would clip the quickdraw on the backpack to the rope while I carried the backpack. It was another hard lesson that had almost killed me in the learning.

Exhaustion and Flying Bombs

The initial plan to retrieve the backpack was vague and still centered on pulling it up to the flat. There was no extra rope, and any attempt to use the 50-foot parachute cord would have shredded my hands. I decided I had only one option: go back down and dig another flat. In my exhausted state, the thought was overwhelming; I sat unmoving. Five minutes later, some ice chunks, snow, and rocks fell, spun, and skittered down the elbow into the narrow ravine below. It was 11:30 A.M. and I had run out of time.

The sun was warming the rocks and cliffs above me. Rays of sunlight were also touching the snowpack near the backpack. Within minutes, the sun would be on me and the crust would turn into slush. Most importantly was what was going on above me. After the weather of the last two days, I was certain all hell was going to break loose up there, and I had just witnessed the prelude.

I threw the shovel over my shoulders and descended to the backpack. With a flat built half an hour later, I was still unable to heft the damned backpack onto my back. There was no way I would disconnect the backpack's quickdraw from the rope. Nevertheless, the new safety setup was preventing me from hefting the load onto my left thigh and shoulder. With anger outdoing my exhaustion, I dug a second and smaller flat, threw the backpack up there, and sat down with my feet planted on the lower flat. I slipped into the load without any further problems. Unfortunately, an hour had passed since I dropped down to the backpack. Worse, I still needed to retrieve the pickets and rope, which meant passing by the dangerous hole two more times. I completed the round-trip in 25 minutes.

At 1 P.M., exhausted, I was inside the open mouth of a carnivore. I had no alternative but to get to the cave on the far side of the elbow before I stopped. The cliff walls were now spitting chunks of ice and rock every two or three minutes. On the naked slope, I no longer had the luxury of taking a break. In the deepest part of the elbow, some of the material that had already fallen would have injured or killed me if I had been there when it came through. Once again I regretted my refusal to bring a helmet, today it might become fatal.

Soon after beginning to build the next leg, I started to make mistakes. I slipped and fell a few times before I changed the way I was going forward. The snow was no longer a crust. Walking with my torso pointed straight ahead had to stop, replaced by turning to face the wall and walking sideways. While more balanced, my already slow travel slowed even more.

Within a few minutes, I entered the trench area, also where the falling debris was most active. It was crucial to keep my eyes on where I put my feet, but I also needed to watch the cliffs and ravine above me. Since I was unable to do both, I relied on my partially deaf ears to warn me of any incoming bombs. As a reminder of the death from above, around me numerous rocks and chunks of ice lay scattered and partially buried in the snowpack.

After I crossed the main ditch, signifying that I was on the far side of the elbow, I encountered water spilling through a small opening in the snow and ice onto the open cliff face. The low end of the cave, though covered in snowpack, was no more than seven feet from the splashing water. There would be water for camp.

Beginning at the trickling falls, I built the next flat approximately five feet in length, and because of the falling debris, five feet deep. As more debris rained down, I immediately turned around and began the three round-trips. Two trips later, I retrieved the large backpack, detached the water bottle, filled, and drank from it four times.

My thirst satiated, I turned around and prepared to begin the final trip when my exhaustion brought about a near miss. I dropped the jumar into the now chewed-up snow at my feet less than a foot from the edge of the ravine. In horror, I stared at the vital piece of equipment lying in the snow and screamed at myself for being so clumsy. Behind my panicked reaction, though, was the realization that exhaustion had caused this, and my physical state was going to continue to deteriorate.

A couple of minutes later, I was 20 feet beyond the deepest ditch when I heard the next crack and the sound of tumbling debris. Terrified, my eyes darted upward, scanning the rocks and cliffs. A pile of debris made up of snow, rocks, and ice tumbled off a small cliff 100 feet above me, with the mass coming straight at me. When the debris hit the snowpack, much of it broke up and scattered across the slope, preventing me from getting out of the way.

Already facing the mass with my legs spread, I prepared to use my only remaining option: try to dodge the stuff when it arrived. After what I had already been through today, I never would have guessed that I would be able to do a dance on that steep slope. My legwork in the next several seconds would have made Carleen proud. For a husband who disliked dancing, my jumps and sidesteps might have put a smile on her face.

Only one fair-sized chunk of ice hit me, and that was on my left thigh. When I saw the hit coming, I knew I would be unable to avoid it and braced myself. The thump could have been much worse, and the pain dissipated within moments. The salve that soothed the pain might have come from the sudden elation of having dodged another bullet. Some of those chunks had been big enough to injure or kill me.

I also took what I had just experienced as another warning of more to come, and so I continued the slow and methodical pace to the other end of the rope. I got back to the newest flat with the rope and pickets without further incident.

The Cave

Now on the far side of the elbow with all the gear, I felt a glimmer of hope. With the steep, 80-degree wall continuing, however, I was still in danger. I was also far more tired, with more digging to do. I was unsure how much work lay ahead to get inside the cave, but clearly the avalanches had done their work well in filling it. I climbed to a small opening with icicles all around it and peered through into the semi-dark space of the cave. What I saw held little promise. Digging it out might take as long as building a snow cave.

I looked at the almost sheer wall of snow that extended out from the cave and spilled down the ravine. With the time now after 2 P.M., the sun was at its strongest on this southwest face, and the snow had deteriorated dangerously. To venture into the slush with the rope and pickets could be fatal. After what had happened a few hours before, the fear of another fall wrenched my stomach. With two falls in three days, I wondered if I had run out of grace.

I peered beyond the slight bulge in the wall and saw no more than 12 feet away what appeared to be a larger opening into the cave. I had seen it earlier on the other side of the elbow and had been almost certain there was a large space in there. If I dug an elongated flat over there, I would also have a path to water. I began digging.

The flat was three feet wide, while the wall on my right was roughly my height of five feet, nine inches. The now almost-constant bombardment from above was the compelling reason for creating the tall wall. One hour later, I arrived at the entrance.

The space was four and a half feet tall between the snowpack and roof. The bumpy surface of the snowpack was the result of numerous avalanches. Until leveled, a large bulge in the middle of the cavern rendered the space useless. Water dripped or poured off the ceiling. Tonight would be like camping in the rain.

I needed a break, but the falling debris outside the entrance and pouring water inside the cave kept me moving. I plodded on, retrieving all but the rope and pickets. I was halfway across the fresh dig with the lighter of the two packs when something slammed into the right side of my head. It hurt, but without ever seeing what had hit me, all I could do was lower my head some more and keep going. Once again, the mountain reminded me of my bad decision with the helmet. I was grateful, though, for the droopy old Stetson hat I had put on an hour before. The thick felt had no doubt dampened the impact. Like the first hit earlier, I used this one as another warning of how much danger I was in.

I pulled out the tent and tried to set it up on the southern exposed slope to dry it out. But the ongoing falling debris and a fresh breeze soon convinced me to abandon the effort. Inside the cave, with water dripping and pouring on me, I dug a level flat two feet deep. I wore the outer shell jacket and pants, but was soaked anyway by the time I was finished. Sometimes the water ran down my neck; if I looked up, I'd catch a downpour on my face. There was also the mystery of how I managed to get water to run upside down in both sleeves.

In my exhausted state, my continued mistakes were no longer as dangerous. They were just damned inconvenient. I brought the tent in and laid it out on the flat. I assembled the tent poles and laid them on the tent in the normal manner. Still wearing the crampons while moving around, I was careful where I stepped. The tent was almost erect when I finally asked myself why I still needed to wear the devices. I could, after all, accidentally step on the fabric of the tent. As if on cue, a moment later, I lost my balance, stepped on the tent at one of the two doors, and put several punctures through the bathtub wall and floor. Nevertheless, I kept the crampons on, only later realizing the wisdom in this.

By the time I got the rain fly on top of the tent, the tent had water pooling on the floor. In the cramped space, I rolled the shelter in an attempt to drain the water through the mosquito mesh. I was only partly successful, but for the time being would go no further with drying the floor. I scrambled to get the gear into the tent, throwing most of it toward the upper end of the tent where the floor was only damp.

Without getting into the tent, I dug into the backpack and retrieved the saucepans, the one-quart jar, and two of the 96-ounce water bladders. I was desperate to get into the tent and sit down, but needed to retrieve the water first. In addition, because I needed to arrange the technical gear at the entrance properly, I found the reason to continue wearing the crampons. Until these last two chores were complete, I would remain outside the tent.

I finally crawled into the tent at 5:40 P.M. Beginning with the dawn scout, 11 hours had passed. Incredibly, in that time I had traveled only 200 feet beyond the previous night's snow cave. Through years of numerous grueling and dangerous trips, where a few had almost taken my life, none matched this day. Beyond the cave entrance, the ice and rock bombs continued to fall. Last September, when I thought about using this cave as a possible place to hole up, I had no idea how critical its location would be.

The extreme exhaustion threatened to overwhelm me emotionally. All that stopped me from breaking down was my organizing the contents inside the tent. Before I could set up the bedroom and the kitchen, I used a terrycloth towel to get rid of remnant pools of water at the foot of the tent.

Hell's Second Visit

I had been inside the tent for less than half an hour when I experienced the second roaring and ground-shaking avalanche on the approach.

What came down the elbow less than 20 feet away made the monster from the first camp on the traverse seem trivial. Having a ceiling and two walls made of rock failed to reassure me. Obviously, a huge force had rammed a lot of snow into this hollow. I huddled helplessly inside the tent and hoped the horror did not jump over here and tear out the snowpack with me in it. If I uttered anything, the thunderous noise would have drowned out any yells or screams.

Although it seemed to go on forever, the nightmare passed. As the shaking receded, I listened to the tumultuous sound for another two minutes on its journey to the canyon floor 2,000 feet below. In the quiet, the dripping sounds on the tent that had irritated me before were now music to my ears.

After I calmed down, I recalled that the tormentor's voice had returned during the onslaught. Once again, he informed me that a real photographer would have gotten up and taken photographs of this in-your-face event. Once more, I responded: then I was no photographer.

A short time later, I gave pause to the question of whether I was willing to do something like this ever again. I reflected on how dangerous the day had become. With increasing exhaustion, I had lost the pattern of repetitious actions and increasingly made more mistakes. Once again, I had found myself now and then off the rope, horrified at my lapses. I had screamed at myself to no avail. If I broke loose up here and fell, there was no one to rescue me. Hell, if I had fallen, a rescue would have been pointless.

As I repeatedly mulled over the day's mistakes, fear and revulsion overwhelmed me. I finally decided that I would in no way step out of the tent without the crampons on and the ice axe in hand. I would also stay absolutely away from the entrance seven feet away.

Utterly exhausted and cold, all I wanted to do was crawl into the damp sleeping bag and go to sleep. The last time I had eaten anything was in the snow cave, and I had no appetite now. Maybe later I would eat a peanut butter sandwich. I crawled into the sleeping bag 20 minutes after the elbow roared and was asleep almost immediately.

Two and a half hours later, I woke up, got the stove going (though only for heat), and prepared a peanut butter sandwich. Every bite was forced, but I had to shove something in my body. Today's troubles stemmed in part from my lack of nourishment over the previous three days. The first 100 feet tomorrow morning was across more near-vertical snowpack. I needed to eat.

Just before 10 P.M., I crawled back into the sleeping bag. The last thing

I did was check the altimeter and barometer. The barometric pressure was steady, which meant that tomorrow morning I would again have hard crust to walk on.

May 19: More Weather and a Rotting Snowpack

While no more moisture got into the tent, everything was already damp or outright wet. The crucial fill power on the sleeping bag was almost nonexistent. It took all the layers of clothing I had to stay warm, and I still had a bad night. The annoying water drops on the tent were worse than being under a tree after a lengthy rainstorm. In spite of being exhausted, I continued to awaken. I finally gave up and crawled out of the bag at 2 A.M.

While sipping the first cup of coffee, the normal sense of security and well-being returned, but this passed when I crawled out of the tent. I saw the thickening cloud cover, which explained the warmth. I visited the moonlight view of the elbow, a sickening sight that would have been beautiful in different circumstances.

Back in the tent, I began to collapse under the rising horror that there was no crust on the snowpack. I needed a crust for at least the first 100 feet! If I stepped onto that near cliff outside the cave entrance, yesterday's narrow escape may yet be undone.

God almighty, it's just one thing after another.

I looked at the altimeter. There had been an elevation gain of 40 feet in the 10 hours I had been in this camp. That led me to assume that the barometric pressure had never really gotten high. How else would the slight drop in the pressure be enough for the clouds to return?

I needed to travel! This was the fifth day on a traverse that was supposed to have taken no more than a day and a half to complete. It was also the 10th day of the trip. I was going to be overdue. Hell, I noted angrily, as far as the 11-day permit was concerned, going overdue had been a forgone conclusion for the last three days. A second date was now looming. Carleen's call to report me overdue was six days away. A quick calculation revealed that, starting today, if the latest revised itinerary went perfectly I would arrive at Polebridge in six days.

So there it was. A perfect trip would have taken 11 days. While I had expected to use a few of the 5 spare days, I had been confident 16 days would be unnecessary. Now after the events of the last 5 days, there was no way I could know where I would be on the 16th day, but almost certainly, Polebridge was out of reach.

Nor would I turn back, especially when I was this close to Hole in the Wall. Besides a tremendous desire to continue the trip, I had an equal desire to stay away from the traverse. I was almost certain the next fall would be fatal. For that matter, how did I survive the first two? If I survived this trip, I was damned if I would ever come back.

I finally concluded that in all likelihood I was going to be in trouble with the park service. I had heard the words before. I was not liberal enough with the number of days on a permit. Right! How does one get liberal with the days when the permit writer wants to know where I will be at the end of each day? With the knowledge that the park service would come looking for me if I went overdue only if Carleen called, I gave them what they wanted as best as I could, while my wife got the more realistic schedule. Obviously, what they wanted was unworkable for most of the winter trips in Glacier National Park, particularly this trip. Hell, I angrily observed, it was unworkable for most winter trips anywhere!

When I told Carleen 16 days, I was unconcerned about her making a phone call. An awful lot of delays would have had to happen to eat up that many days. Now, too late, I realized how wrong I had been. Unable to tell what was in front of me, three weeks might pass before I returned to Polebridge.

As I resigned myself to probably going overdue, I realized Carleen was going to be more worried than she already was. Clearly, she was going to experience much bigger doubts about her husband's mortality in less than a week. A lump formed in my throat as I realized there was nothing I could do to prevent what was coming. I was unwilling to move any quicker in an attempt to alleviate the pain she might have. Any haste up here could become my death knell, particularly in the first 100 feet.

Nor was I certain I could prevent my dying. I could do everything right on that slope this morning and still die just for attempting it in its present condition. If I attempted to complete the final 100 feet in this rotting snow, the elbow's mouth was wide open and waiting. If I stayed here today however, I absolutely would go beyond the 16th day.

With clarity, I realized I had two more things working against me besides the steep slope and warm temperature. After the exhaustion created by yesterday's events, I had slept only four hours. On its own, the lack of sleep was sufficient to cause me to make a wrong move. I was also malnourished.

Though I was unable to detect it, the little eating I had done was insufficient for the coming exertions on the remainder of the approach. I needed sleep and food to regain good judgment.

A Decision to Stay Alive

At 5:30 A.M., I made a final decision. In addition to the bad condition of the snowpack, my exhaustion and weakness became the final reasons for staying put in the awful dripping cave until the next day. I was asleep within minutes.

I woke up hungry four hours later. Like an old friend come for a visit, I joyously welcomed my appetite and consumed the remaining stew, more fruit, and some peanuts. In less than an hour, I began to regret my decision to hunker down. Too late—the bombs had begun to drop in the soft snowpack around the entrance.

The barometric pressure was also rising. The altimeter showed that since arriving here the elevation had dropped 89 feet. If this kept up, there would be a crust to walk on tonight.

At 11 A.M., I thought about what the next day meant for Carleen and me. It was going to be our 22nd wedding anniversary. (Exhaustion had the better of me; our anniversary is actually May 21.) I began to cry. The tears ceased and then returned with the memories from the day before. Unlike previous bad trips when the memories waited to haunt me after I got home, or at least in the vehicle, on this 10th morning of the trip they came for a visit inside the tent. A part of me knew that the combination of idleness, exhaustion, and lack of food was spiking the emotional roller coaster; nevertheless, it felt real.

Shortly after waking from another nap around 4 P.M., I put the boots on and headed for the entrance with the camera. I took photos at the entrance for 10 minutes. Later I would discover that moisture in the camera and lens had fogged the photos.

Back inside the tent, I cooked a second stew and ate most of it. Before I crawled back into the sleeping bag, I checked the altimeter. The reading showed a loss of 171 feet in 24 hours. A high-pressure ridge with cold nights and sunny warm days was coming. Uncertain of its strength, I was sure that I would need to be off the south- and southwest-facing slopes before it arrived. Somewhere out in front of me, the real springtime avalanches were coming. I was asleep before 6 P.M.

25 • into hole in the wall

May 20: The Longest Day

Five hours later, the 11th day began. Horribly afraid of what could happen today, 40 minutes later I created another message for Carleen. Less than an hour later, I recalled it was our anniversary and broke down again. A few minutes later, I grasped that I needed to focus on the task directly in front of me, otherwise my thoughts could distract me enough to make the worst I was imagining happen. At this point, preparing for the day became my sole focus.

At 1:30 A.M., most of the kitchen was packed. I was ready to go to the next level of preparation, synonymous to two hours remaining in this camp. The continuous activity minimized the fear. Shortly after 4 A.M., I was ready to go.

The outside temperature was hovering around 32 F., not enough for a hard crust, but far colder than 24 hours earlier. I still mistrusted the snowpack and used two snow pickets as an anchor at the cave entrance. While I might die on this trip, I needed to do all I could to avoid it on this day. I enlarged the flat at the entrance. With a wide and deep gash between the snowpack and the rock face that paralleled the direction I was to go, I extended the flat another 10 feet. Nearly one hour later, dawn was breaking on a heavily clouded day when I returned to the cave for the two unused pickets.

The route I chose dropped several feet toward some dirt and rocks. The plan was to rope off on a 10-foot Douglas-fir sapling on the edge of the snowpack, 65 feet beyond the cave entrance. Grateful for the hardened snowpack, I had no trouble getting to the 25-foot mark where I planted the first picket. As I neared the open ground, the snowpack softened and

I punched through. Attached to the rope, I continued the small descent and extended the distance from the cave. I got to the tree without further incident, although I encountered small ledges, loose rocks, and mud.

Unwilling to take the loads through what I had just gone through, I changed the route. I climbed back onto the snowpack, tied a knot in the rope 30 feet from its end, and planted the last picket. Back at the cave, with renewed confidence in the snowpack, I repositioned one of the two anchors and headed back out, dragging the final picket. A short time later, I got the fourth picket planted and dug the flat.

I also discovered I was no longer alone. Punched into the snowpack were two sets of fresh grizzly bear tracks, one large and the other small. A sow and her yearling cub had approached to within 100 feet of the camp. Curiously, they had turned around and headed back into Hole in the Wall. Was it because of my sometimes-loud presence, or the steep slope just beyond their tracks? Either way, the tracks were disturbing. What were they eating?

The area of the tracks also marked where the angle of the approach eased by at least 15 degrees, and there were several midsized pine trees immediately on my left. I returned to ferry the first load at 6:35 A.M. From when I had begun to dig the initial flat until I started to ferry the first load, two and a half hours had passed. As disgusted as I felt with the pace, it beat the hell out of the progress of the day before. And I was still alive.

I finished the two ferries and retrieved the rope and pickets by 7:20 A.M. It had begun to rain. I took a break anyway. Beginning at the second leg, I broke trail without using the sideways shuffle, and my pace increased.

At 8:43 A.M, I took the last photos of the first 100-foot ferry, the cave, and the elbow. While the second 100 feet was still dangerous, I was no longer in the terrifying near-vertical terrain. I wondered, though, how it was that I was no more than 100 feet beyond the cave. With my once again tired mind, it was frustrating. At this pace, would I make it to Hole in the Wall today? The question was almost nonsensical. I intended to spend no more nights on the approach. Besides, the next 100 feet, including the second flat, was ready for the first ferry.

Less than an hour later, in a steady light rain, a bluebird on top of a dead snag tweeted as if it was one glorious spring morning. He lifted my spirits as I wondered whether he knew something about today that eluded me. After a few minutes, the bird flew off, and I continued extending the rope and pickets in the third leg.

Growing Hope

Another 20 minutes had passed when I dropped the first ferry at the end of the rope. For the first time in the six days that I had been on the approach, digging a flat was unnecessary. In its stead, I used a 12-inch-diameter tree that provided a small flat for the loads. On the other side of the tree was the torn-up snowpack from numerous recent avalanches. Uprooted trees, dirt, and boulders were scattered across the 200-foot-wide avalanche chute. Beyond it was a thin line of trees.

The chute was obviously dangerous, but also came with a second and more soothing message. The angle of the mountainside had dropped some more and was probably no more than 45 degrees. Hole in the Wall was 1,000 feet beyond that next line of trees!

God almighty! Am I actually going to make it off this mountainside today?

In the next two and a half hours, I traveled another 300 feet and dug two smaller flats. On the other side of the next row of trees, I faced yet another avalanche chute, most of which overlooked the flat of Hole in the Wall. The next line of trees was 500 feet away, except I no longer was headed in that direction. From where I stood, I would begin what at first would be a gradual descent above what remained of the cliffs on my left. In another 100 feet, the Hole in the Wall flat would be below me. From there I would start a strong descent.

The way I had been traveling for five and a half days would now drastically change. I would anchor the rope in the normal manner and extend it 100 feet. At the other end, I would decide whether to use the rope, pickets, and harness any further. I would also bring the first ferry and camera bag. In addition, I would carry one of the ski poles.

Several minutes later, with two pickets still in my possession, I had fully extended the rope. I lengthened the ski pole, and for the first time in six days walked on a mountain slope off the rope. At first, I felt naked and vulnerable, although there was no longer a cliff below me. Within minutes, the fear had ebbed enough that I increased my pace.

Although the sun was behind the clouds and the rain had let up considerably, my fear of the avalanches continued. Too many had roared off the mountainsides of Bowman canyon and Hole in the Wall today. The best I could do, though, was to descend nonstop to the flat.

Hole in the Wall Achieved

During the last 10 minutes on the slope, the fear was overwhelming as I questioned whether an avalanche would get me now when I was so close to safety. Nevertheless, the 300-foot descent went quickly and I arrived on the flat 30 minutes later. The feeling I had was familiar, as was the surreal shock that came with it. Stepping off a jet and onto American soil after leaving Vietnam, twice, had been similar. Today, too much had happened over the last several days. The relief was almost nonexistent as I became the first to walk up on this flat under these conditions.

I was halfway across the treeless flat, 300 feet north of the southern edge and near a dead six-foot sapling, badly bent and limbless, poking out of the snowpack. As I dropped the load, I decided this was where the camp would go. Still in a near stupor, I surveyed the snow-covered flat and the peaks that soared above Hole in the Wall.

A few minutes later, as reality set in, I realized that the huge mountainside I had just descended could still let loose an avalanche that would overwhelm the spot where I was standing. The lifeless snag was a testimony to that truth. Exhausted, and with a climb still to be made to retrieve the main load, I nevertheless moved another 400 feet north to the approximate center of the flat. There was another, though larger, dead sapling at this location, accompanied by several strongly leaning but living Douglas-fir saplings. While avalanches had reached this far, between the mountainside and the small rise I was on was also a wide depression. I began to build camp.

The main load was still unsafe on the mountain—I could waste no time on the turnaround. Anchoring the tent with the two pickets, I set it up in 30 minutes, and then placed the camera and remaining gear from the ferry bag into the tent.

A Stealthy Avalanche

Armed with only the ice axe and crampons, I headed back into harm's way. In the late afternoon, the crust on the snowpack had almost disappeared. Although the clouds prevented the sun from coming through, there was a warmth that no winter day would bring at this elevation. With each step, I dropped between four to six inches into the snowpack. Already dragging in exhaustion, I slowed even more.

As I trudged back into the avalanche-damaged snowpack, I noticed that my tracks from the previous ferry had vanished, buried by a fresh slide. This slide had been silent when it came down. As I looked around, I spotted chunks of snow, little islands created by previous avalanches that this one had gone around. It would still have been big enough to pull me down and over the cliff. More ominous than the recent slide were the huge cracks in the snowpack; they had not been there two hours earlier. Like so many previous incidents, I took this to be the latest warning that I needed to get off the mountainside.

Without a load, I still needed 45 minutes to return to the backpack. Half an hour later, the gear and I reunited with the tent. The approach was finally behind me. It was only temporary, but for the first time in six days, I felt a margin of safety. Exhausted, I nevertheless strengthened the anchors on the tent with the ice axe and final two pickets before I crawled into the tent. Still feeling insecure, I took the shovel and piled snow around the edges of the tent. At an elevation of 6,300 feet, a winter storm was still possible on May 20.

Finally, inside the tent sitting in the chair with the bedroom and kitchen set up, I relaxed. Once more without running water, I was back on a diet of cold food. I pulled out the pistachios, peanut butter, and the last two English muffins. I also brought out the partial bladder of water and drained most of it, though too late to stop the dehydration cramps, which appeared soon after I became idle.

The thermometer and humidity gauge showed a temperature of 42 F. outside and 53 F. (and a humidity of 91 percent) inside the tent. I opened both vents and vestibules, and the humidity dropped to 79 percent. To dry the sodden gear it needed to be much lower.

I had been up for 19 hours, 12 of them for travel. I'd covered a mere 3,095 feet, but that was a third again greater than the previous five days combined. On the surface, both numbers together seemed derisive. Hell, in the summer a person could crawl from one side of the approach to the other in half a day. In reality, I had just experienced the most dangerous mile of my life.

During the final two hours of travel, I had observed the southwestern wall where I would be ascending toward Boulder Pass the following day. Inside the tent, I mulled over what I had seen. The amiable-looking slope during the scouting trip of last autumn had avalanched, and there was no alternative route. Any attempt to follow the summer trail would be suicidal, something that had been obvious the previous September. The lost count of small avalanches on all sides of the bowl today had abundantly confirmed that.

The previous six days had done its work well on the state of my well-being. I was relatively safe on the huge flat, but my fear returned, albeit at a lower level. I was unable to stop questioning whether I had gone through the horrific last six days only so I could die on this flat or during the ascent the next day.

Inside the camp, I now had no doubt that I would be unable to exit on either the 15th or 16th day. I recalled with disgust the blissful period of naivety through last fall all the way into this trip. A part of me had thought that if I could get through the approach and into Hole in the Wall, the rest of the trip would be easy. With the approach now behind me, immediately in front of me was a route that was no cakewalk. I had heard that there was no rest for the wicked. Might there also be none for a fool, who suddenly has discovered the truth? After my final arrival in camp, it took another two hours to fall asleep.

May 21: Sunshine and a Mental Breakdown

By "dead-of-winter" standards, the night stayed warm. I would never know, however, what the temperature fell to overnight. The wire on the new indoor-outdoor thermometer that extended outside, like the one it replaced, had broken.

When I got up at 4 A.M., the temperature inside the tent hovered around 30 F. That meant the outside temperature was closer to 25 F. That, in part, was why I had slept borderline cold in the damp sleeping bag. The rising barometric pressure had opened the door for cold air. Simultaneously, it shut off the avalanches and provided me with excellent hiking conditions. I refused to give a damn, though, until the stove was lit, providing me with the much needed heat and a cup of coffee.

Soon after the stove was running and the coffeepot was on, I noticed the dimness in the head lantern's light. I knew what had happened. I thought I had learned my lesson of stuffing the recently purchased lantern inside a pocket of the photo vest, jacket, or pants. The on-off button somehow always switched on, yet under the same conditions was unable to switch back off, thereby draining the three AAA lithium batteries. Yesterday I had stuffed the lantern in the voluminous 800-cubic-inch pocket on top of the backpack, thinking the problem solved. As I emptied the backpack in camp last evening, I pulled the lantern out and found the light on. Only one day earlier, I had put the third set of lithium batteries into the lantern, leaving me with two unused AAA batteries.

Spewing venomous rage, I figured that if there were any grizzlies around, which there were, they would easily hear my roars in the darkness. If that sow and cub came to see me about it, I was going to pepper spray the hell out of them—someone was going to pay.

After I calmed down, I began to look at my options. For starters, I would use the lantern only when necessary. I would exchange the two unused batteries with two of the nearly depleted batteries in the lantern. (Later, I would discover that old and new lithium batteries are unmixable. Within a disgustingly short time, the device ceases to function.) Inside the ditty bag, there was also a spare and different model head lantern. The backup had proven its reliability in past trips, and it had three unused AAA lithium batteries in it.

Not knowing how much longer I would be in the backcountry, particularly where traveling in the darkness was concerned, I was down to minimal use of the lanterns. I also determined that this more expensive model would never go into the backcountry again. While the phrase "you get what you pay for" normally applied to gear, it did not fit the lantern. The cheaper backup model from the same company had never turned on when packed away. (To their credit, the Princeton folks, hearing about my troubles with one of their lanterns, sent a replacement along with an accessory semi-hard carrying case, designed specifically for these types of conditions. That cooled me off, and I continue to use their lanterns.)

In spite of the angry outburst shortly after I woke up, the nine hours of sleep had done me well. As I slipped into the comfort zone of sipping hot coffee, I realized my body felt great this morning. On further reflection, I wondered how well I would have been doing if I had eaten properly. I had forced myself to consume a single peanut butter sandwich for supper, while this morning I had yet to eat.

With the little food as I had consumed, several days of supplies remained. While comforted that I was in no danger of running out of food, I also had less stamina, plus a backpack that should have weighed a lot less. More than that, in front of me was a strong and in some areas dangerous 1,200-foot ascent to Boulder Pass. Would it take three days to get to Boulder Pass Campground?

More Delays and Bad News

Just after 5 A.M., I had almost completed the second cup of coffee, which meant I would be going to the next level of preparation, eating and personal hygiene. With the stove off, I was cold again, while the thermometer read 35 F. I reasoned there could be only two reasons why I felt the chill: either I had cancer and was near death, or all the gear was wet.

An hour later, the altimeter showed that I had gained 95 feet since I arrived at camp. More bad weather was on the way. What would it do to the snowpack on the slopes in front of me? While uncertain, the last week had given some dangerous hints.

At 6:30 A.M., I recalled a vital decision I had made back in the snow cave four days earlier. If I made it to Hole in the Wall and there was sunshine, I would dry the gear before continuing the trip. Ignoring the cold, I opened the left vestibule and took the first photographs of the day. There were a few high clouds on a beautiful, blue-sky morning. The moon was two-thirds full and waning. It hovered in the deep blue to the southwest between 9,843-foot Mount Carter and Bowman Lake. The sun was also on the peaks. Like a magnet, the beautiful contrast of the blue sky, sunlight on the snow-covered peaks, and the snowpack in camp, held me until my fingers were burning with the cold.

After I shut the vestibule door, I placed the camera in a plastic bag near my body to warm it. When the sun arrived, condensation would instantly cover the cold gear. More moisture on the gear would have the opposite effect of what I sought with the delayed departure.

As the minutes slowly passed, doubts crept in about the wisdom of my decision. Still raw from my experience with the weather and terrain, I trusted neither to wait nor to travel. Numerous avalanches would be dropping around me today, while incoming weather would likely create more avalanches. I began to feel like a target on a firing range waiting for the bullets to arrive.

I thought about the phone call Carleen was going to make in four days. Would my pace increase enough to get me to the trailhead at Kintla Lake in that time? Surely, there would be a park ranger there with a two-way radio. If the damned sun could just get over here and dry the gear, I might be able to get at least halfway up the wall today before the crust turned to slush.

Sitting and waiting while pondering my circumstances, I finally broke down and started to cry. I recovered quickly as I forced myself to re-realize that only I could make the call of what was the right thing to do. There was great danger in letting my actions be affected by what was happening in civilization. Safety was paramount, and that meant I must dry the gear.

Today's sun was a two-edged sword. I needed the heat to dry the gear. On the other hand, I needed a crust to walk on with minimal avalanches to deal with. Had my luck run its course on the approach?

I thought about things that I missed.

I want to eat a bag of potato chips, shake my fist at another driver, and see my wife and the dogs, then go mow the lawn—sitting here is kicking my ass.

I started to cry again.

Damned crybaby!

At 8:20 A.M., I predicted the sun would arrive at 9 A.M.

If the call is made, they will come looking. I am not missing! I'm just delayed. They don't know that. If it goes out into the media, that will be detrimental.

The first rays touched the tent 19 minutes later, and it was finally time to go to work. My head immediately let up on me. I spread everything out on the poncho and the tent fly, and then rotated the gear for greater exposure. With the hope that the gear would be dry by noon, as each item dried, I placed it in the tent.

The Avalanches Continue

The avalanches began by midmorning. As the sun rose higher, new areas on the mountainsides were exposed and the number of avalanches increased.

At 2 P.M., the sleeping bag, the last bastion against the cold, was also the final piece of equipment to dry, four hours too late for me to break camp. Besides the impossibility of traveling with the ongoing avalanches, the crust had turned to slush before noon.

By 3:30 P.M., the altimeter showed that I had gained 150 feet in 23 hours. That was enough to bring more moisture. I doubted it would arrive by tonight though. The pressure drop was too gradual for a sudden storm.

The revised plan included an early to bed and early rising at perhaps 10 or 11 P.M. I would begin climbing by 3 A.M. In that way, the strength of the crust would be more certain, and I would need the lantern for less than two hours after I left camp.

Except for the ice axe and crampons, I was uncertain whether there would be any further need for the mountaineering gear. Just in case, I placed all the gear in the ferry bag for easy access. If at some point I needed to use the gear, I would have to break open the backpack to get at the bag. But a balanced backpack took precedence over easy access to the climbing gear. The backpack still weighed over 100 pounds. In the type of terrain in front of me, balance was vital. With my options further narrowed by the bear canister, I had to get everything else as perfect as possible.

In the late afternoon and early evening, I began to feel better about the trip, something that had been almost foreign during the afternoons of the previous several days. The combination of sunshine and dry gear was behind this feel-good mood. I knew it was temporary, but I would take it anyway.

The down sleeping bag was back to its original fill power rating of zero degrees F. As I crawled into the bag, the nearly six-inch deep fluff was luxurious and comforting. I delighted with the thought that tonight I would wear only a shirt, pants, and socks. Nor would I have to jog to stay warm. The avalanches were still dropping when I fell asleep at 6 P.M.

26 • boulder pass

May 22: Another Ascent

I was up after six hours of sleep with the first cup of coffee warming my hands 20 minutes later. Still tired, the numbness in my hands had interrupted my sleep throughout the night. I was certain that the ski pole use had brought on the extra discomfort.

I needed to leave early enough to get some elevation before the crust became slush. With the late rising at midnight, however, I revised the plan to begin traveling by 4 A.M. As the minutes passed, the fear of what was coming grew. Yesterday had been a blessing for drying the gear, and except when my thoughts wandered over to what was coming the next day, had been good for me with the one-day respite from the danger of the slopes. Like R&R (Rest and Recuperation) the U.S. Army provided for their soldiers in Vietnam to such places as Taipei Taiwan, the day passed too quickly, and now that next day and whatever came with it was here. It was time to go back into God only knew what.

Yesterday's avalanches reminded me of the rattlesnakes on the trail of the Selway River canyon, 10 years earlier. In a single day, there had been too many to count, and I had eventually almost ignored them. Some of the snakes had been within a few inches of my boots while walking down the trail. I stayed out of their space and they left me alone.

Before I began to pack, I once again revised the trip itinerary. I had at least seven days of supplies and as much fuel remaining. I could use four to arrive at the campground of Upper Kintla Lake and another two to arrive at Kintla Lake's trailhead. If I could do better, I would. By now, though, I had no confidence in any revised plan. The most reliable itinerary I possessed was the one that said do as much as I could each day, with safety being the main goal.

As the time to leave closed in, the fear and doubt increased. With all the trips taken since February and years of winter travel, I was unsure if my experience was enough for what this trip had become. The three prior trips were supposed to have brought me into this challenge with both eyes open. Maybe they had, but for now, I had trouble believing it. At 2:30 A.M., as I began to pack, I decided I had been physically and mentally unprepared for what had transpired thus far. Right behind this thought a rhetorical question rose. If that's the case, then how did I access Hole in the Wall?

The topographic map indicated today's travel would be nothing like the approach. Sure, and those incremental contour lines on the maps had an elevation difference of 80 feet, more than enough to hide small but extreme angles. I saw one such area 300 or 400 feet above this flat. Directly below was the roughed-up snowpack from at least one avalanche, small compared to some of the massive avalanches around this bowl, yet big enough to take me down. That small area had an angle that was at least 50 degrees.

At 5 A.M., I was ready to go. Although I still needed the head lantern, there was a hint of daylight to the east. The moon was in the southern sky. Its light revealed high clouds to the southeast. I had seen this moon and high clouds during the April trip. On that occasion, the bad weather was on me before the day ended.

I had gotten used to ferrying two loads. Broken down they were reasonable. Now combined, the weight was almost unbearable. As I began a slow arc to my left at the base of the climb, it was light enough to see some details on the trees. I glanced to the right. Somewhere over there was the summer campground. During the scouting trip last September, I had spotted the outhouse, which gave me the general direction of where the camp was located. At first, all I could see in the field of white was the silhouette of trees. Then I spotted something about 150 feet away that at first glance made no sense. There was a 10-foot-long object lying horizontally above the snowpack. For a few moments, I thought I was looking at a stock hitch, while unaware that the campground was off-limits for stock. In this much snow, how could the stock hitch be at the surface? Finally, it struck me what I might be looking at. Was that the pole used to hang food? The snowpack was no more than a foot below the object. Except for my heavy load, I would have gone over and verified what I saw, but was unwilling to drop it or carry it 300 feet round-trip. I needed every bit of the time and energy I had for ascending the mountainside.

I climbed 240 feet in 40 minutes and was at the base of the sharp climb when I dropped the backpack. From there I scouted the steep ridge for a safe route. I began with a series of switchbacks inside the avalanche chute on the left side of a scattering of trees. I would have entered the trees sooner except for a high, long snowdrift that separated the slope from the trees. All I carried was the camera, but even that was too much as I made my way through the torn-up avalanche zone. Once I gained access into the trees, I stayed in them for safety. At the top of the avalanche, I got around a 20-foot cliff and crossed the final snowdrift onto a large and almost treeless 25-degree slope. Several minutes later I stopped, well within a safe area with more up ahead. It had taken an hour to ascend 300 feet above the backpack's location.

During the return trip to the backpack, I altered part of the route to avoid the avalanche area. With a hard crust, I was unconcerned about a slide, but I was anxious about breaking a leg or blowing out a knee in the rough-and-tumble avalanche area when I came through with the load. It had been over two hours since I left camp when I reunited with the backpack. The sunlight was crawling down the slope, but I needed to rest. I brought out the food and water and took a 40-minute break.

The sun's rays were almost on my location when I hefted the load and began the ascent. In spite of the weight, I made the climb in 45 minutes. When I stopped at the end of the earlier trail, the snowpack was already soft. The time was 8:30 A.M. and the sun was warm. The snowpack was going to get worse, and soon. With 700 feet still to ascend to Boulder Pass, it was obvious I would arrive there no sooner than tomorrow.

I could feel the weakness in my muscles brought about by the 500-foot climb with the monstrous load. I was in good shape, but I figured what I had just done would have worked a young man over. Unlike me, however, a 15-minute break would have had the younger man ready to continue.

More Relief

The area of the ascent that had me mortified yesterday and last night was now below me, and there were no visible sharp inclines above my position. From what I could see, there was no chance that even the farthest-reaching avalanche would touch me here. Not even Hole in the Wall had afforded me that level of safety. A wave of relief spread through me. Within moments, the delight and relief at still being alive after this last ascent, combined with all the incidents of the last week, overwhelmed me. Tears blurred my vision while the sobs shook my body.

For all I could see, the terror of this trip was finally behind me. I continued the climb without the backpack an hour and a half later, taking only the ice axe, a ski pole, the camera, and the Stetson. In another hour and a half, I came to a stop on a small knoll. In front of me, Boulder Pass was three-quarters of a mile to the west on the other end of the small, 500-foot-wide valley I now stood on the edge of. Boulder Peak dominated the left side of the magnificent view. Along the length of its summit was an ominous snow cornice perhaps 100 feet deep. The wall on the right was an unnamed peak whose ridgeline, at 8,528 feet, the same elevation as Boulder Peak, ran 700 to 1,100 feet above the valley floor.

I stood motionless for several minutes as I took in the incredible 360-degree view and regretted I would be unable to return with the gear today. Plowing through this wet snowpack with the heavy load had been out of the question even before I left it behind. The crampons had sunk six to eight inches with every step since leaving the backpack.

Beyond the view to the south and west was a large mass of clouds. I had no doubt wet weather would be on me before the end of the day. Though it would begin with rain, at this elevation, how long would it remain that way?

I headed back down to the backpack. Forty minutes later, the seven-and-a-half-hour travel portion of the day ended at 12:30 P.M. By the time I arrived, I had no qualms about stopping for the day, having run out of energy in the wet snowpack.

Yet Another Storm

I took a break before beginning to dig the flat for the tent. By 2 P.M., I was still unfinished with the digging and was well into another break. An hour later, camp was complete and I was inside the tent. The rain arrived an hour after that.

Inside the dry and comfortable cocoon, I was unconcerned. My mental state in the tent for the remainder of the day was the opposite of what I had experienced for a week. It almost felt like sanity had returned in my life. The threats and fear from as recent as this morning were gone. While there was still danger, the worst was likely behind me. If the weather allowed, tomorrow I would arrive at Boulder Pass Campground. With a crust to walk on, I would likely arrive on the flat above me with the backpack in two hours. I might even use the snowshoes once I was up there.

After crawling into the sleeping bag in the early evening, I had trouble falling asleep. Once I did, I kept waking up. I woke up hungry at 10 P.M., which was unusual. I ate some peanuts and fruit and went back to sleep. Throughout all of this, the rain continued its light pattering sounds on the tent shell.

May 23: A Tough Exit of Hole in the Wall

After a short and restless night, I got up for the day at 1 A.M. The rain stopped 3 hours later, but in the 15 hours at this camp, the altimeter had gained another 39 feet. Although I could see stars when I stepped outside, more wet weather was in store. Worse than that was the warmth. The snowpack was still soft, and I was suddenly grateful I had built a trail the day before.

With most of the gear packed by 3:45 A.M., but the sleeping bag and pads still out, the short night of sleep caught up with me. I knew it was a bad idea, but crawled back into the bag anyway. I would rest for just a few minutes before I finished the final pack.

I woke up almost three hours later. Alarmed at the late hour, I scrambled out of the bag. As I packed the rest of the gear, in the quiet I suddenly recalled that during the three-hour nap I'd woken for a moment to the sound of more rain hitting the tent. A thick fog bank greeted me when I crawled out of the tent 30 minutes later. Since it was no longer raining, I had no complaint. During a brief interlude of packing the remaining gear, I stepped in the snowpack beyond the camp and confirmed it was still soft. I was going to take a beating getting to the top.

Unlike the seventh day when I left the gear and backpack unprotected, this time I bagged everything. While the extra care took more time, when I got to the next camp at Boulder Pass Campground, the gear would be dry.

At 8:30 A.M., the fog temporarily lifted and revealed part of Boulder Peak. I hefted the load and began walking. Getting through the snow was all I thought it would be, plus a little more. As I slogged up the slope, I stepped into the holes from the day before without plunging much deeper. After 20 minutes, I had to stop, remove the backpack, and take a break. I had only ascended 140 feet. With the clouds continuing to lift 20 minutes later, I continued the slow climb.

The next 20-minute break, which included removing the backpack again, happened 25 minutes later. Disheartened, this time I only ascended

120 feet and was far more tired than I should have been. The next 20 minutes of travel rewarded me with 80 feet. My legs were beginning to feel like rubber. At 10:45 A.M., I began the final 100-foot ascent to the flat. I arrived at the end of yesterday's tracks 15 minutes later. In another flood of relief, after almost eight months, Hole in the Wall in its entirety was behind me.

The Flat Below Boulder Pass

The day had continued to get brighter and warmer as I climbed. When I finally arrived on top, however, I reentered a cloud bank. Unable to see beyond 50 feet, the valley in front of me was invisible. Knowing avalanche walls were on both sides of the valley, I was unwilling to continue until I could see the flat. I dropped the backpack and sat down.

For two and one-half hours, I had ascended a southeast-facing slope through some of the worst snow conditions I had experienced since February in the Belly River canyon. By the time I reached the top, I was exhausted and considered stopping for the day. I was also back to thinking about my age and how little I had eaten in the last nine days.

A gusting northerly breeze created a fast-moving, swirling fog in the valley and around me. A few minutes after I sat down, the cloud lifted briefly, revealing the valley, including splotches of sunlight on the western end near Boulder Pass. Northeast of my position, bathed in a mixture of clouds, blue sky, and sunlight, Mount Custer emerged out of the clouds, the last I could see of Hole in the Wall. The change in weather over the previous 24 hours created a different flavor, but no less beautiful.

At noon, I picked up the backpack, gave a cursory test of the crust, and kept the crampons on. I traveled for three minutes, punching through with every step before I stopped again. In a fit of anger, I dropped the load to get at the snowshoes. I should have put the damned things on while I was idle. Several minutes later, I continued.

Straight in front of me was a patch of blue ice in the middle of a huge field of white. A small picturesque lake had begun to emerge through the heavy snowpack. Snaking lines in the snowpack created by the near constant winds arced around the bowl of the iced-over lake and continued eastward toward me and beyond. Hovering over all of this was stalwart Boulder Peak, all but the eastern end smothered in a cloud. The scene was jaw-droppingly gorgeous.

Even with the snowshoes, the crust was too weak to hold my weight. I broke through the crust with each step and then dropped a couple more inches. Desperate to get some distance, the ragged travel coupled with my already exhausted body was maddening.

For heaven sakes, in two days Carleen is going to call the park service! I need to get more distance! This is the flat where I can finally do some traveling!

It was no use. Fifty feet beyond the lake, near the base of the cliff on the northern edge of the valley, I dropped the load. The day's travel was finished. Discouraged and exhausted, I sat on the backpack.

Nowhere in the valley was it safe from the monstrous snow cornice on top of Boulder Peak. If it let go, it could cover the entire valley floor. Since I could go no farther, my alternative was to hope it stayed put for the next 16 hours. A small knoll 300 feet south of my present position near the summer trail looked like the safest location to build camp.

A Scout Toward Agassiz Canyon

Nor was I going to build a camp and spend the night wondering what was on the other side of Boulder Pass. I left the backpack where it lay and headed west.

Small masses of the cornice on Boulder Peak 1,300 feet above me would drop from time to time, releasing some of the rage the main cornice would if it suddenly broke loose. I was in no danger from them, but if that entire overhang broke loose I would be dead in seconds. To fertilize my fear, much of the time as I traveled the length of the elongated peak, the cornice lay hidden inside the clouds like a hungry carnivore lying unseen in the bushes next to the trail.

Almost 50 minutes passed before I arrived at the 7,480-foot summit of Boulder Pass. The top of 9,944-foot Kinnerly Peak, overlooking Upper Kintla Lake, had been in view for 12 minutes. I made it to the western edge of the Boulder Pass flat 30 minutes later. North of my position 1,000 feet and 250 feet below me was Boulder Pass Campground. Upper Kintla Lake was two and a half miles northwest as the crow flies and 3,200 feet below. More importantly, I could see the snow line on the north face of Kinnerly Peak! It was somewhere between 1,500 and 2,000 feet below me.

Shortly after beginning the turnaround, my appetite returned, but not for the disgusting peanuts and fruit. God, I missed the stew! A few moments later, I recalled that the south-facing wall had water running off a few of the cliffs. My next thought was that I should go get some. Right, all I needed to do was bring out the technical gear and have at it in the avalanche-torn-up snowpack, and maybe break a leg. No, I would go without. I had come too far and been through too much to let down my guard now. Although I had the growing sense that I had completed the trip, there was still plenty of room to get hurt, or worse. There would be no stew tonight. The thought was frustrating as hell, but I had to stick to the plan. Besides, the fuel was getting low, and I might still be several days from civilization.

Yeah, I thought derisively, I was so hungry I could almost eat that dehydrated stuff straight from the bag. Then it hit me: why not give it a shot. If it were unpalatable, I could put the mix away and wait until I had running water. The idea seemed to reenergize my tired body, and I picked up the pace.

I reunited with the backpack two and a half hours after I left it and arrived at the camp location at 2:40 P.M. I had been moving for over six hours. Rather than heft the entire backpack, I retrieved some of the external gear, including the tent, shovel, and snow pickets, and carried them to the campsite.

One hour and 40 minutes later, it had just begun to rain and I was inside the tent, comforted by the chair, and with the sleeping bag draped across my legs up to my waist. The experiment of mixing and eating the dehydrated stew ingredients was a delicious success. I had munched and crunched my way through two-thirds of the bag of yummy stew and was thinking about mixing a second bag.

The quiet voice in my head reminded me that normally one of the stew packages made two meals. Perhaps I ought to consider how much swelling that dehydrated stuff was going to do inside the shrunken cavity that used to be my stomach. Shut up, I told myself, I was going to eat as much as I could stand.

Several minutes passed, and the need for sleep caught up with me before I could dig into the second bag of stew mix. As I crawled into the sleeping bag, I realized there was no water for tomorrow morning. Suddenly desperate for sleep, I reluctantly crawled out of the bag, got the stove going, and began melting snow. An hour later the rain had just stopped when I finally got back into the sleeping bag. Sleep was once again pulling me under when I heard a faint and familiar sound. I opened my eyes, looked at the roof, and saw the landing snowflakes. I thought I ought to close the two vents and was still thinking about doing that when I fell into a slumber.

I woke up several times through the night to roll over or reposition myself. Each time the wind was slamming into the tent. After all I had been through, I was unable to bring myself to believe that the storm was anything more than a lark and went back to sleep.

May 24: The Final Delay

After 11 hours of sleep, my rise to consciousness was quick. I awoke with the strong need to get out of the sleeping bag, grab the toilet bag, and head outside immediately. I resisted for less than a minute before I realized I was going to lose this one, and scrambled out barely in time.

Forty-five minutes later, I had just finished my first cup of coffee, which I had downed rather quickly to get warm, and was ready to start the second cup, but in a more leisurely manner. Although alone, I was embarrassed from the near accident. It was easy enough to figure out what had happened: I had downed the equivalent of two high-fiber meals the afternoon before. My body was so desperate for those thousands of calories it rapidly digested everything but the fiber. That done, that same system continued its high-level activity, which in this case meant an evacuation of an awful lot of fast-moving fiber 12 hours later. As a result, I was compelled to use most of the supply of moist bath tissue. Strict hygiene held a clear precedence over saving the paper for later. With three terrycloth cotton towels and three cotton handkerchiefs in the gear, I had plenty of other options. It was not an option to be negligent and get sick from improper hygiene.

Once resettled it was time to pay attention to the weather. Even given the late date, winter had made a comeback in the park above 7,000 feet. With the snow swirling around outside, I was grateful I had inconvenienced myself by melting all that snow the evening before while it was still wet from the warm day.

Warm and comfortable, I considered the circumstances of what was happening. For starters, the weather had penetrated the tent. Tremendous gusts threatened to flatten the tent while snow blew through the mosquito mesh and inside. I recalled with regret one of the rare shortcuts I had taken during this trip. Regardless of the weather, it was normal to pile snow around the base of the entire tent, leaving only an air vent on the leeward vestibule. I had failed to do that yesterday and had even left both vents on the roof open. Now I was paying for my negligence. The hard-won dry gear was getting wet.

A few minutes later, I realized that any travel today was a bad idea. The gear and I were up to the task of moving in these conditions, although the heavy load on this crust would no doubt have me breaking through with every step. The problem, however, was the avalanche conditions from the wind stacking on the ridges and peaks on both sides of this valley. There would be no travel today.

There was also no denying the lack of energy in my body. After yesterday's harsh climb, my muscles remained weak. No more than one mile from here, a 3,000-foot descent was waiting for me and my 100-pound load. One of the most dangerous conditions in the mountains was a descent, particularly with a heavy load in a rotting snowpack.

Panic and Tears at Going Overdue

I thought about the other consequences. This was the 15th day, and in 24 hours Carleen was going to make that phone call. A small part of me, the piece that was perpetually tired, stood up and said, "Good, bring that helicopter in and get me the hell out of here!"

Like relishing the thought of murdering someone, once I stepped back and saw the horrifying consequences of the act, so too became the helicopter ride. The runaway thought drowned in the more realistic supposition of what a helicopter extraction meant. It could take away the accomplishment of this trip along with the preceding trips leading up to this one.

Panic arose. For several seconds I threw aside the thought of safe conduct with the wild idea of packing and getting the hell out of here. I forced myself to sit back. Regardless of what day it was and the impending consequences, I had to treat today as though it was one more day of needing to do the right thing. Somehow, I felt some relief and was able to relax briefly.

In another hour, I had eaten a second bag of stew and even given it a derisive name: "New-age-munchy-crunchy-mountain-man stew." I also swallowed one ounce of olive oil.

With the wind still pushing snow into the tent from the east, at 7:15 A.M. I exited the tent and piled snow around the base of it. Back inside 15 minutes later, the interior was calm and it was no longer snowing on the gear.

By 8 A.M., I was back to wanting to pack up and head out. While the right thing to do was to stay put, part of me was saying that the real danger ended yesterday, that I could move forward without such a heavy cloud of peril hovering over my head. I resisted the thoughts.

I need to stay put and wait 24 hours even though people are going to come fucking looking for me. This is why they won't be looking for a body. They will find me alive, in good shape, and still moving. I must take care of my equipment and myself to progress.

I continued arguing and questioning my decision to stay put. I even entertained the thought that when they came, I would hide. By 8:15 A.M., I was in tears.

A trip like this, a man should walk out on his own two feet.

I broke down some more. My head kept hammering at me. Relief came only after I began the realistic planning for the next day of travel.

With the barometric pressure beginning to rise, there was the possibility for good travel conditions tonight. In spite of the last 10 days, when the measurement of my forward progress was in feet, I planned on an arrival at 5,600 feet of elevation tomorrow, the edge of the final avalanche chute, three miles from here. If I could get there, early the next morning I would cross the chute and arrive at Upper Kintla Lake Campground or possibly Kintla Lake Campground on the 17th day. With a still heavy load, I planned to arrive at the trailhead no more than two days later.

At 9 A.M., the strong wind from the east continued with a heavy, horizontal snowfall. In another 45 minutes, the moisture became driving snow pellets in the wind. I wondered how that huge snow cornice on Boulder Peak was doing. Was it really 100 feet thick? Perhaps it was thicker than that. Meanwhile the barometric pressure continued to rise. At 10 A.M., the altimeter had lost 46 feet since I arrived the day before. Half an hour later, the snow pellets quit, replaced by large snowflakes smacking against the east vestibule. I stuck my head outside. The brightness coupled with the blowing snow made it impossible to see the foot of Boulder Peak several hundred feet away.

At noon, I sealed the data-filled audio and camera cards in a ziplock bag and stuffed the bag into the bottom of the bear canister. If I died, the bear canister would be the safest place for what would become irreplaceable material for Carleen.

By 1 P.M., the altimeter had lost 75 feet. The weather was well on the way toward another blue-sky day, and better, a clear and cold night. In the early evening, I ate a third bag of dehydrated stew, noting that the honeymoon was over with the stew. This last one I forced myself to eat. As I prepared for bed a little after 5 P.M., the altimeter read that I had lost 125 feet. Tonight or tomorrow, there would be open sky. The plan was to get up at midnight and be on the trail by 3 A.M.

27 • success and defeat
in agassiz creek canyon

May 25: A Harsh Descent

I was up by 11 P.M. It was only a short sleep, but between the five hours of sleep and the two-hour nap I had the afternoon before, it would suffice.

Having eaten heavily in this camp, I re-inventoried what was remaining. In an interesting coincidence, I learned that in three days the food and moist bath tissue were going to run out at about the same time. The fuel and coffee grounds would be gone in four or five days. In short, at my present rate of consumption, which had increased 30 hours earlier, it appeared I could arrive at the Kintla Lake trailhead fresh out of food.

Depending upon how far I traveled today, I might have to redo the daily rationing. Right! At this point rationing the food was a bad idea. If I ate insufficiently, I would run out of energy long before the traveling portion of the day was finished. On the other hand, if I failed to make good progress today, enough to get me to the trailhead in 72 hours, I would have no alternative but to cut back on the daily amount of food I was eating. What was worse than insufficient nourishment was getting none at all.

Would I run into the first backpackers of the summer season at Upper Kintla Lake? I wondered if a crew had cleared the trail to the campground. It would be nice to see some people and to have a cleared trail on the canyon floor.

A park employee had informed me that the cable bridge crossing at Kintla Creek had remained in place through the winter. Normally disassembled during the winter, that had been pleasant news. On the other hand, this same fellow had talked about snowpack on the trail along Bowman Lake, and that for the trip I would need crampons and an ice axe only at the elbow on the approach. While I wished for the bridge, I might need to count on the technical gear to get across. I doubted I would be able to wade the stream this far into the spring runoff.

I also figured that today I would run into other issues where running water was concerned. At some point, I would be walking on a rotting snowpack that had rising streams beneath it. A weakened snowpack over water was a great way to break a leg. On the upside, the dangerous condition would be found only on the steep mountainside and fast descent into the snowless region. The key was to be careful, something exhaustion liked to ignore.

I began packing at 1:30 A.M. The altimeter now read 157 feet lower than 36 hours earlier. At 31 F., the temperature was a disappointing indicator that there was still cloud cover; the crust would be unable to hold my weight.

Wearing the snowshoes, the day's travel began at 3:44 A.M. Sure enough, the snowshoes broke through with every step. Nevertheless, the huge quantity of food I ate in camp did its job. An hour later, I arrived at the edge of the lip that overlooked Boulder Pass Campground and the descent into Agassiz Creek canyon. Encouraged, I realized that with half this pace I would be in camp by 9 A.M. I might even be able to get across that last avalanche chute before the heat arrived and then down to the lake today.

Under an overcast sky, and in the half-light of dawn, I cheerfully hollered an apology at the campground for failing to visit, and then began the descent with a growing lump in my throat. Damned near none of this trip had gone according to plan.

Cliffs and Bad Snow

With five minutes and 50 feet of descent behind me, I came to another stop. There were small cliffs everywhere. I remembered them from last autumn, but thought I had circumvented that area enough to get on the summer trail. What I saw in the heavy snowpack perplexed me on where to continue. I also had trouble staying upright with the snowshoes as I descended. With what lay in front of me, I had no trust in them. Would the crampons work in the deep powder I was now traveling in? I dropped the load, took the flotation devices off, and replaced them with the crampons.

With the backpack on, I tried to travel southwest, the general direction of the trail below the campground. The semi-flat I was on with a scattering of trees on the edge of it looked right. I was wrong, though, and turned back less than 50 feet later. Next, I headed into the scattered trees straight west and soon saw that another cliff had me blocked.

The crampons were the only thing going right on the precarious slope. The deepest they penetrated the snowpack was eight inches. Since my direction included descending, the posthole travel was only a small hindrance. I still tired quickly, and halted again after a descent of 140 feet in 8 minutes to take a 20-minute break.

Although the pace had slowed down, I stayed hopeful, knowing that the cliffs would end in half a mile. I traveled 20 minutes and dropped another 125 feet before being brought to a stop. An hour had passed since beginning the descent. In that time, I had dropped a mere 325 feet, with no end in sight through the cliff area. The terrain had gotten so hazardous I reverted to scouting and packing a trail. The time was 6 A.M., and it had been full daylight for 45 minutes.

I traveled through another scattering of trees for the next 100 feet, bracing against them to stay upright as I packed the trail through the deep powder. On the other side of the trees, 60 feet below the backpack, I encountered the most hazardous area yet. For 30 minutes, I packed the trail over what had to be a small cliff. I finally arrived in an open area about 15 minutes later, where the summer trail changed directions and headed north. I turned back to retrieve the backpack.

Back at the small cliff area, not trusting my earlier work, I rerouted the trail. Another hour had passed by the time I reunited with the backpack, where I took another 20-minute break. I was perched at 7,200 feet, still 1,600 feet above the elevation of tonight's camp. I now wondered if I would make it there today.

Exhaustion and Anger

I arrived at the end of the trail a few minutes before 8 A.M., dropped the backpack, and continued north, descending toward the ravine directly below Boulder Pass Campground. I dropped 70 feet in five minutes in a mostly open area before turning around at the edge of the forest. This last scout appeared to have been a waste of energy. Frustrated and tired, I returned to the backpack with the decision that there would be no more scouting or trail-packing trips. The knowledge that I was now below the cliffs and in easier terrain backed my resolve. I took another 20-minute break at the backpack before I continued.

Although tired, I dropped 360 feet in 20 minutes. I stopped at the ravine and took another break, this time for 30 minutes.

Where in the hell is all that energy I was supposed to have accumulated in the last camp?

The combination of powder and rotting snowpack had taken a big toll. In four hours, I had traveled less than one mile and dropped 800 feet. Discouraged and exhausted, I was still more than 1,000 feet above where

I wanted to set up camp. Although I knew a helicopter threatened to appear at any minute, I had to treat this day as no different from the previous days.

As I sat on the backpack and regained my energy, I began to pay attention to more than just the travel. There were birds chirping inside the forest I was now in, and I could hear a stream running beneath the snowpack. The day was shaping up to be a mix of clouds and blue sky. I was at the base of an unnamed peak and 500 feet below Boulder Pass Campground. The sun was also on that peak and slowly moving down its side toward this ravine.

A few minutes after I started moving again, the gurgling water below the snowpack broke into the open at another small cliff. Already aware of the change in the terrain, at 6,600 feet the tumbling water emphasized it even more. The rotting snowpack was only going to worsen as I dropped lower. With sunlight now filtering through the branches of the forest, it was also warmer.

Soon I crossed the avalanche chute where I knew the summer trail went. Back inside a series of cliffs, I figured the best thing to do was stay as close as possible to that route. Once out of the trees, the slushy snowpack slowed me even more. I was back in the trees 40 minutes later, with the stream gurgling below me, when I stopped again.

Typical of this type of travel, I was uncertain how near I was to the trail, but knew that I needed to stay as close as possible. Below and to the right of the area I had just come out of were many cliffs. I had but one direction I could go, into the same area as the summer trail, entering the thick forest along the side of a steep north-face bowl.

Like all the travel since dropping off the lip earlier in the day, none of the area looked familiar despite having hiked here in the fall. I used the map, altimeter, and distant landmarks such as 10,101-foot Kintla Peak and 9,944-foot Kinnerly Peak to try to orient myself. Just before I got to the far side of the steep north face, I almost brought out the technical gear for a 25-foot traverse of a 70-degree slope. Instead, I stepped sideways as I had done in the elbow on the approach.

I popped out of the thick forest and into the sun several minutes later. Some of the Douglas-firs in this area had a base diameter of six feet. I pointed the crampons in the direction of one 30 feet away, and headed down what remained of the north face. The crampons lost their grip in the slush. I fell and slid on my rear down the slope toward the large tree. Rather than attempting to stop, I controlled the descent with the ski poles and crampons, straight into the tree. I came to a jarring stop, thinking I had done quite well. Since I was already sitting, it was time for another 20-minute break.

The Final Camp

With the altimeter reading 6,131 feet, my relief was enormous. I was near the area where I would be building camp. I needed only to cross the large forested flat and find the trail that descended toward Kintla canyon. The topographic map indicated a large swath of open terrain less than a quarter mile to the southwest. To maintain my bearing, it may have been better to go over there. In spite of the exhaustion, though, which gave me a strong desire to take shortcuts, I needed to do everything I could to be near the summer trail. In the early morning darkness of the next day, the last thing I would need was to try to find the summer trail on a steep and snowless mountainside smothered with bushes, tanglefoot, and timber fall. Unsure of where the snowpack would end, the trail needed to be close by. Irritated, I wondered why this trail was so indiscernible through the forest compared to the trail in Bowman canyon.

I dropped to the flat and arrived on the other side 40 minutes later. I entered a small opening and decided I would be unable to get much closer to the avalanche chute and still find a flat in the sun. I figured I was no more than one mile from where the dirt trail would emerge from the snowpack. The altimeter read 5,965 feet, while the map indicated I was at 5,854 feet. I was unaware that the barometric pressure was falling once more, creating the disparaging difference between the two guides. The time was 12:34 P.M.

I dropped the backpack and sat down to remove the slush-covered crampons, except there was only one to remove! I was so tired that the first thought was to just abandon the goddamned wayward device. It only took a moment to recover from that ridiculous idea. In the last week and a half, the crampons had been critical in keeping me alive. When retired, their place would be on a wall of honor in our home. They kept me safe; I had an unspoken promise to reciprocate. Besides, I doubted I could make it safely off this mountain without both crampons.

I found it lying in the snowpack beneath the big tree I had slid into an hour and a half earlier. I picked up the crampon, apologized for being careless, and promised to do better.

Back at camp, I set the tent up in five minutes. In spite of my exhaustion and the thought that a helicopter might appear at any minute, there would be no shortcuts taken. Aside from the large drop in elevation and exorbitant three and a half miles I had traveled, today was no different from the last two weeks.

The Helicopter

At 1:30 P.M., I was yanking the gear out of the backpack and throwing it into the tent when I heard the muffled yet familiar sound of helicopter rotors. I stood up straight, stared through the treetops, and waited. Maybe this was nothing more than one of the tour helicopters I had seen flying around during the rare non-stormy days. Yet none of those had approached Hole in the Wall and Boulder Pass.

Within seconds, the helicopter popped over the lip precisely where I had been that morning at daybreak. The aircraft was no more than 300 feet above the snowpack and was moving slowly toward the southwest, the same direction I had traveled off the lip. Without a doubt, they were following my tracks. The trip was over.

While unsurprised to see the helicopter, this being the 16th day, spotting it was almost surreal and came as a shock. The exhausted part of me from the last camp raised his head and expressed delight, while the rest of me bowed in abject defeat. All the work and all the danger I had gone through on the approach had beat me to a pulp physically and mentally, but I was undefeated. Spotting the helicopter—that finished me. The distance of one mile or less from the dirt trail, perhaps only two hours away, was now out of reach.

The helicopter disappeared behind the treetops as it continued southwest. Less than a minute later, the sound of the beating rotors changed as it turned and paralleled the Agassiz Creek drainage. It appeared again less than a fifth of a mile away and slowly headed north for less than a minute before banking once more. This time it headed straight for my camp and in a minute was 500 feet directly above me. The aircraft slowly continued southward for a minute or two before it arced to the right and headed north again. That was when I figured they knew I was in these trees somewhere. That meant they would keep circling until they spotted me or landed the aircraft and searched for me from the ground. I was sure they would leave only when they found and extracted me, whether I was willing or not. (I knew from previous experience that, once the searchers found me, extraction was the only option.) Once on the snowpack in the nearby open area, they would soon intersect my tracks and follow them to this camp.

Looking to offset the side effects of what was about to happen, I reasoned that perhaps a little assistance from me would go a long way later. With that in mind, while suppressing the urge to hide, I picked up the red jacket and waved it. Several seconds later, the helicopter came to a near hover above me before it sped off toward the open area.

Still in shock and revulsion at what was unfolding, I went to work breaking down camp. There was no need to leave it in place while I prepared what would be a futile argument. They were here to extract me. Moreover, being active would help keep me from breaking into tears.

I was still breaking camp several minutes later when I heard the signal whistle through the trees. I hollered back, stepped over to the edge of the clearing, and waited. A few minutes later, three snowshoe-clad men emerged from the forest 100 feet away.

Officer Gary Moses, Kyle Johnson, and David Smith walked into camp. As it turned out, I knew all three men. Kyle informed me that we had talked on the phone a number of times through the winter when I called looking for information on the park's weather and snowpack.

Officer Moses was in charge as the incident commander. I had already encountered him in March and May 2006, both times for being overdue. During the second meeting, he cited me for the two days I was overdue during the successful crossing of Ahern Pass. Like this trip, weather had delayed me and Carleen had called.

The last time I saw David, who also had to remind me that we had met, was on Chief Mountain Highway. He and three other people had been cross-country skiing to Belly River Ranger Station to do some wolverine studies.

Once the introductions were complete and they had established that I was fine, we began to talk a little more freely, perhaps a mistake. They were friendly enough and offered to help break camp. Although uncomfortable with others handling my gear, I was quick to be amiable with the offer and expressed my thanks.

Asked how the trip went, I responded with one sentence. A trip like this had no other answer.

"I got my ass kicked."

David asked if I had a GPS. I said no and asked him why.

"We do," he answered in a matter of fact tone. "Did you know your camp is on the trail?"

I said no; anyway, just how close was I?

"The trail is beneath your tent. How did you do that?"

All of them stopped what they were doing, eyed me curiously, and waited for the answer.

How does one explain navigation techniques to someone holding a GPS device? Until the damned machine broke or ran out of battery juice, I was outgunned.

"I have a lot of experience," I said.

I thought all three of them nodded in agreement. As we continued to pack, I got the impression that these men were impressed with what I had just accomplished.

When I made the observation of what the helicopter extraction was going to do to the four trips and my recent accomplishment, Officer Moses disagreed.

"The press release may actually do some good for getting your name and the trip known to the public," he said.

Perhaps the helicopter ride would be less destructive than I thought.

(Later in West Glacier, David would volunteer the information that he knew of no one who could complete the trip I had just done, even though the men he had in mind, including himself, were at most half my age. With as much trouble as I had completing the trip, there was not much bragging room left over, so I thanked him and said no more.)

At the helicopter, I relinquished the backpack, then stood by and watched helplessly as the last of my fuel was scattered over the snowpack.

Oh God, that's the last of my fuel!

The lump in my throat that had been coming and going since I first spotted the helicopter returned. I had carried that fuel for 16 days through hell, only to watch it poured into the snowpack two and a half miles and 1,500 feet above Upper Kintla Lake Campground. More than the helicopter and the four men's presence, that small act told me the trip was indeed finished.

Each man who handled the backpack commented on its still heavy weight. Gary even ventured that the load was about 100 pounds. Having lived through the consequences of the crushing weight, I said nothing.

Once airborne, within a few minutes I had a bird's-eye view of the final camp and the avalanche chute 300 feet beyond. On the ground, I had been uncertain of the camp's location in relationship to the chute. Now I breathed in silent relief. The camp's location had been perfect for beginning the descent the following morning.

Then I spotted the shocker: the camp was half a mile from the dirt trail! Without the ride, I would probably have arrived at the trailhead in no more than 48 hours!

Suddenly glad I was still wearing the sunglasses, I kept my head turned so the two men sitting back there with me would be unable to see my tears. After a minute, I casually wiped my face, turned back, and faced the interior of the helicopter.

epilogue

28 • Aftermath

Back in Officer Moses' office in Apgar, I was encouraged to call Carleen so she could know I was safe. After the call, I was debriefed. I showed him precisely where my camps were located on the topographical map and when. At the conclusion, I asked Officer Moses about the assumed citation I would receive. I also expected that I was going to pay for the helicopter extraction. He said no, this time the government would cover the extraction. He further added that I did everything right up there to stay alive and get through. Hearing his words, a heavy weight dropped off my chest. I was almost certain the cost would have been many thousands of dollars. This was far different from my experience with him five years earlier.

Two of the park's law enforcement officers gave me a ride back to my vehicle at Polebridge. During the course of our conversations, I mentioned that I had known from the outset that the 11 days on my trip itinerary would probably fall short. At no time did I have anything to hide; I was under the impression that Officer Moses had made that clear. Nevertheless, this conversation would resurface three months later on August 24 in a courtroom.

After picking up my vehicle and then later during the drive to Helena, there was a sense of emptiness, an incomplete trip. What I had accomplished was a first, and yet there remained the feeling of having fallen short.

The following day, Officer Moses' statement in my camp came true—the park service's press release appeared in newspapers around the region. I received a few congratulatory e-mails from those who knew what I had accomplished. Then there were the other comments.

"Make him pay for it," one said. "They should have left him there. That way we would have one less fool in the world."

Most of the newspapers simply ran the park service's press release, which gave a one-sided version of events. A newspaper in Spokane,

Washington, captioned the story with "No Love Lost between Glacier National Park Personnel and This Hiker." The release gave the impression that I waved the red jacket seeking help. In all, the media releases were heartbreaking. I remembered what it felt like as a kid, staring at the people around me and knowing full well that a fair shake was out of reach. The pain, the hurt, and then the anger emerged. There was more to come.

On June 25, exactly one month from the date of my extraction, Officer Moses issued a citation and a summons to appear at a court hearing in Apgar on August 24 at 9 A.M. I did, and pled guilty to the charge of not being where I said I would be when I said I would be there. The penalty was the cost of the court hearing and all the rescue costs incurred.

In addition, I was required for the next 24 months to carry a satellite locator device anytime I was in the backcountry of Glacier National Park. Ironically, I had tested the device with satisfactory results in the extreme conditions of the Selway-Bitterroot Wilderness in July 2011—one month before the court date and consequent penalties.

Two issues came out during the trips of 2011. It pained me continuously to have Carleen not know if I was okay. The personal locator device I now own makes it possible for her to know where I am and whether I am all right. Had I known of its utility prior to the 2011 trips, I would have had the device on my person the entire time. (The literature I had read previously, regarding the first generation of such gizmos, led me to distrust the locator device. A second-generation personal locator, the one that I purchased, has all but eradicated the problems of the original device.)

The second issue remains unresolved. My aging and the deterioration of my body continue. The best I can do is to stay as fit as possible through continuous exercising, brief backcountry trips, and a proper diet. I am painfully aware that the end is in sight. Is it even possible for me to carry 90- to 120-pound loads today? If not, the lengthy winter trips will be finished.

Outside the courtroom on August 24, 2011, Officer Gary Moses informed me that thereafter the park would require only that I give the route and the length of time on the itinerary for these types of trips. It was a step in a direction I gladly welcomed. The challenge I seek is on the snowpack, rather than conflicts with people. I have always lacked the necessary skillset to win a fight where people are concerned. Nor do I see anything that would indicate this condition is about to change.

Will I return to Glacier National Park? To answer that, I can say that the real purpose of accessing Hole in the Wall under these conditions was to determine the viability of completing the trip I started working on in 2009. My original intent was to say nothing about this trip until I decide to start it. However, my plans have changed given the incident in the backcountry office in Apgar at the beginning of the final trip, continuing with the red-jacket signal and my so-called desire for a rescue, which culminated in the court appearance on August 24.

I confess that the strong memory of the four trips initially caused me to falter. Apparently, though, it was not permanent. My resolve where the main journey is concerned has never been stronger.

The Continental Divide route within Montana, from Wyoming to the Canadian border, is 950 miles long and far lengthier during the winter. That distance does not include the often high-mileage exits to resupply. To complete it, I have no alternative but to travel 140 miles through Glacier National Park from Marias Pass to Polebridge. The route will include another traverse into Hole in the Wall.

Whether thrust upon me or by volition, I believe that a challenge is synonymous to fear. I also believe that walking through a challenge and fear is the story of everyone's life, regardless of the circumstances we face. I do not consider myself unique. One such challenge is building as I write this. The preparations are already underway. When the actual trips begin, and I am out there alone once more, that is when the fear will pounce, inevitable but utterly unpredictable, again and again. As each one of those scenes and events unfold, my thoughts and sometimes even my words will be a replay from my past.

God almighty! What the hell have I got myself into?

Once again, that is when I will be forced to pay attention, to simply take the next step, and then the next, and then another.

Richard Layne

Richard Layne was born in 1951 at home in Arkansas, on the edge of a cotton field where his father was a sharecropper. He grew up in western Montana with much of his time spent outdoors. A Vietnam veteran, he spent several years in the U.S. Army.

Richard travels in Montana's backcountry, including Glacier National Park, primarily during the winter. Some of his trips have been noted in newspapers and on radio and television news. He has published three short stories and photos in three Montana regional magazines: *Montana Magazine, Distinctly Montana,* and *Montana Headwall.*